THE OCCUPIED GARDEN

ALSO BY KRISTEN DEN HARTOG

Water Wings
The Perpetual Ending
Origin of Haloes

THE
OCCUPIED
GARDEN

A FAMILY MEMOIR

of WAR-TORN HOLLAND

KRISTEN DEN **HARTOG**

&

TRACY KASABOSKI

THOMAS DUNNE BOOKS
ST. MARTIN'S PRESS
NEW YORK

THOMAS DUNNE BOOKS.
An imprint of St. Martin's Press.

THE OCCUPIED GARDEN. Copyright © 2008 by Tracy Kasaboski and Kristen den Hartog. All rights reserved. Printed in the United States of America. For information, address St. Martin's Press, 175 Fifth Avenue, New York, N.Y. 10010.

www.thomasdunnebooks.com
www.stmartins.com

Library of Congress Cataloging-in-Publication Data

Den Hartog, Kristen, 1965–
    The occupied garden : a family memoir of war-torn Holland / Kristen den Hartog and Tracy Kasaboski. —1st U.S. ed.
        p. cm.
    First published in Canada by McClelland & Stewart, 2008 with Tracy Kasaboski as the primary author.
    Includes bibliographical references.
    ISBN-13: 978-0-312-56157-4
    ISBN-10: 0-312-56157-1
    1. Hartog family. 2. World War, 1939–1945—Personal narratives, Dutch. 3. World War, 1939–1945—Netherlands—Biography. 4. Netherlands—History—German occupation, 1940–1945. I. Kasaboski, Tracy. II. Kasaboski, Tracy Occupied garden. III. Title.
    D811.5.D3728   2009
    940.53'4920922—dc22
    [B]   2009002957

First published in Canada by McClelland & Stewart Ltd.

First U.S. Edition: May 2009

10   9   8   7   6   5   4   3   2   1

Voor Tante Rige
En ter nagedachtenis van Cor en Gerrit

Contents

Significant sites in *The Occupied Garden*

Prologue

WHEN THE SECOND WORLD WAR erupted over the Netherlands, our grandparents were in their early thirties, raising their family in a town outside The Hague. Opa was a market gardener who grew vegetables on two and a half acres of rich black earth, but by the time we visited sixty-five years later, long after their deaths, only a small corner of the garden remained. A horse was pastured beside the fence, and the rest was an expressway full of roaring cars. In a curious twist of fate, someone had spray-painted a dove on the cement embankment, and written, in heavy red letters, *Always in our harts*.

We stood together, trying to picture this place as it must have been, alive with tall bean stalks and rows of endive. The garden was Opa's livelihood, but also the family's lifeline while the country suffered five years of occupation. In the final months of the war, death from starvation was common.

Our grandparents rarely spoke of those times, and never – to us – of the explosion that cast a shadow over the rest of their lives. So what follows comes not from them but from clues left behind, like ghosts' footprints. A grenade on the mantel. Snatches of letters and diaries. A cache of photographs, some hazy, some clear. We were compelled to search out their story when we realized it was disappearing, and to re-create their experience based on the remaining fragments. As we pieced the remnants into a narrative, we began to understand the silence that bound those years and nearly erased them.

THE OCCUPIED GARDEN

ONE

Twilight
1927–1940

FOR ALL THE YEARS AFTER THE WAR, Gerrit dreamed – sporadically, without warning – of being chased by German soldiers with guns, but back in the crisp winter of 1927, as he skated on a willow-rimmed pond in South Holland, he had no such demons. Warm in his wool cap and coat, he sped along under a cloudless sky, breath pluming in the bright winter air, his plaid scarf flapping behind him. He had just turned eighteen, and his life would change in moments.

On either side of him, the flat landscape of Overschie stretched into the distance, and underneath the snow, bulbs lay in wait for spring. Gerrit loved spring, a time of beginnings, but at this point he still loved winter too. He was an exceptional skater, and stood out even here in the

Netherlands, where skating and bicycling came almost as naturally as walking. He'd never have boasted, but his skates cost more than he could afford: long metal blades that locked on to black boots, they were fancier than the wooden tie-on kind most people wore.

Savouring hot anise milk under a tent on the ice, a slender young woman watched him go by, noticing both the skates and his accomplished style. Gerrit caught her eye but looked quickly away, red as beetroot. She smiled, and admired his languid figure eights as he skated backwards, then forwards again, and glided off, pushing from side to side with grace and agility, his hands clasped behind his back. She sipped her rich, sweet milk, and had turned to say something to the young couple with her, a woman and an uncommonly tall man gobbling almond cake, when suddenly Gerrit appeared again in her peripheral vision. Without seeming to watch him, she saw his every move as he made his way towards her and away, and towards her again. Her heart raced under two sweaters and a heavy blue coat, and she pulled the collar close around her neck and shivered. She knew the blue was lovely with her eyes – a blue like cornflowers – and while there would come a time when she'd stop thinking about such things, it was far away from this moment, when she was still young and attractive, freshly aware of her new admirer. She lifted her head and looked at him. From the side, anyone could see how they matched; how their noses must have pulled them together – strong, bony noses of equal character, ready to be passed down through the generations.

The den Hartogs hailed from the Alblasserwaard region of the Netherlands, a large rural stretch east of Rotterdam, and bordered by wide rivers that continually overflowed their banks. As a child, Gerrit's playmates were the squelching mud and the moving waters of the river Lek, though he never learned to swim. He was the youngest of three children – he had a sister, Marrigje, and a brother, Nico. His father Rochus had once been a salmon fisherman, and his back was bowed from years of hauling the heavy nets, and pulling barges as he walked the canal's narrow footpath. Gerrit's mother Arigje hated fish – the taste, the smell, the slipperiness – and was glad enough when Rochus became a *tuindersknecht*, or gardener's hired man. It was a fine job in the provinces of North and South Holland, which grew most of the fruit and vegetables for the country, and Rochus taught their sons the same trade, moving the family from village to village as opportunities arose.

Gerrit was twelve when he left school and apprenticed with his father and brother as a *tuindersknecht*. Kneeling among the plants, the smell of the turned soil in his nostrils, he felt more at ease here than he ever had in a classroom, though he was already curious about the world and enjoyed reading. It didn't hurt that the *tuinder*, Willem Quartel, had a son Gerrit's age, called Jaap, and the boys became friends. They were close in stature and both had open, friendly faces and easy smiles, so were more often mistaken for brothers than wiry Gerrit and the heavy-set Nico.

Vegetable gardening was an honest trade, but like fishing, dependent on the whims of the buyer. The vegetables were sold at an auction house to which the *tuinders* belonged as part of a co-operative, and middlemen sat on bleachers surveying the produce as it floated past them on barges. A big clock hung on the wall, counting down the time that the buyers had to make a bid. If they liked what they saw, they bought, and if they didn't, the co-operative paid the *tuinder* a minimum amount and gave the vegetables to the cows. It was a living – sufficient in Rochus's eyes. He was a modest man, devoted to his wife and proud of his three children. Arigje thought the income of a *tuindersknecht* meagre, and her husband's contentment with their life was a source of irritation for her. She loved fine things and kept bits of ribbon and lace tucked away in a drawer, as if one day there might be room for them in this life she hadn't chosen. The marriage, while not unhappy, was somewhat lopsided, in that Rochus loved Arigje from the beginning, and Arigje came to love Rochus over the years – he'd been her second choice, when her first fiancé changed his mind, and the disappointment never quite left her. In spite of Rochus's devotion to her, she was a severe woman who ran her household and the lives of her family with more than the necessary diligence. His parents, of course, were Gerrit's precedent for marriage, and unwittingly he gravitated towards a woman whose backbone rivalled his mother's.

Like Rochus, who escaped his wife's displeasure in the world of books, Gerrit was an avid reader, and when his queries about Cor revealed that her family, the Posts, owned a bookshop on the Zestienhovensekade in Overschie, he became a regular, if nervous, customer, doing his best to peer intently at the neat rows of books, to choose one that might especially impress, but all the while trying to keep his eyes from darting around for her, a small young woman with sharp features and a quick step, always busy. Sometimes it was her older sister Truus, plump and dark-haired, running the shop – the same girl who'd been skating with Cor that day on the pond – and Gerrit's disappointment showed on his face, until Truus called, "Co-or!" And Cor would appear, while Truus slipped away. Gerrit passed her his selections, aware of his rough hands and her smooth ones as she wrapped the books in brown paper.

A year after they met, Gerrit's family moved again for work, this time several towns away to Leidschendam, a community with roots in the fourteenth century, situated on the perimeter of The Hague, where the queen sometimes resided. Once, twenty windmills had pumped water off the land on the outskirts of town, drying it and creating the flat, green fields called polders. Now, only three mills were needed to do the job, and the polders provided fertile pasture for grazing and farming. Renting land at the edge of the Tedingerbroekpolder, along the tracks that ran from Rotterdam to The Hague, the den Hartogs became self-employed gardeners rather than hired help. But each week, Gerrit made the trip back to Overschie, near Rotterdam, on his bicycle or skates, braving not just the weather but Cor's close-knit family: Truus and the little sister Maria, brothers Gerry and Tom, and parents Neeltje and Jacobus. In winter, he knew the villages by their church steeples, each one different, and counted them as he zipped by on his fine steel skates. Through open barn doors, he glimpsed farmers milking cows or feeding their pigs. Dogs raced to the edge of the canal to bark at him. In summer, horse-drawn carts clattered over brick streets, and on his bicycle Gerrit pedalled around them, calling a greeting and lifting his cap. Finally, Overschie, where Truus's towering fiancé Jacques, who claimed aristocratic ancestry, laughed and said, *"Hier komt de boerenjongen"* – Here comes the country lad – at the sight of skinny Gerrit hurrying towards Cor with his worn pants tucked into his knee socks, face shining with anticipation.

Each of them came from a long line of Gerrits and Cornelias. The Posts and the den Hartogs followed the Dutch custom of naming the first child after one of the father's parents, the second after one of the mother's, and so on, and if a child died – an all too common occurrence in those days – the next to come along took the same name again. Thus names cycled through family trees in a repetitive, ever-increasing spiral.

Traditions like this were important, and respected, within both the home and the larger nation, and they carried through to the army – little more than a patriotic display – where enlistment was mandatory. And so with other young men following in the footsteps of previous generations, Gerrit acquired his army training at nineteen, proud of his uniform and his part in the custom. A photograph from this time shows him posing on the Post balcony in Overschie, the clay tile roof slanting beside him. He wears his soldier's uniform, the hat tall and boxy with a small visor, the high-collared jacket extending to his thighs and closing snugly with showy buttons. Cor stands beside him; fine-boned, slim-waisted, she rises just past his shoulder. Their arms link – as in the wedding portrait yet to be taken – and she gazes at him rather than the camera. In this rare, candid shot, Cor looks happy, and even some-what coy, with her foot placed forward and her skirt swinging. Gerrit in all his finery leans into Cor and stares at the lens, his hat doubling the size of his head. Below, the canal waters form a ribbon through the busy town. So close to Rotterdam, Overschie would be blackened by the explosions' clouds six years hence, but at this time, no one suspected Gerrit would actually wear his fine uniform in combat.

Their engagement ran alongside the Depression, called the "crisis years" in Holland, a period preceded by mounting economic strain that stemmed from the Great War. The Netherlands had stayed neutral, and so hadn't the debts that other countries accumulated through battle, but Germany was its major trading partner, and its economic collapse burdened the Netherlands. Early in Cor and Gerrit's engagement, social unrest was brewing, and long queues of the unemployed report-ing for assistance were a common sight. Both the Posts and the den Hartogs had money troubles – Gerrit's family had more vegetables than they could eat, but little else, and Cor's had only books upon books, and the thread to bind them – so the couple was urged to postpone their marriage until they could make a proper start.

Gerrit continued to grow vegetables with his father and brother in Leidschendam, and several times a week, a barge arrived, pulled by men who looked like Gerrit's stooped father. Once the crates of vegeta-bles were loaded, one man pulled the barge with a pole, as Gerrit's father had in his fishing days, while a second jumped aboard and pushed his pole through the water; together they steered the yield to auction. More often than not there was a glut of produce and too few buyers. As in Overschie, the unsold vegetables – termed *doorgedraaid*, or "turned through" – went to the cows, or got tossed on a heap where they rotted back into compost. As compensation, the auction house gave the growers one cent for every head of lettuce thrown away. When Gerrit's brother Nico married, it was obvious the *tuin* couldn't support the family he'd start, so he moved to nearby Voorburg and got work as a mailman and part-time janitor at the Christian Emmaschool.

Unlike the den Hartogs, the Post family had roots in Overschie that went back more than a century. Cor's opa had been a carpenter, and her father a house painter, on occasion taking big jobs like the painting of canal bridges in Overschie, but the fumes strained his asthmatic lungs and he had to quit, so the bookstore and binding shop upstairs provided the family's main income. Cor and Truus also ran a library, charging a small fee for borrowing. Both the store and the library emphasized religious books, which was all Cor read, but Gerrit's tastes spread wider. He read everything he could about plants and flowers, about far-flung places, and travelling by plane above the clouds.

By 1931, Gerrit's sister Marrigje, called Mar, had already married, and that year Truus did too. Cor and Gerrit assumed they would be next, since they'd been engaged several years now, but their parents continued to dissuade them. As the years crept by, Truus and Mar started families, but nothing changed for Cor and Gerrit. The couple grew frustrated, and suspected more than money lay at the centre of their families' objections. The den Hartogs were members of the Nederlands Hervormde Kerk, or Dutch Reformed Church, to which Queen Wilhelmina belonged, and the Posts were devoted to its stricter offshoot, the Gereformeerde Kerk, which had returned to the name used by the religion in Reformation times. Both Churches were rooted in the Calvinist tradition, but the Gereformeerde denomination of the Posts was dedicated to a rigid dogmatic interpretation of the Bible, while the Hervormde denomination of the den Hartogs put more emphasis on the grace and beauty of God's word, honouring its mystery. Cor was descended from a founder of the breakaway faction, and religion was paramount in the Post family. Among them, she in particular had an analytical approach to the Bible, and a natural intelligence, and those two traits combined made her fierce in her belief, rather than calmly faithful, like Gerrit.

Yet in spite of the Posts' dour Calvinism, laughter floated in Cor's home, usually instigated by Truus or brother Gerry, who could both find humour in almost any situation. Once, Cor, Truus, and Maria practised a *tableau vivant* for their church's Christmas celebrations – the still poses the closest thing to drama Calvinists would allow themselves to enjoy. Cor stood draped in a white sheet, arms raised, embodying Faith; Maria knelt beside her as Charity. Truus, representing Hope, stood similarly clad, head turned sharply towards her sisters, chin lifted. Cor watched the clock on the wall, seeing the second hand tick, wondering how long they could hold the pose this time, for so far they'd not done very well. From the corner of her eye she saw Truus's eyes bulge and cheeks balloon as she held her breath as well as her pose, and then the three collapsed in hysteria, sheets puddling around them.

The den Hartogs were a less boisterous lot, sister Mar kind and soft-spoken like Gerrit, and brother Nico slow and plodding, in Cor's view. But religion was equally important in their family, and Gerrit sang in the choir of the Hervormde church he attended with his parents, where men and women sat on opposite sides. Cor went once, feeling awkward and out of place, everyone staring at the obvious outsider as she entered with Gerrit's parents. Rochus offered her a small reassuring smile, but Arigje looked straight ahead, giving nothing. In Dutch society, known for both racial and religious tolerance, a loose, voluntary segregation deter-mined which butcher, green grocer, and milkman people patronized, so a Catholic housewife bought milk from a Catholic milkman, and a Hervormde boy married a Hervormde girl. Sitting beside Gerrit's mother, Cor felt her disdain and sent a sliver of it back. The women had not warmed to each other over the eight-year engagement – Cor liked Gerrit's father, but his mother sent wordless messages of possessiveness where Gerrit was concerned, and offered no sense of welcome to Cor, though the invitation to church had been her idea. Cor knew Gerrit's mother hoped she would join the church once she married Gerrit. She listened to the sermon, hands folded in her lap, and noticed that several elders wore black from head to toe. The reverend had a rich, lyrical tone, but she enjoyed Gerrit's voice more – she was sure she could distinguish it from the many others singing.

Despite Cor's visit to their church, Gerrit's mother sensed her son would bow to Cor's religion rather than Cor to theirs, for the young woman, slight and plain as she was, already exuded a quiet power, and Gerrit seemed content to please her. Furthering the likelihood, his mother thought, was the fact that his gardening friend Jaap Quartel, who had recently moved to Leidschendam with his sister and widowed mother, was also Gereformeerde, and played the organ at that church on Sundays. The conversion would be an easy one, she knew, with both wife and best friend beckoning.

Ultimately, it was Cor who set things in motion. When her brother Gerry announced *his* engagement, Cor told her parents that, poor or not, Gerrit was the man she loved and she was determined to marry him. She knew it was bold to speak out, for even though she and Gerrit were in their mid-twenties, they were bound to their parents' wishes, but she thought of Gerrit's last visit, when they'd sat together under the big willow by the water. They'd kissed, and their hands had strayed, and Cor knew that next time they might not stop. Her parents hesitated, exchanging a quick glance, and Cor wondered what excuse could come next. As they stood frowning in front of her, she blurted that she wanted to enter her marriage while still chaste. She flushed with embarrassment, for such things were never mentioned, and though her father glowered and her mother pursed her lips, the wedding was quickly set for May 3, 1935.

On the day Cor married Gerrit, narcissus blooms tinted the countryside white and yellow, and tulips paraded across meadows in a kaleidoscope of colour, but Gerrit chose lily of the valley for Cor's bouquet. True to the Dutch tradition, he brought them to her home on the Zestienhovensekade, and he stood staring at the door knocker as if he might glimpse the future in its highly polished brass. He held the small posy in his hand, listened to the canal water pressing slowly by behind him – and suddenly doubted his choice of flower. Would the Posts equate the simple stems with a simple man, one not good enough for their daughter? Would Cor be disappointed? He thought of the photo that sat on the hutch in the Post home: bride Truus beside her groom, only slightly taller than Jacques though he was seated, her arms filled with a spray of lace and fern and plump carnations. He'd read about carnations in a horticulture book he'd borrowed from the Post library, and knew they were one of the oldest cultivated flowers, admired for their ruffled beauty and faint clovelike scent. Dianthus was the botanical name, and meant "divine flower." Exceedingly popular and showy, they may have been fine for Truus, who was outgoing and vivacious, but Gerrit knew they were not right for Cor. The slender lily of the valley, surprisingly fragrant and with a weed's endurance, was more suited to his bride. His doubt evaporated. Thinking of the way she ran the backs of her fingers over his cheek, he lifted the knocker.

Inside, the Post household was a flurry of activity. Truus had come to do Cor's hair, knowing that the bride-to-be would be anxious about it. Cor had lost her hair at age seven after a bout with typhoid fever, and what had grown back was thin. Forever after, Cor refused to cut it, preferring braids that wrapped over her head, saving what came out in the comb. On this important day, Truus helped wash and comb the fine, dark blonde tresses until they shone, then wound the hair into delicate coils on either side of Cor's head. The youngest, Maria, fussed with the hem of her wedding dress, a plain ivory gown of heavy crepe sewn by Truus, and when little Nel, Truus's daughter, peeped beneath it to see if Cor wore stockings, Maria laughingly slapped her hand away.

Cor's mother Neeltje bustled from room to room, pausing to flick a piece of lint from husband Jacobus's jacket and to straighten her youngest son Tom's tie. Her critical gaze passed to Gerry, her other son, and when she saw that one pant leg, pressed earlier by Maria, was not as neatly creased as the other, she made a mental note to remind Maria of the value of a job well done.

Neeltje's tiny, round-faced mother lived in the house on Zestienhovensekade too. With quicksilver intelligence, she was both spirited and ladylike, but these days some of her spiciness had cooled. While she pined incessantly for her youngest son Marinus, a military officer stationed in the Dutch East Indies who hadn't been home on leave in nine years, now she was newly widowed as well. A portrait on the mantel-piece offered a small reminder of her husband Teunis, but it wouldn't save him from fading in the memories of others – eventually he'd be known only as a small man with a glass eye who was born in a windmill.

Oma Cornelia, called Kee by the family, always dressed in black lace, with a matching hat tied beneath her chin and set on her head like an inverted dish. This day was no different until she misplaced her elbow-length gloves, and ran frantically about the Post household shouting, "Where are my arms? I cannot find my arms!" Cor suspected it was her husband she was missing, and she wondered what it was like to live with a man for so many years, and then to lose him. The family, used to Kee's dramatics, took little notice.

Cor's father sighed and went to the window. Just as he parted the curtains for the third time, looking for the bridegroom, Gerrit knocked.

In their wedding photograph, Cor hooks her arm into the crook of Gerrit's elbow and holds the flowers in her left hand. A sprig of fern decorates her hair, and her dress, which someday will be cut apart and fashioned into christening gowns for her babies, falls in neat folds around her, with more lilies pinned to the train's hem. Gerrit stands beside her, slender in the new black suit he'll wear every Sunday for years to come, making the most of a costly purchase. How proud he feels, dressed in something so fine, and not his corduroy pants that sag with age, his faded jacket, wooden shoes, and the cap that keeps the sun off his head. The portrait shows his wavy hair combed back from his face and two cowlicks swooping above his high forehead. A single bloom is pinned to his lapel. There is some glimmer of their later selves here already: Gerrit's enthusiasm shows in his raised eye-brows and dimpled chin, his big ears standing at attention; and Cor seems to be wary, and planning the future. She clenches her square jaw and her lips form a thin straight line, as though she knows that happiness is precarious.

Gerrit paid an Overschie boy with lettuce to move Cor's belongings to Leidschendam on his family's barge, and as the vessel floated along the Schie, Cor rode by train with her new husband, travelling away from home with mixed emotions. The Posts were a *klit* family, meaning its individual members were entangled like knots in the hair, so pulling herself free was difficult, as much as she craved independence. In Leidschendam she'd have Gerrit's family – his brother Nico in Voorburg and sister Mar in Rijswijk, their three villages positioned one after another along the edge of The Hague – but it was a poor substitute for her own, and Cor's home-sickness, spurred on by the chugging train, increased with distance. She looked at Gerrit, and with a twist of guilt remembered her father's words to her mother when they thought she wasn't listening: that Gerrit was a good man, but the den Hartogs were common folk and she could do better. Cor raised her hand to Gerrit's face, and reminded herself that her parents might just as well have deemed Jacques "unworthy" for Truus – whether or not he had aristocratic roots, his immediate ones were as plain as their own. She eyed Gerrit riding happily beside her, and felt a rush of devotion. He was a good man.

At Leidschendam, she disembarked, just a step ahead of her husband. The breeze spilled over her, smelling of spring flowers, but the fragrance was lost on Cor until Gerrit pointed it out. Her connection to the natural world was different from his, though she was aware of the orderly pattern of the country, and how each region depended on the others: cattle in the northern province of Friesland, grain in the remote northeast, fish from the many rivers and the North Sea. And throughout the lowlands, canals criss-crossed in a dizzying pattern, one part of a complex system that kept the Netherlands from sinking into the sea.

From the train, they walked along the busy Vlietweg, which fun-nelled traffic from Leidschendam to Voorburg and beyond. On one side, horse-drawn carts clattered over the bricks and the odd cattle truck chugged past, cows peering through the slatted wood of their enclosures. On the other lay the wide canal, where barges laden with produce were poled to the auction house. Cor watched them pass as she stepped neatly along beside Gerrit. These were the kinds of boats that pulled his vegetables, and so they were part of her new world, but also her old, since her belongings were travelling on a similar craft. Only a glance away, beyond the sweaty, sinewy labourers on board, green lawns stretched up to imposing mansions, each surrounded by a manicured garden. She'd be living, now, in one of the wealthiest parts of the country – close to the *bekakt*, or the stuck-up, though the word was so coarse that Cor flushed when it passed through her mind. She recalled Jacques's tease that she would fit in here, next to the scholars, diplomats, and noblemen, with her prim manners and her exacting diction. It was meant as a jab, she knew, but she was not ashamed of being proper.

She and Gerrit turned away from the Vliet, with its bank of mansions, towards the working-class, largely Catholic subdivision where Gerrit lived, the straight and tidy streets branching off the Vlietweg like teeth in a comb. Cor had been here many times before, but today she saw it anew, with a wistfulness she hadn't expected. Filled with plain, two-storey brick houses attached in blocks of four, the area was set apart from the old, curving streets of Leidschendam. The houses here were almost brand new in 1935, and lacked the charm and unmistakably Dutch flourishes of older architecture – decorated cornices, shaped gables, ornate brickwork. Each flat, unadorned facade along the Tedingerstraat was nearly identical; the paint on a door, the fabric of window curtains, and the plants growing in the tiny front gardens created the only distinctions. They passed the milkman's home and business at number 15, where the milk cans were lined up along the house, and Gerrit nodded to the *melkboer* in his white jacket and cap preparing to make deliveries with his cart. Across the way was the butcher shop, with its cool marble interior and carcasses hanging from steel hooks. The sweet smell of tobacco and cedar wafted from the open door of the cigar shop, and a white poodle yapped at them as they passed. A man wheeled his barrel organ over the brick road and stopped at the corner to crank the handle that made music spill out of the ornately painted contraption.

Soon Cor stood before Tedingerstraat 61, the house of her in-laws. A low fence abutted the sidewalk, and behind it were flowers planted by Gerrit's mother – her Moeder den Hartog now. She saw the woman pull aside the curtain and peer out at them; Moeder and Vader had come from the wedding on an earlier train to prepare for the newly-weds' arrival. Cor glanced away, pretending she hadn't seen her, and looked at the yard instead, where flowers bloomed. Cor took no notice of their variety. As she approached the entrance, her gaze moved to the upper-floor windows, wide, rectangular panes that would let in lots of light, but already she was thinking, *How will I ever live my whole life here?* Just then, the door was pulled open from the inside, and Gerrit's father spread his arms wide to hug her.

"*Welkom!*" he said, kissing her cheeks, and she noticed the fruity pipe-tobacco smell of him.

"It was a good journey?" asked Moeder as they came through the door, but the words seemed directed to an invisible someone, and Cor let Gerrit answer.

His mother bustled about, bringing tea and biscuits, and Cor – not knowing whether to offer her help – sat wishing they could excuse themselves and go upstairs. But her mother-in-law prattled on, and not for the first time Cor noticed her river dialect. Gerrit's father spoke the Alblasserwaards dialect too, but it sounded less obvious to Cor, and she'd never heard him use words like *allez* or *enfin*, as his wife did. Moeder called Gerrit "Gurt," drawing out the long *u* sound, and while Cor would come to mimic the pronunciation, by then an endearment, today it seemed another oddity in a day filled with them.

One comforting sight was the portrait of Queen Wilhelmina that hung on the wall, ermine cloak trailing from her shoulders. Even topped by a crown, her face was kind and matronly rather than regal – round, with small features and happy eyes that sat a touch too close together. Good Christians revered the royal House of Orange, since they believed the right of rule was God-given, so the same portrait hung in the Post household on otherwise sparsely decorated walls. Here there were prettier things than at home, though the family was poorer: Moeder den Hartog's Delfts Blauw china graced the mantelpiece and the eyes of peacock feathers looked out from a delicate blue-glass vase. The feathers always surprised Cor, because she thought of Gerrit's mother as superstitious, and she knew that feathers indoors were said to bring bad luck. Cor wasn't superstitious about much outside the Bible. Even if the aura of bad luck became visible around the vase, if it emanated in blue waves from the feathers, Cor could ignore it – thunderstorms too. One had just begun to rumble over Leidschendam, and Moeder den Hartog rushed through the house, closing it up. "God's wrath!" she exclaimed, looking out at the rain bouncing up off the road, her eyes darting nervously. Cor knew it was no such thing, though she was equally devout.

Later, as she unpacked her suitcase, she came across two photographs Truus had tucked in with her belongings – in one, Cor looked out from the bookstore doorway, and in the other she stood inside, with the books on their shelves behind her. In the years to come, the features of her face would fade from the photographs, though the books and the storefront remained. But even now, when the photographs were crisp and new, they suddenly seemed like mementoes. One of Cor's favourite cousins – another Cornelia – lived in Schiedam near Overschie and would take her place at the bookstore on Saturdays, while Cor's duties would begin here. From now on she would awake in these rooms. She'd have her babies here, and in the not-too-distant future, stand on the balcony with her husband and children watching green and red tracers light up the sky.

That night, Cor lay in bed, observing the shapes of her new surroundings by moonlight. She thought of Gerrit's parents downstairs, asleep in their twin beds, framed photographs of the previous Moeder and Vader den Hartog hanging on the wall above their heads. The pictures were a reminder, she knew, of the importance of tradition and duty, but Cor didn't intend to follow the custom and hang the likenesses of

Rochus and Arigje in her bedroom. Nevertheless, listening to her husband's steady breathing, she already understood she'd become part of the tapestry of this family, and that she and Gerrit would continue the weaving.

When she finally slept, she dreamed of the street-life in a place that seemed to be Overschie and Leidschendam at the same time – the milkman pedalled past in his short white coat, as did the fish vendor, the cigar vendor, and the *schillenboer* who collected potato peels and old bread to sell to the farmers. Each of them had his special cry, but the most joyful was that of the flower vendor, who called "*Bloemeninallekleuree!*" – Flowers in all colours! – the words echoing as he disappeared, and sung even in the rain and wind. There was so much wind in this flat land reclaimed from water that Cor dreamed of it roaring across her husband's garden, picking up all the seeds they had just planted and scattering them uselessly into the sea.

In the middle of this restless sleep – two hours, or three? – Moeder den Hartog called upstairs with a loud "*Gurrrrrt!*" and rapped on the wall. Cor started awake in the darkness, wondering at first where she was and why. She could see Gerrit open his eyes beside her, and just as she moved to kiss him, the rapping came again, along with a louder "*Gurrrrrrt!*" Cor bristled, and knew she must express to her mother-in-law, however wordlessly, that it was Gerrit who'd taken a capable wife, rather than his bossy mother who'd acquired a fourth child. She urged Gerrit out of bed and drew the sheets up without a wrinkle. It was four in the morning, and the workday had begun.

Cor joined the den Hartog family during Gerrit's busiest time, when the first crop of cucumbers, planted months earlier in the clay- and straw-walled hotbeds, was ready for picking. May's chores lasted from the dark morning of each day until ten o'clock at night, when the sun sank into the low horizon and mirrored Gerrit's exhaustion. Alongside his stooped father he spread the composted manure, turned the heavy black soil by hand, two spades deep, and planted summer crops like beans, melons, potatoes, endive, carrots, beets, and cabbage. Soon, after the seedlings appeared, he began the back-breaking job of fertilizing and watering. For this he walked on planks between the rows, and, carrying a yoke hung with two twenty-litre cans that held water or wet manure, he showered the plants that had sprouted in the two-and-a-half-acre garden. He had a thin frame, and his veins bulged with exertion.

Through the spring and summer, while Gerrit worked eighteen-hour days in the *tuin*, Cor took up the task of wife, silently asserting her role to Moeder den Hartog. Dressed in a traditional white apron that crossed at the back, she spent her days cleaning, cooking, washing, and mending. At harvest time, she salted vegetables, or preserved them in jars. The beans, cucumbers, and beets that lined the shelves were grown by her husband and prepared by her, and the glass jars packed full with colourful, homegrown food were proof of their now seamless bond – tangible evidence of happiness. But she was still restless. Having been raised in a bustling town at the edge of Rotterdam, she found her new home oppressively quiet. Since the age of twelve, she'd been used to daily contact with customers in the bookshop and library, and she missed the smell of the books, the lap of the canal outside the door of the house, and the giddy company of her sisters, Truus and Maria. Neither she nor her sisters had a telephone, and the letters they sent back and forth did little to bridge the distance. She even missed Truus's husband Jacques and the jokes he repeated ad nauseam, dou-bling over with laughter. Jacques could fold himself in half and still be almost as tall as Truus, who had thick black eyebrows and a happy, heart-shaped face. Their rows were loud and frequent, and the making-up just as exuberant, but however much Cor disapproved of such outward displays, she adored her sister. She knew she ran the risk of for-getting to laugh if she spent long stretches away from home, and that she had a tendency to take things too seriously; two creases had already formed between her eyebrows, and she was only twenty-six. Gerrit had noticed them, and often smoothed them with his finger. "I think you'd like to visit your family," he said one day, and his expression held a kind of apology for the things he couldn't give her. After that, once every two weeks, Cor spun through her chores and hurried for the train to Overschie. The tracks ran alongside the garden, and she liked to take a seat on that side, so she could see Gerrit from a distance in that great plot of land, turning to find her in one of the many windows rushing by.

Back home on the Zestienhovensekade, she caught up with Truus and Maria, and visited her childhood friend Marie Zandbergen, and her husband Dick. In the first hours, the visits were just what she'd craved, but by the middle of her time away, she wanted to be back in Leidschendam, settled into the routine that gave her days an undeniable purpose and a constancy that was in sync with the world around her: Gerrit's work and the auction, as well as her own visits to the baker and the dry-goods store. She prided herself on the efficiency with which her days unfolded, waking early each morning, seeing Gerrit off, soaking her whites in scalding water, scrubbing everything until it gleamed, and then standing back to inspect the whole. Each day, at lunch and at dinner, she removed her apron, hooked a basket over her arm, and walked the short distance to the end of the Tedingerstraat. Here, she turned right, passing the busy Stalen-Ramen-Koop factory that manufactured steel-framed windows, and crossed the Broekweg to reach the *tuin*, where she would find Gerrit tending the vegetables. She brought him strong, hot coffee and sandwiches, and kept him company while he ate, and the garden stretched out before them, an expanse of black soil to which they entrusted their future. On the slight rise beyond the field lay the railroad track joining The Hague to Rotterdam, Cor's link with Overschie but also her passage back again.

Gerrit had a similar desire to connect with the world beyond Leidschendam, but the draw for him was news. Much as he loved to read, books and newspapers didn't bring current events to life the way radio broadcasts did, so before long, the rich wood cabinet of a multiple-band radio graced a small table in the living room. It was a costly purchase, but for Gerrit, news was as necessary as food and water, and in the evenings when he switched the radio on, its warm yellow glow filled the room. He liked the fact that he could tune in to stations from across Europe, but the Dutch and Belgian-Flemish broadcasts were the only ones he understood. So while Cor worked in the kitchen, cleaning up from the day and preparing for the next, Gerrit relaxed near the radio, and listened.

By now Cor had arranged her own things in the half of the house she shared with Gerrit, and like her mother in Overschie and her mother-in-law downstairs, she hung the standard portrait of Queen Wilhelmina on the wall, dusting and straightening it as she went about her daily chores. Wilhelmina had inherited the crown in 1890 from her dead father, Willem III, when she was just ten years old. A special law was passed to allow it, since the right of accession had not previously included women, and there were worries that the related German royal house might try to claim the throne. Her German mother Emma, Princess of Waldeck-Pyrmont, ruled as regent until Wilhelmina turned eighteen, but the girl's gilt-edged childhood was nonetheless cut short by the looming responsibility. Wilhelmina grew up in what she herself called "the cage" – not the actual palaces her family inhabited, but the regal confines that had existed since birth, when she escaped from the womb only to find herself equally hemmed in by protocol and expectation.

In an attempt at normalcy, little aristocrats were often invited to play with Wilhelmina in the palaces' ornate drawing rooms, but at heart, the girl was a lonely, deeply religious child whose best friend was her mother. She preferred riding around the flower-laden grounds of the royal residence Het Loo with Queen Emma in a wicker horse-drawn carriage; or in winter, skating at the palace of Huis ten Bosch under the guidance of one of her father's aides-de-camp. King Willem, two generations removed from his daughter, believed skating was an indecent pastime for a girl of high breeding, and was unaware of the lessons she took in his last sickly years. Wilhelmina was told it might kill him to know. Shrouded by trees, cheered on by her mother, she stumbled and then careened along the ice. She grieved when the king died – for the loss of a father, and for the weight that loss placed on her – but at last she could openly speed around the moat at Huis ten Bosch, a child queen clad in fur-lined velvet.

Situated a short distance from Leidschendam, Huis ten Bosch nestled in an ancient forest that gave the palace its name, which means "house in the woods." *House* is a relative term, and doesn't usually imply grandeur, but in her day, Queen Wilhelmina was the richest woman in the world, and the castle had a Green Room, a Blue Room, and an Orange Room, and each window opened out to lush, rose-covered grounds ringed with moats in a symmetrical design. The bridges that arched over the moats led to a forest of lofty elm, smooth beech, and old oak with rippled bark. This dense forest would turn thin over the course of the German occupation, as trees were cut and burned in makeshift stoves, while at the palace, bullets punctured walls, and the gardens were upturned and destroyed. But in the early years of her reign, Wilhelmina's surroundings were still pristine, and the country itself was, by her own admission, like a nation asleep. The times seemed unimportant; "life was a pond without a ripple," as she wrote in her autobiography.

Fond as she was of its grounds, she didn't like the inside of Huis ten Bosch until she grew up and married Duke Heinrich Vladimir Albrecht von Mecklenburg-Schwerin, a "countryman" (not to be confused with a country *lad*, like Gerrit) and a German who decorated his villa's walls with elephant heads. In the Netherlands, Prince Hendrik, as he became known, satisfied himself shooting deer and geese in the palace woods, or simply wandering the grounds with his little dachshund Helga, arm in arm with Wilhelmina as together they admired the wild anemones that spread as far as the eye could see. Indoors, Wilhelmina and Hendrik began to refurbish the palace, the walls of which had long been padded with dark, dusty upholstery that matched the plush sofas and chairs. Bit by bit, they made the place their own, much as Cor and Gerrit did the upstairs rooms of the Tedingerstraat house, though of course in more extravagant fashion.

In her autobiography, Queen Wilhelmina paints her marriage near blissful, and writes that Hendrik followed God's example in his love for mankind. Other sources suggest Hendrik – whom the people nick-named *Zwijnen Heintje*, or Porky Henry – was a wayward boozer with a wandering eye, not unlike Wilhelmina's father, Willem, whom the *New York Times* called "the greatest debauchee" of his era. Hendrik was purported to have fathered many illegitimate children while married to Wilhelmina. The queen herself suffered several miscarriages, and it seemed a miracle that Princess Juliana was born at all.

An only child like her mother, she arrived in April 1909, just months after Gerrit and Cor were born in nearby villages, he in December and she in January. Princess Juliana spent a large part of her childhood at Huis ten Bosch, not far from Cor and Gerrit. While Wilhelmina abhorred the restrictions of her own childhood, she made the classic error of motherhood and repeated Queen Emma's mistakes by placing those same bars around Juliana, whose carefully selected playmates were instructed to address the young princess as "Mevrouw," or Madame. Yet in other ways, Juliana was lucky. She caught frogs in the pond, and skated openly on the moat.

According to Wilhelmina, this domestic tranquility lasted for years, punctuated only now and again by a recurring fear of uselessness that started early in her reign. Raised all those years in the cage, she was pre-pared for the important role that awaited her. But when it came, she dis-covered that the country ran smoothly regardless of the body on the throne, and she felt more alone than ever. The Dutch constitution had been rewritten during her father's time to shift power from monarch to government, and Wilhelmina could have ruled benignly. Instead, in 1899, the nineteen-year-old queen made a gesture that would characterize the future of her reign, offering Huis ten Bosch as the meeting place for the First International Peace Conference – though her efforts must have felt futile during the Great War that broke out fifteen years later.

A year before Cor and Gerrit married, Wilhelmina's mother Emma developed a barking cough, and died of complications from bronchitis. And that summer of 1934, before the grief could lift, Prince Hendrik suffered a heart attack at Noordeinde Palace and died in hospital. To underscore what she thought of as the heavenly beauty of Hendrik's final journey, Wilhelmina saw to it that a white carriage, pulled by eight horses draped in white cloth, carried his coffin through the streets. As she and her daughter followed the carriage in their white dresses, she had no awareness of Cor and Gerrit among the anonymous mourners who watched from the sidelines; rather, the individuals must have seemed to her as parts of a whole – two dark ribbons of commoners ever-present in her periphery, and accentuating the whiteness of Hendrik's procession.

Emma's and Hendrik's deaths marked the beginning of many difficult years for Wilhelmina, who watched Adolf Hitler's rise with growing dread. During the Great War, she'd heard the sounds of the front in Flanders from her home, Het Loo, and felt relieved that Germany had not invaded her own country. But she'd found herself in a curious position: anxious for the Netherlands, and also for her mother's family in Germany. The countries' blood ties had made the situation exceedingly delicate. In November 1918, Kaiser Wilhelm II, the last of the German emperors and a relative of Wilhelmina's, had abdicated and turned up uninvited on the Dutch border, asking for sanctuary. Wilhelmina had admitted him, but thereafter never visited him at his residence in Utrecht. Still, the queen had incurred the wrath of the Allies when she cited the rights of asylum and refused to extradite the old Kaiser so that he could stand trial.

By war's end, relationships had been damaged on all sides, and the severe conditions of the Versailles Treaty had caused a festering wound throughout Europe. Germany had been brought to its knees, limited to a military of one hundred thousand men with no conscription, no tanks or heavy artillery, and no air force. Almost as soon as the ink had dried on the treaty, and even before Adolf Hitler's rule, Germany had begun covertly rebuilding its military. Creative minds found loopholes to make advances: denied planes, they used gliders; forbidden tracked vehicles, they used motorcycles and multi-wheeled armoured cars.

Hitler's Nazis came to power in 1933, promising a disillusioned people change and retribution. Wilhelmina was anxious, but privately unsurprised. She later wrote in her autobiography that "together with the misery of war and defeat, [it was] understandable that the influence of Nazism and fascism grew rapidly." And her feeling of foreboding was quickly justified. Within two years, the regime had openly flaunted the rules of the Versailles Treaty, conscripting one hundred thousand new soldiers per year to its defence force, the newly termed Wehrmacht, whose members were well trained, disciplined, and aggressive, pledging unconditional loyalty to Hitler. Staging enormous spectacles, the Nazis began wooing the German people and renewing their national pride. During the Nuremberg Rallies, battalions of brown-shirted storm troopers goose-stepped through the banner-decked streets, and hundreds of thousands filled the parade grounds. At night, the crowds watched open-mouthed as 150 anti-aircraft searchlights striped the sky.

Invariably, Hitler presided at the festivals and parades, exciting the masses with rousing speeches that attacked Jews and communists and the nations that had signed the Versailles Treaty. But while his words thrilled the Germans who turned out to cheer him, next door, Queen Wilhelmina's eyes narrowed with suspicion. A keen observer of politics, she later wrote that, for her, the Second World War lasted ten years rather than the five her country experienced. "What a burden it was to live in the knowledge that we were heading for a catastrophe, and to be gradually enveloped by the dark shadows of the future."

Gerrit and Cor sensed the tension. In August of 1936, as Hitler prepared to host the Summer Olympic Games in Berlin – the last of its kind for twelve years due to the war that would follow – they stood on the balcony at the back of their house, Cor big with her first pregnancy. Despite the late hour, the west retained faint traces of daylight, and pink clouds streaked the sky. Before dinner, the Dutch radio station had reported on the exclusion of Germany's Jewish athletes from the upcoming games, and during the meal Cor had watched Gerrit move the food around on his plate. He wasn't a big eater at the best of times, and his mood could easily spoil his appetite. She knew without asking what was wrong, but it wasn't until they stood outside, in the waning light, that they each confessed their misgivings about bringing a child into a dangerous time. Like most, they'd thought Hitler's hold on Germany couldn't last – but what if they were wrong? Cor pressed her stomach against the balcony's brick wall and felt the baby move inside her. She looked down at the small yard where their child would play, and saw her father-in-law coming home along the path. She waved hello, then turned to observe Gerrit's profile – she loved to study his face when he was looking elsewhere. The baby kicked again, and she reached for Gerrit's hand so that he could share the sensation. These were the moments that brought back clarity and courage.

The discomfort Cor and Gerrit felt over Germany's display of bigotry was echoed around the world. There were heated debates about whether countries should boycott the 1936 Olympic Games, but ultimately, a record forty-nine nations took part, the Netherlands included. The Dutch were so tolerant, some would say, that they even condoned intolerance.

Berlin's stadium dwarfed any built before it. The city was swathed in bold red and black swastikas, and extensive spit and polish reinforced the image of German prosperity. Propaganda Minister Joseph Goebbels – once a journalist himself – warned newspapers to watch what they printed, stressing that the Wehrmacht's barracks should be referred to only as the "north section" of the Olympic Village. Berlin's streets were "cleaned" of its Gypsies – some eight hundred arrested and put into a camp, out of sight of foreign tourists. And at the insistence of the International Olympic Committee, the IOC, the JEWS NOT WELCOME signs dotting Berlin and the surrounding towns were removed.

On the day of the opening ceremonies, the weather turned broody and drizzle dampened the city, but the display went on. More than a million people lined Berlin's streets, anxious for a glimpse of Hitler's black motorcade. Still more, like Cor and Gerrit, tuned their radios to the big event, and listened to the fanfare of trumpets that signalled the führer's arrival, and the orchestral rendition of the Nazi Party's anthem, "*Horst-Wessel-Lied*." Over the heads of spectators inside the roofless building, the bloated *Hindenburg* airship unfurled the Olympic banner. Athletes filed past Hitler like so many soldiers. Clad in his military uniform, moustache brushed to precision, he moved to the microphone and declared the games open. The sky overhead erupted with the release of thousands of pigeons, caught in flight by an IOC newsreel and said to be "carrying a message of peace to the world."

Cor and Gerrit exchanged doubtful glances as they sat next to each other in front of the radio, and Gerrit watched Cor pick up her knitting from the basket beside the chair. Cor had the same hunger for information that he did, but could shut it out when it became disturbing. He watched her work the wool over the needle with her finger again and again, completing each stitch so quickly that his eyes couldn't quite catch how it was done.

In September, news broke that Crown Princess Juliana would marry His Serene Highness Bernhardt zur Lippe-Biesterfeld, a German aristocrat and a member of an elite branch of the Nazi's paramilitary Schutzstaffel, or SS, though he would later claim to have joined only in order to graduate from law school. His brother Aschwin belonged, as did other relatives and friends of Bernhardt's, some of whom would come to the wedding. The union meant trouble for Wilhelmina, though she announced her approval in a radio address. Hitler, too, sent congratulations – but he was at the core of her misgivings. Told of the engagement in his one and only meeting with Bernhardt, which custom required, Hitler now held the news aloft as proof of a Dutch and German alignment that was strengthening all the time. The words curdled in Wilhelmina's belly. These last years, she'd continued to ignore the exiled Kaiser Wilhelm, and she went out of her way to avoid Germany, and thereby Hitler, when she travelled in Europe – though each spring she fulfilled the loathsome duty of sending him birthday wishes. Publicly, she announced that her daughter was marrying the man she loved, and that the Netherlands was not marrying Germany, though as a precaution, an inquiry investigated Bernhardt's alleged anti-Nazi sentiments. The prince officially resigned from the SS, took Dutch citizenship, and changed the spelling of his name from *Bernhardt* to *Bernhard*, just as Wilhelmina's Heinrich had changed his to Hendrik, but the international press still referred to him as "Nazi Prince Bernhard," while the German papers scorned him for denying his roots. Two days before the ceremony, at a party celebrating the nuptials, the Nazi anthem was played, and some of the German guests offered the Nazi salute.

But as the wedding day drew near, Bernhard's easy charm and white carnation boutonnieres swayed many opinions, and brought a brief reprieve from the disapproval over Juliana's choice, almost as if everyone wanted to believe in the curative properties of love. On January 7, 1937, oranges hung in the trees to honour the House of Orange-Nassau, and the crowd tossed back traditional nips of *jenever*, Dutch gin, as Wilhelmina's golden coach rolled by, taking the couple to The Hague's town hall for their civil marriage ceremony, to be followed by a church wedding in the Grote Kerk. The prince's German relatives flanked Wilhelmina as they posed for photographs. The women wore long gowns, white gloves, and feather-trimmed hats, and the men sported costumes heavy with gold braid and epaulets. Prince Aschwin,

Bernhard's brother, wisely left his Wehrmacht officer's uniform at home, and turned up in a plain black suit that drew little attention.

Two in a sea of well-wishers yet again, Gerrit and Cor joined the throng on the streets, and shivered from the cold as they waved to the heiress and the nobleman with eight middle names. In this place and time, allegiance to the queen – and to the future queen, who was Cor and Gerrit's contemporary – could be likened to a Catholic's allegiance to the pope, which meant that thousands turned out for the celebration but none of them saw the details: Juliana's sash of orange blossoms, or the diamond bracelet that fell from her wrist during the ceremony and was quickly, almost imperceptibly slipped back on by her polished young groom. It was enough to be there in the crowd, close to the momentous event, a flock of strangers but a people too.

Soon the gossip began, enriched by the gin, and Cor overheard snippets of speculation about when the first royal baby would be born and if Juliana would have the same trouble her mother had had, both conceiving a child and carrying it to term; would handsome Bernhard, someone asked, be faithful? Cor lifted her chin and turned away, sending out waves of disapproval that were only heeded by her husband beside her. He glanced down and found the expression he'd expected: lips pursed, eyebrows raised ever so slightly. To ease her discomfort, he whispered, "I wonder how *our* baby's doing." Cor smiled. Their daughter, Arigje, called Rige, had been born on the eve of the Berlin Olympics, as the sweet melons ripened in the garden. Just four months old, she was at home today, being rocked to sleep by Gerrit's mother, the oma she was named for. Moeder den Hartog doted on her new granddaughter, and had even warmed to Cor now that a baby linked them. It would take Cor longer to return that warmth, but she'd begun to feel it, seeing how natural the older woman was with Rige, how effortlessly she cradled her and sang lullabies that transfixed the girl, who watched her oma's moving mouth in wonder. Privately, Cor tried for the same response: she held Rige close and sang, but her words emerged less convincingly, and also off-key. Sometimes when Rige looked up at her, she had a terrible feeling that the child expected something Cor couldn't possibly give.

After the ceremony, the crowd strained for another glimpse of the bride and groom, and Cor's eyes followed the princess in her gilded coach. She didn't notice that Gerrit watched her rather than elegant Juliana. More than ten years had passed since they met, and he'd become a husband, father, and accomplished *tuinder*, but he could still feel enchanted by the strong line of her jaw, and the way the sunlight sparkled in her hair. Because of the significance of the day, he thought of the importance of his marriage to Cor – how it had brought him so much more than he'd anticipated: there was his obvious love for Cor, which had existed long before they'd wed, but also a desire to protect and provide, and strangely, a feeling of security. He kept his hands on her slight shoulders as the crowd dispersed, and they moved in unison through the throng. As Juliana and Bernhard prepared for an incognito honeymoon in Poland – before the infamy of Auschwitz, Sobibor, and Treblinka – Cor and Gerrit returned to the canal's edge, where Gerrit kneeled and tied the blades to Cor's shoes. Arms linked, they skated back to Leidschendam.

More than ever, Gerrit pored over newspapers and tuned in to his radio in his scarce free time. He heard how Queen Wilhelmina had opened the Moerdijk motor bridge that arched over the Hollands Diep, providing a much-needed link from the southern provinces to the big cities of Rotterdam and The Hague, where before the only connection for vehicles had been a ferry. The radio also reported the startling news that Prince Bernhard's Ford had collided with a truck and slid under it, the accident breaking his neck and crushing his ribs. Reporters stressed his daredevil nature and the calm devotion of Princess Juliana, who sat by his bed in the hospital during the months of recovery. But the overwhelming news items covered the Netherlands' volatile neighbour, Germany, and the fighting going on farther afield.

Gerrit learned that faraway China and Japan were at war, Italy had invaded Ethiopia, and Spain fought within itself, aided too eagerly by Germany and Italy. There were reports on all fronts of children and innocents suffering. Come spring, as he hoed in his *tuin*, he mulled over current events, instead of daydreaming, as he normally did, about flying in an airplane or drifting slowly over the land in the basket of a hot-air balloon. He liked to picture the *tuin* from above, with its long, precise rows of green foliage stark against the black soil, and then to pull back farther, to an impossible perspective that took in the parcels of water and land fitting together in an elaborate puzzle. He'd been working in gardens since he was twelve, and felt lucky that circumstance had pushed him towards a job for which he was so well suited, though the work was physically hard and his back ached often. His education was sparse, and he hoped one day to study horticulture formally, yet it was difficult to see how that would be possible anytime soon. Still, his work afforded him long hours of contemplation, at the same time busying him to such a degree that it exorcised his worries, however temporarily.

He believed the garden was good for Rige in the same way – sometimes when she had trouble sleeping and Cor was ragged with frustration, he brought their daughter to the *tuin* and pointed out spinach in the moonlight, carefully repeating the word *spinazie* so that she could take it in. He let her finger the leaves of a Brussels sprout and showed her the small corner she could have for her own garden when she was older. Rige grinned at that, though she couldn't possibly have understood him. She had bright blue eyes like Cor's and his, and white-blonde curls that sprang out in all directions. He carried her through the rows, back and forth, back and forth, singing softly with his rich voice, until her head drooped and fell to his shoulder and her breath warmed his neck.

He and Cor learned their roles as parents quickly. Rige was just one-and-a-half in February, when Cor gave birth to Jacobus, called Koos with a long *o*. He was born two days after Princess Juliana's daughter Beatrix, and days before Truus had her third daughter. During Cor's labour, Gerrit leaned over the sink, bleeding from his sizable nose, just as he'd done when Rige was born, and just as he'd do three more times for the boys to come. But with this baby, there was perhaps good reason for his nervous bleeding. In no time, the first-born son would show signs of the kind of mischief that makes a parent's heart clutch in panic.

Because of his baby boy, the celebrations in the streets to welcome Princess Beatrix were more invigorating for Gerrit than they would otherwise have been. He joined in the festivities and the nips of gin, privately toasting his own son and Truus's girl, while others toasted the new royal daughter. In an ideal world he and Cor would live closer to Truus and Jacques, and raise their children side by side, even if the sisters didn't always agree on how the job should be done. He recalled Truus and Maria's visit soon after Rige was born, when the aunts had cooed over their niece. Truus had looked up and asked, "Just one name?" Her own girls had multiple, grand-sounding names like Antoinette, Jacqueline, and Phillipine, due in part to Jacques's high-born ancestors but also to Truus's decision to string several names together. "One is sufficient," Cor had said, not explaining that she preferred starkness and simplicity, and thought Truus's choices had a Catholic ring. They were surrounded by Catholic families on the working-class Tedingerstraat, and Gerrit knew it was important to Cor to assert their difference.

Yet today, looking down the bustling street, it pleased him to see how many good people lived in the neighbourhood, religion aside: the Bloms next door had a girl Corrie and a boy Piet, old enough to look out for Rige and Koos; across from 61 were the van Kampens, Mevrouw somewhat hot-headed and Meneer unusually quiet, but they were kind people and their girl Jeanne was well behaved; the milkman Piet Rehling and his wife were expecting a child any day, a playmate for Koos perhaps; and Jaap Quartel, church organist, fellow *tuinder*, and Gerrit's childhood friend, lived farther down with his old mother and his spinster sister Paulien. These people were like an extension of Gerrit and Cor's own families, and today, regardless of the gloomy newscasts, there seemed a safety in that, a hope brought with the birth of a royal baby. If in the years to come there were no princes born, baby Beatrix would be queen.

With Jaap Quartel and Theodoris Blom, Gerrit toasted the princess once more, and laughed when the neighbourhood *dronkaard* sidled up to them, lifting his glass and then weaving on down the street to find a free refill. Gerrit watched him go – a small man with florid skin and watery, bloodshot eyes. Cor disapproved of him, but Gerrit thought him harmless enough, and today he was funny too, curtsying to the different groups he approached. Gerrit sipped again and accepted congratulations on the birth of Koos, then hurried home to his family, a little dizzy from the gin. Unlike the *dronkaard*, he didn't drink often, or much, but he liked the resulting hum of happiness, and the way the alcohol made him notice the snowflakes disappearing from his coat sleeves as he stepped inside. He thought of how quickly spring would come – soon he'd plant the flat, white seeds of the cucumbers and keep them warm under glass and reed mats, coddling them until the vines grew ropy and strong.

Around this time, support for the increasingly anti-Semitic Nationaal Socialistische Beweging, or NSB, sank below 3.9 per cent, though it had enjoyed a slight surge in popularity during the crisis years. The council of Gerrit and Cor's Gereformeerde Church spoke out against this staunchly right-wing party, decreeing its mandate clashed with the Church's fundamental beliefs. The party's leader, Anton Mussert, was an ambitious man who would do what it took to acquire power. At its inception, his NSB was modelled largely on Benito Mussolini's fascist party, and had little to do with anti-Semitism – in fact there were Jewish members – but as the thirties pushed on, and Nazi strength grew next door, Mussert aligned his party more closely with Hitler's, and eventually Jews were no longer welcome to join. In the Netherlands, few took Mussert seriously, and his political opponents often ridiculed him for reasons that had nothing to do with politics –

years before, at twenty-three, he'd married his mother's forty-one-year-old sister. Hitler himself had little interest in Mussert, a soft-looking man with full cheeks and girlish eyes, but knew that Mussert's willingness to co-operate with the Germans, and the fact that Mussert's brother was a lieutenant-colonel in the Dutch army, could prove useful before long. For his part, Mussert was an ardent nationalist, and didn't want the Netherlands folded into the German Reich, but he naively believed these "allies" could help him in his ultimate goal to rule the Dutch nation.

By 1938, thousands of German Jews had already fled to the Netherlands, regardless of the laws set in place to discourage them: to protect Dutch jobs, foreigners could only work with a permit, and their stay on Dutch soil had to be short. Some moved on to other places soon after arriving, but more kept coming, and by spring, there were so many refugees that the conservative government closed its borders amid a flood of protests by the communist, social democrat, and liberal parties. Events outside Dutch borders added pressure as well. When a Polish Jew killed a German official in Paris, glass flew in Germany. A violent rampage that would come to be called Kristallnacht, or Night of Broken Glass, spread throughout the country and in annexed Austria. Vandals smashed the windows of thousands of Jewish-owned shops, littering the streets with glass; they set synagogues ablaze and desecrated Jewish cemeteries. Jews were hauled into the streets and beaten senseless, or to death. The SS took thirty thousand to concentration camps at Buchenwald, Dachau, and Sachsenhausen, ostensibly to protect them from the people's wrath. Sachsenhausen sat just outside Berlin, and was a formal, geometrically designed institution that until now had housed mainly political opponents of the Nazi regime, and served as a sort of training ground for concentration camp personnel. From here on its role would expand. Set into the iron-grid gates were words that would become infamous: ARBEIT MACHT FREI – Work Makes You Free.

Following the havoc and these subsequent imprisonments, a new stream of refugees entered the Netherlands, with the Dutch government's stipulation that the Jewish community support them. To contain the swell, the government erected a camp near Westerbork in the northeastern province of Drenthe, uncomfortably close to the German border but complete with shops, schools, and facilities for sport and agriculture. The Committee for Jewish Interests footed the bill for the camp, which totalled more than a million guilders. The surrounding fields blazed with lupines in summer, but the bare heath turned to soup when it rained, and the camp was quite purposely set far enough from towns that the refugees' presence wouldn't affect people's daily lives. Even the queen could be accused of a not-in-my-backyard attitude: a more southerly location for the camp, in the beautiful Veluwe region, was nixed because it was just twelve kilometres from Het Loo. It seemed tolerating guests was different than embracing them.

Despite Hitler's promise to respect the Netherlands' neutral position, the Dutch government began to store away great quantities of rice, beans, and sugar. Cor, too, was preparing. She took Gerrit's uniform from the closet and aired it outside, brushing the fabric smooth and buffing the buttons. Next door, Mevrouw Blom beat her carpet, and a cloud of dust motes sparkled in the sunlight as she wryly called over, "Let's hope that won't be necessary," motioning to the uniform. Cor bristled. "What's good for the fatherland," she answered stiffly, "is good for all of us," and she hurried inside with her chin raised.

Upstairs, she hung the uniform in the bedroom and stood back, observing the empty body and sleeves. From here she could see the edge of a fancy framed certificate that hung in the hall, awarded to Gerrit for his exemplary sharpshooting skills for the Bijzondere Vrijwillige Landstorm, an organization formed in recent years to keep peace in case of uprisings or riot. What brooded over Germany was more menacing than scuffles in the streets, and while she'd disapproved of Mevrouw Blom's comment, she didn't want war any more than her neighbour did.

At times on the Tedingerstraat, Cor felt smothered by nonconformity. The Bloms at 63 were friendly enough, but Mevrouw made herself more attractive than was necessary, in Cor's view, and the family

belonged to no church, though they were raising a son and daughter. The
Catholic children on the street tended towards wild behaviour, and
the parents didn't seem to realize the need to be rigorous in every aspect
of life – not to drink it away like the *dronkaard* everyone found so
amusing. She had high hopes that fall when the house on the other side,
59, emptied and was made ready for new tenants. As it turned out,
Henny Cahn and Bep van der Weele didn't fit Cor's mould any more than
the other neighbours – and perhaps less. But Bep clowned over the fence
and Koos laughed and gurgled, responding to her happy, comical face
framed by dark hair. Bep's smile drew Cor, too, and hooked her before she
knew that Bep was divorced from her first husband, that she and Henny
weren't married, that Bep had no interest in church, and in fact had not
even been baptized. Henny was a graphic designer and a photographer –
an artist who'd strayed out of his territory – but his camera wasn't the only
thing that made him an anomaly: the Netherlands had had a large Jewish
population for centuries, but in Leidschendam there were relatively few
Jews – twenty-six out of a population of roughly nine thousand – and now
Henny was one of them. He stood out on the Tedingerstraat, as did Bep,
who was ten years his senior and had two nearly grown children: a daughter, Carla, who lived with her, and a son, Hans, who'd stayed with his
father in The Hague. Though Bep frequently took work as a housekeeper,
she and Henny ignored their own piles of laundry and rolling dust-balls
because there were always better things to do, and Bep's nose was often
stuck in a book.

"My husband hated that," she once told Cor, grinning.

When Bep pressed a book into Cor's hands, Cor accepted it, but
kept it next to her bed, pinned down by her well-thumbed Christian
guide to motherhood. After a suitable time she returned it unread,
along with something more virtuous that she hoped Bep would read.

"God will always wait for you," she told Bep.

"Good," Bep answered. "I'm always late for everything."

Cor let the joke pass, but her will to evangelize stayed strong. She
owed it to God, and to Bep and people like her, though even Gerrit said

she sometimes went too far. The church elders approved of her approach, and said as much at their family visits to Cor and Gerrit's house. Elders of the Gereformeerde Church – a district elder accompanied by another – made the rounds annually, checking in with members of the congregation and encouraging personal disclosures along the lines of a Catholic confession. There was no absolution for one's admissions, but they were kept confidential. In her first years as wife and mother, the meetings were difficult for Cor. She rushed around the house, washing dishes and dusting, eager for the men to arrive but dreading it too. She had the utmost respect for the Church's tradition, and understood this process as an integral part of her faith, but personal conversations did not come easily for her, especially with elders. After they arrived and were seated, she poured tea into the good china cups and passed them around, then took her place beside Gerrit, drawing strength from his nearness.

Around this time patches of eczema appeared on Koos's skin, and Cor became convinced this meant he'd have asthma, like her father and her brother Gerry. Gerrit told her she worried too much, but she knew the difference between fretting without cause and being vigilant. She paid attention to what she saw, and unlike Gerrit, she'd witnessed asthma attacks up close. She rubbed cream on the rough skin, and listened for the first wheezing breath. When the weather was cool and dry, she placed Koos in his bassinette on the balcony so that the fresh air would invigorate his lungs.

When Koos was just one-and-a-half and Rige almost three, Cor delivered a second son. The new baby was named Rokus, which meant "Rough One," but again the name was given only with tradition in mind, since it was Gerrit's father's turn to be *naamgenoot* in the cycle of namesakes. By now, Cor was practised at giving birth, and accustomed to caring for young children, but having Bep next door made her busy life easier. Bep had trained as a nurse, and though she hadn't completed her studies, Cor admired her efforts and respected her opinion, even when it didn't conform with her own. At Bep's insistence, Cor dropped the proper "Mevrouw" she used for most women outside the family, and called her by her first name. Rige called her Tante Bep, and liked that she got down on her knees to play, which was something Cor never made time for. Bep switched easily from chasing a hysterical Koos with a pot on her head, to sitting with Cor at the table, discussing women's rights over hot tea. As a young woman in Middelburg, Zeeland, she'd fallen in with the SDAP, the social democratic labour party, and pushed for women's right to vote. Cor exercised that right to vote for a different party, the more conservative one her Church supported, but she knew it was because of women like Bep that she could choose to do so. Bep was older than Cor, Gerrit, and Henny, and while Cor would never have made the same life choices (divorce, cohabitation, and a life outside the Church), an honest friendship had grown. She felt she could talk with Bep all day, and realized she'd been starving for this sort of interaction since leaving her sisters and friend Marie in Overschie. She wished she could bring Bep around to God. The closer their friendship, the more vital this seemed.

Henny was an enigma, and quite unlike anyone Cor had ever known. He'd once been a busker – he played the guitar, and like Gerrit, had a beautiful singing voice. He said his family had hoped he'd be lead singer in the synagogue one day – but he'd long ago shunned the strict rules of his faith, and claimed he felt like a Jew but "in my own way." Cor turned those kinds of comments around and around in her mind, as they made no sense to her. But she liked this peculiar man. He was an idealist whose critical thinking she found fascinating, even if she often disagreed with him, and he had an intense, challenging gaze that attracted women wherever he went. Cor watched the coquettish behaviour of her neighbours in the Tedingerstraat, and frowned upon it, but Bep found the women amusing. "Look – even *de prater* loves him," she told Cor, nodding towards the street, where a coarse, thick-set woman had stopped to pose for Henny's camera, smoothing her greasy curls with one hand. Cor grimaced. "The prattler" lived one block over on the Broekweg, but she was a fixture in the neighbourhood, like the *dronkaard*. Distinctly unladylike, she waddled from street to street in wrinkled clothes and a dirty apron, talking too loudly and too long with anyone she met. She'd earned her nickname, as had the drunkard and the long skinny boy everyone called *komkommer*, or cucumber – the monikers were full of truth and not meant to be malicious, but even so, Cor didn't use them.

Henny played along with *de prater*'s antics, Cor noticed, and snapped her likeness. He was an accomplished photographer, happiest when his camera was within reach, and she'd become accustomed to seeing him on his belly, the viewfinder pressed to his eye – as often as not, one of her own family was the focus of his lens. There would be no photographs of baby Koos had Henny Cahn not moved in next door. With his treasured Leica camera, he zoomed in on Koos's big round head and dimpled cheek, on his chubby body clad in a sleeper Moeder den Hartog had made. A toy elephant on wheels was hooked over the edge of his playpen, and Koos looked past it and grinned up at his new friend. Henny winked. The laws that would forbid him to enter this house had yet to take hold in the Netherlands.

In August, Juliana and Bernhard welcomed their second daughter, Irene, the Greek name for peace. Bernhard's new best friend – a paid companion named Willem Röell, whose family had worked for the royal house for generations – had a wife and child who got on well with Juliana and Beatrix, and the two couples often discussed the troubling times. Though worlds apart from Cor and Gerrit in status, they had similar parental concerns, and wondered how the coming years would affect their children. Already, Germany had followed its annexation of Austria with that of most of Czechoslovakia, and tension was mounting in Europe. The Dutch government had mobilized its forces, and surveillance posts would soon appear in unlikely places, including the small tower that graced the roof of Emmaschool. Gerrit's brother still worked there, and now Rige attended the school's kindergarten. A Luchtbeschermingsdienst, or Air Protection Service, had been organized in every municipality; it acted as a round-the-clock watch for air raids, and loosely policed a nationwide blackout meant to deter potential bombers. Though the blackout was not yet strictly enforced, at nighttime, most blinds and curtains were pulled closed to the outside, where street lamps remained unlit and the moon and stars provided the only illumination. From the balconies at Bep and Henny's, the den Hartogs', and the Bloms' next door, the three distant windmills in the Driemanspolder could barely be seen in the darkness.

Near month's end, Queen Wilhelmina and King Leopold III of Belgium offered to act with other leaders as mediators between the Germans and the Poles, whose border disputes threatened to explode, but later Wilhelmina would admit, "Our good intentions only annoyed our future allies." Two days following, as the queen celebrated her fifty-ninth birthday, Germany's invasion of Poland seemed imminent. She eyed the high officials who'd joined her for dinner and asked who'd read Hitler's book, *Mein Kampf*, the sales of which had made him a millionaire. They should know, she suggested, what Hitler thought of Poles, among others: the *untermensch*, he called them, an "inferior people." The next morning, Hitler's soldiers brutalized Poland from the west, north, and south, while the Netherlands lay "asleep on the pillow called neutrality," as the queen would later write. Soon afterwards, Britain and France declared war on Germany, drawing most of the Commonwealth into battle. But still the Netherlands refused official alliances and advanced promises of aid. If an invasion came, the country would stand alone.

When Gerrit's regiment was mobilized in preparation for war, he kissed Cor and the children and bade his parents goodbye, leaving the *tuin* in the care of his father. Wearing the uniform Cor had painstakingly brushed and cleaned, he was now a corporal in the Twenty-Eighth Infantry Regiment, part of a makeshift army of gardeners, fishermen, and peddlers, and one of many who rationalized that no shots would be fired. Nevertheless, fear and sadness knotted in his stomach and stayed with him all the way to his post near Utrecht, where he billeted with a family in Tuindorp. The children there reminded him of Koos and Rige, young enough that they grew and learned daily, and he was sick at the thought of missing such changes. Rokus was only a few months old and would seem like a different boy each time Gerrit returned on leave for short visits. Cor was still waking with Rokus several times a night, and he knew from the rings beneath her eyes that she was exhausted. He was glad Bep was next door, and that his mother was just downstairs. Cor sometimes interpreted Moeder's help as interference, but he hoped she would see her way past that. The two women were more stubborn than was good for them, and he wondered if little Rige, such a gentle child, would follow in their footsteps.

Thirty years old now, Gerrit belonged to the "second army," full of men well past the draft age. For years, their uniforms and all things related to war had been packed in mothballs, kept at home in readiness for something they never expected to happen. On balding heads, their caps looked less jaunty than they once had, and their jackets and pants strained at the seams and buttons. As fall turned to a particularly severe winter, and the men huddled together playing cards and betting on the games, Gerrit stood apart, observing as some lost weeks of wages, and wondering what their families would do when no money came home. With Rige's school picture safe in his pocket, he took his turn on sentry duty, watching the moonlight play on the water and alert for the enemy.

While the rest of Europe had been holding its breath, a tradesman with a shock of black hair had toiled quietly in the heart of Munich. Working alone over the course of a year, the wiry, determined little man, Johann

Georg Elser, repeatedly visited the cavernous Burgerbrau beer cellar, eating his dinner amid the smoky revelry, paying his bill, and then slipping through the cloakroom and into a broom closet, where he waited until closing time. For each visit, he wore dark clothes that rendered him innocuous in the crowded, dank surroundings. After hours, when the Burgerbrau grew silent, he inched forward his plan, prying the wood cladding from one of the brick pillars inside the hall and painstakingly boring a hole. By November, the hole was large enough for his creation: into the hidden cavity he placed explosives concealed in the workings of old clocks.

While Elser put the finishing touches on his plan in Berlin, across the border in the province of Groningen, a German intelligence officer made a large purchase of Dutch army uniforms and was arrested trying to smuggle them into Germany. Dutch newspapers ran cartoons lampooning the corpulent Hermann Goering, Hitler's second-in-command, disguised as a policeman and a streetcar driver. But the caricatures were bluster, and the revelation of the latest Nazi outrage was discussed at auction, after church, and on every street corner. Prince Bernhard's friends in Germany warned him that Hitler planned to invade the Netherlands and Belgium any day, and in The Hague, Wilhelmina and Leopold consulted into the wee hours at the queen's palace, again determined to mediate talks between the Allied powers and Germany before the violence spilled into western Europe. France and England agreed they'd consider the offer for talks, and Hitler was expected to do the same, though the German press, now entirely under Goebbels' meticulous control, played up what it called the Netherlands' spineless neutrality. Ears pricked, the optimistic waited for Hitler's response, expected on November 8, when he would deliver an annual address to old-guard Nazis at the Burgerbrau.

He entered the beer hall to loud German marching music and the cheers of thousands. Framed by swastika banners, Hitler mouthed his anti-England sentiments from the podium, and his words were broadcast across German airwaves. He said nothing about Wilhelmina and

Leopold's offer – as Georg's clocks made their countdown in the pillar beside him – and because of the heavy fog that night, he cut short his speech in order to take the train rather than the plane back to Berlin. So when Georg's bomb exploded, the hall collapsed, killing a waitress and seven Nazis, and injuring sixty-three more – but the target was already far from the scene of the crime, on board the train with Goebbels. Worse still for the would-be assassin, Georg Elser was detained at the Swiss border because his passport had expired, and the contents of his suit pockets betrayed him: a postcard of the Burgerbrau's inner rooms, pieces of a fuse, and a pair of pliers. But even under torture, he insisted he'd acted alone in his attempt on Hitler's life.

Wilhelmina gritted her teeth and penned a courteous message to Hitler, congratulating him on surviving the explosion. But SS Chief Heinrich Himmler, along with Goebbels and the führer himself, soon announced a convoluted theory that the Burgerbrau incident was really a British plot pulled off with Dutch assistance. The Hague, they charged, was the headquarters for the British Intelligence Service for Western Europe, which had undoubtedly funded the attack. How could the Netherlands be neutral, they asked, if it harboured the BIS? In the pages of his diary, Goebbels relished the anxiety building within the Netherlands, and the "twilight of the neutrals."

The country's precarious position had become glaringly obvious. Days after Elser's attempt, as Wilhelmina's peace offer evaporated, the queen received a telegram from President Franklin Roosevelt, a man of distant Dutch ancestry who now offered the royal family safe haven in the United States. But such a drastic move didn't yet seem necessary. The invasion Bernhard's friends warned him of didn't happen when they said it would, although the likeliness grew alongside the tension. Within weeks, the queen made her second appearance in full regalia on the cover of *Time*. Four years earlier the magazine had recognized her as the world's wealthiest woman. Now the headline read WORRIED QUEEN.

After a long winter in the Tuindorp area, digging trenches, building artillery platforms, and generally preparing for battle, Gerrit and his unit were ordered south in mid-April. Every ditch and tree on the Tuindorp terrain had become known ground to the men stationed there, and Hoekse Waard island was very different territory. With his fellow soldiers, Gerrit stayed at a farm, bunking in the barn, but it wasn't the accommodation that disheartened him. The island was clearly not battle-ready; it lacked defence works and concrete shelters, and so the soldiers set to work building bunkers and platforms for heavy artillery. But shortly after they began, the command came to stop, and the men sat idly.

The time passed slowly, and made Gerrit miss his family more. He thought of Cor at home, probably saying goodbye to Bep and Henny, for on his last weekend leave, he'd discovered a small scandal had erupted on the Tedingerstraat: the landlord had found out Bep and Henny weren't married and evicted them. The couple had secured a place in Voorburg, but while their new apartment on KoninginWilhelminalaan was only a few kilometres away, he knew Cor would miss seeing them every day, and that she'd fret they'd somehow go further astray without her. "If Bep would accept Jesus," she'd told him, "marry Henny, and bring him to the faith, God would protect all of them." Gerrit smirked, recalling her words. He remembered Henny saying that he was a Jew in his own way, and he knew it was wishful thinking on Cor's part to expect some grand Gereformeerde conversion. But it was a sentiment he'd heard her express many times, and he could see the couple now, smiling at Cor as she lectured, thinking she meant well but was mis-informed. He chuckled to himself imagining that they'd left town to avoid her incessant evangelizing – a joke he'd never share with Cor. Of course there was a serious side to the move. He liked Bep and Henny, and it had comforted him knowing they were next door while he was away from his family. His parents were still there, and Cor had even told him, "Your mother comes up often," but the full stop that followed the sentence implied not much had changed between the women.

But back at home, upstairs and down, both wife and mother prayed for Gerrit, and for the thousands of other inexperienced soldiers guarding the country. Cor had only recently realized she'd become pregnant on Gerrit's last leave. Her body had barely had a chance to recover from the last child, Rokus, before the new one took root, but this was no time to distract Gerrit with the information. She wondered if the men at their posts knew how easily Norway and Denmark had been invaded weeks before. She herself had heard it on the radio, conscious of how strange it felt to listen to Gerrit's prize possession alone. When he was seated there with her, she let her mind wander if the news was grim, knowing he'd summarize later; but in his absence she listened intently, as if it were a responsibility, one of many she'd taken on while he was gone. He didn't know it, but she surprised herself by feeling glad of her in-laws' company, their presence reassuringly normal in abnormal times. They left her alone, though, while she listened to the radio, sensing that it was her connection to their son, and therefore private. Sometimes Cor sat, one hand resting on the warm cabinet, wishing that some message from him could reach her over the airwaves. *Cor, I'm fine. Stop worrying.* There was of course no such message, only scraps of bad news that foreshadowed more bad news: the Dutch government had declared a state of emergency and arrested leading members of the NSB, but the slippery Anton Mussert had gone into hiding. The Germans were powerful, everyone knew, with or without his help.

In more prestigious circles, warnings sent again by Bernhard's friends took on a new urgency. After months of alarms that had come to nothing, Bernhard doubted his sources were trustworthy, but as clusters of German troops ringed the border, it seemed prudent to move his young family from Soestdijk Palace near Amersfoort to The Hague with the queen. As they pulled away from the palace, his friend Willem Röell stood on the steps, waving. They'd already agreed that in the event of an invasion, their wives and children would leave the country, but Bernhard and Willem would take up arms.

On the evening of May 9, 1940, the population listened to the prime minister's much-anticipated radio address. There would be no invasion, he stated. Hours later, as dawn approached, four thousand paratroopers dropped out of a clear sky onto railroad bridges and highways, and the Wehrmacht moved over the border. The worst fears of Westerbork's seven hundred German-Jewish refugees had come true. Terrified, they followed an evacuation plan previously set out by the camp's home secretary, and boarded a train to the southwestern province of Zeeland, near the Belgian border, where they hoped to sail for England – but the rail bridge en route was blown up before they could cross it, and the refugees raced due north, getting as far as Leeuwarden before the fight was lost. They were housed temporarily with families in the area, but by the end of May, they'd be back in Drenthe province at Camp Westerbork, at the mercy of those they'd tried to escape.

In the Leidschendam area, bombs fell in the meadows by the Vlietweg. Windows rattled; houses shook from the impact. Parachutists fell to their deaths on the pavement, or landed safely and moved into action. At first people didn't understand the danger, and asked each other if it meant war. Peering out their windows, they wondered if they should go to work, or if the trams would be running. An old woman stormed out of her house and scolded a soldier for traipsing through her garden and wrecking the flowers blooming there. And two boys in Voorburg ran to help a German parachutist who had landed in the Vliet, but he hollered at them – German words they didn't understand – and they hurried away.

At the house on the Tedingerstraat, Rige stood on the stairs in her nightgown, watching her Opa Rochus, who'd been ready for the day in his gardening clothes when the parachutes descended. He sat at the head of her baby brother's cradle in the front room, pipe in his mouth, hands resting on the arms of his chair. He said nothing, but watching his calm, determined expression made Rige feel better, as her mother, upstairs, paced the floor, moving from window to window with Koos following. Her oma was making coffee and laying out an early breakfast, since all of them were up now except baby Rokus. Rige looked at the intricate smocking and the tiny flowers embroidered on the cradle's cover, and the pockets that held a soft hairbrush, ointments, and powders. She wondered how a baby could sleep through the drone of the planes and the sudden airless quality of a house that vibrated with fear. She padded through the kitchen to the back door, and her oma stroked her hair as she passed. The planes were like giant birds, flying so low that Piet and Corrie Blom, watching from their yard next door, ducked as they passed. Rige thought of her father. Already the one visit she'd made to "the army place" back in the fall was a distant memory. She and her mother had been driven by Oom Tom in a black car. The chocolate milk in the trunk was a treat for her father, but the jars had broken and the milk spilled out. She remembered herself in a sandy trench, and then again at a long wooden table, eating red beets and bacon from an aluminum plate. She'd given him her first school photograph – an image of her at a desk, holding a cloth ball, but not smiling because she missed her father. And he had put it in the pocket of his uniform and winked. "For safekeeping," he'd said.

In Leidschendam and throughout the country, sheets of coloured paper fluttered to the ground alongside the paratroopers. The messages, printed in a clumsy mix of Dutch and German, read:

> Warning!
> To the People of the Netherlands!
> Do not join a war you did not enter!
> Do not destroy your own beautiful land, but preserve
> peace and order!
> Citizens, if you are caught in acts of sabotage, you will
> receive the death penalty!
> People of the Netherlands, we warn you!

Few had time to stop and read. At Huis ten Bosch near The Hague, the palace guard shot at an aircraft and it crashed nearby, but the woods ringing the palace were already dotted with German soldiers. One elite group of paratroopers had a special purpose – to float into Huis ten Bosch and capture the queen – but Wilhelmina and the royal family had heeded the advice of military Commander-in-Chief General Henri Gerard Winkelman, and in doing so, slipped the trap. They were whisked by car from the palace's dangerous seclusion to Noordeinde, the royal residence buried within the city. With the acting skill of a good mother, Juliana joked with Beatrix as they drove, keeping her distracted, though Bernhard rode beside them with a sub-machine gun in his lap. It was, the queen later wrote, "an adventurous journey; confusion everywhere, crowds and traffic jams and bewil-dered soldiers, who after their first experience of battle with the enemy paratroopers were hardly able to distinguish between friend and foe." People recalled the reports last year of huge quantities of Dutch army uniforms being smuggled into Germany, and though the suspects had been arrested, panicky gossip persisted that German sol-diers were arriving incognito, dressed not just in Dutch uniforms, but as priests and nuns.

Once in town, Wilhelmina chafed at being restricted to Noordeinde – or rather the two small rooms that formed their shelter within the palace, unusual accommodations for a queen. That night, she, Juliana, and Bernhard would sleep fully dressed on mattresses on the floor, along with Willem Röell's wife Martine, the children, and their nanny. She wondered what good she could do from here, and only half-believed the reports of skirmishes still taking place in the streets. It was her duty to be seen in town, to go out and offer encouragement to her people, to visit the wounded, as she had done so often in times of disaster, and she was known, by now, for a lifetime of pulling on her rubber boots and wading out to commiserate with victims of floods. But when snipers shot from the windows of a café across the way, the gravity of the situation crystallized. A bullet narrowly missed the nanny, and Bernhard ran with his gun to the second floor of the palace, firing back and smashing the café's windows.

During a quiet spell in these tense days, Bernhard photographed the queen in the back garden with Juliana and the little princesses. Wilhelmina sat on the ground in her coat, slumped against the wall. She fully expected to be at her post in Noordeinde until England answered her appeal for help in turning the Germans back, but the military's commander brought bleak reports, and Wilhelmina decided to send her family to safety across the English Channel. Martine Röell and her daughter would go too, but Wilhelmina would stay behind; she harboured a romantic image of herself as a warrior queen, fighting alongside her soldiers in the tradition of her forefather, Willem of Orange. It was he who had adopted the motto *Je Maintiendrai* – I will maintain – a sentiment passed down through the royal generations. Bernhard, too, claimed that he preferred to stay – fulfilling his plan with Willem Röell – but in the end, the queen insisted he accompany his wife and children to England. Packed in a cardboard box, the crown jewels went with them on the risky journey, and as the boat left the harbour for England, a bomb dropped yards away. Still, with his movie camera, Bernhard filmed their departure, and caught Beatrix giving him a chubby thumbs-up.

In the early hours of May 13, the queen's commander reported that a German tank column was just hours from Rotterdam, The Hague's neighbour. He advised her to flee to Zeeland, just as the Westerbork refugees had tried to do. At half-past nine, preceded by a single police car, and with only a few belongings crammed into a suitcase she'd packed herself, Queen Wilhelmina departed in an armoured truck. She boarded a British destroyer for Zeeland, but its commander couldn't make contact with the allies stationed in that region, which turned out to be under heavy attack by the Germans. As Wilhelmina recounts in her autobiography, she held a "miniature war council in lifejackets" and decided to go to England. She knew that news of her flight would be fodder for Nazi propaganda, and that some of those she left behind would believe she'd willingly deserted them. Furthermore, she understood the tremendous consequences for her country should the Germans take control. But she saw few options. She'd already asked her secretaries general to stay on as heads of their ministries in the event of a takeover, and to help maintain peace and order for the people's sake, and with that in mind, Wilhelmina set out into the North Sea, a helmet crushing her signature hat. Just that week she'd been declared the longest-reigning monarch in the Dutch dynasty, and today it seemed her throne had been pulled out from under her.

TWO

The Lettuce King Soldier
MAY 1940

VERY LITTLE IS LEFT of Gerrit's time as a soldier, but in the handful of photographs he kept of his section, he is easy to find because his cap angles insistently to the left, and his ears fan out beneath it. To those who knew him, the uniform looks strange on this peaceful man, but the face and stance are proud, and show a gardener in a soldier's disguise: *de Sla Koning* – the Lettuce King – or so the other growers had called him at auction.

Aside from the pictures, there's a small booklet that lays out the rules of combat, and wound around its spine, the rope of his ID tag, which lists his particulars above and below perforations in the metal. There is also an official document that shows he enlisted at nineteen, the year after he first skated past Cor. A small metal lockbox contains a piecemeal collection of coins and three bullets, though Gerrit's children never saw him shoot a gun. Looking through the box triggers a memory of a grenade that sat on the living room mantel after the war, but none of the siblings knows the story that went with it, or what became of the strange memento. Also missing among Gerrit's own possessions is probable evidence of his resistance work, found in the town's archives long after his death. In a booklet called "Resistance in Leidschendam 1940–1945," Gerrit's name appears on a list of men from a local branch of the Binnenlandse Strijdkrachten, or BS. This was the underground organization headed by Prince Bernhard, charged with assisting the approaching Allies during the final months of liberation. Gerrit's name is third from the top, beside the title Section Commander, but his children never knew of his official involvement. Likewise, throughout their lives they wrongly assumed that he saw no action at the beginning of the war, when the Germans invaded.

His regiment formed part of Group Kil, named for the river that separates Hoekse Waard from Dordrecht Island, and was responsible for guarding the ferry crossing between the two. The Moerdijk bridges were a short distance south, providing the only southern access to so-called Fortress Holland, the western part of the country that contained its biggest cities. They spanned the Hollands Diep, a place where the rivers Maas and Waal converged to spill out to the North Sea. One was an old rail bridge, the other the new motor bridge recently opened by Queen Wilhelmina. It stretched like a braid of steel over the water, a harsh addition to the leafy trees and verdant plains of South Holland. To the northwest, in a zigzagging line, lay Overschie, Rotterdam, The Hague, Rijswijk, Voorburg, and Leidschendam. Gerrit's entire family was there, in those inner-fortress rooms he'd been charged with protecting, and he knew the importance of his position.

Before the battles began, the flat, rural terrain around him was green with new spring grass. Sheep grazed on the tops of dikes, and buttercups nodded in the breeze. From the stone watertower, their

lookout, Gerrit could see the tidy farmhouses across the Kil, and fields
that brought to mind the garden in Leidschendam, where his father
worked alone through the busy spring – too much work, he knew, for an
old man whose muscles were starting to wither. Gerrit's own backaches,
likely caused by rheumatism, were bad enough, and he was more than
thirty years younger. He pictured Vader, pipe resting in the perpetual
groove it had caused in his lip, ear nibbled away from too many years in
the sun. Gerrit thought of how Vader had told him not to worry, using his
best stern-father voice, which no longer worked now that Gerrit had one
of his own. The *tuin*, and more importantly the family, would be fine in
his absence, Vader had assured him on his last furlough. Cor had said the
same, but too briskly, with her spine too straight and her jaw clenched as
he'd kissed her goodbye. For her own sake he hadn't held her too long; he
knew how important it was to her that she keep her composure – she had
never expressed that in words, but he understood her better as the years
wore on, and saw how she protected herself from the pain of too much
tenderness. So she hadn't said, *I'll miss you*, and neither had he.

His eyes strayed to the houses across the Kil, inhabited, like his, by
women, children, and men too old to fight. Throughout the area, people
had dug crawlspaces into which they'd retreat if the fighting began. But
in such marshy land, cellars could only be so deep before they'd pool
with water. Faces here had become familiar in the last while: the
teenage son of a farmer who billeted some of the men; and an eleven-
year-old rascal who rode on the motorcycle of the soldier delivering the
mail. He hoped both these boys would lose their curiosity if a war
started, but he told himself it was unlikely the Germans would attack.
After all, a month had passed since the Denmark and Norway inva-
sions; no furloughs had been cancelled, and there was no ammunition
in Gerrit's gun. Soldiers' cartridges, carefully counted, lay in neat
rows in a locked storage shelter.

On May 6, after weeks of idleness, Group Kil received orders to
resume the work that had been halted earlier on the bunkers and artillery
platforms, and the very next day, before much had been accomplished,

the command came to place obstructions and heavy machine guns at strategic points on Dordrecht Island. Gerrit's eyes searched the sky for enemy planes, and he and the men around him grew nervous. They set explosives beneath bridges, but no order came to wire them, and while the High Command notified other groups to be on strict watch, this warning never reached Group Kil. The tension settled.

By this time, the Netherlands had not fought a war in 145 years, and there was a natural inclination to believe none would be fought now. After the Great War, popular opinion had held that the newly formed League of Nations would maintain peace, so many in the Netherlands had argued for the dissolution of the military altogether – an idea that luckily was ignored. Still, by 1939, the Dutch forces were woefully inadequate, with much of their equipment dating back to the last century. And though the rise of the Nazis had at last forced dissenters to recognize the need for improvements, the Netherlands had no armaments industries, and foreign factories were overrun with orders. Naively, tenaciously, the Dutch clung to their declaration of neutrality, and counted on honour to protect them. The hastily cobbled army possessed twenty-six armoured cars, no tanks, and a mere fraction of the anti-aircraft guns that the government had deemed essential for war.

Dutch commanders recognized the army couldn't defend all of its territory, and thus concentrated their defence at a series of natural barriers consisting of bridges and dikes, wide bodies of water, and forested hills. The northernmost was the Afsluitdijk, a thirty-kilometre stretch of dike that sealed off the Zuiderzee, an arm of the North Sea. The centre was Grebbeberg, forested high-ground with plenty of options for defence. The southernmost was the area surrounding the gleaming steel of the twin Moerdijk bridges, near where Gerrit waited with the other men of his regiment. Water was the age-old defence of the Dutch; they'd flood the dikes to push back the enemy, and then they'd hold the bridges. They never suspected that the Germans would fall out of the sky.

When that moment came, the soldiers were unprepared. While troops close to the border reported suspicious activity on the German side throughout the evening of May 9, the Dutch High Command didn't extend these warnings to its interior commanding officers in Fortress Holland, who after all were far from the border, their troops forming a last line of defence. The German planes crossing in great numbers early that morning seemed to be headed for England, and the troops were not told to go to full readiness. When the planes turned back, strewing bombs and paratroopers over the Netherlands, Dutch soldiers were still in their pyjamas. One among many, Gerrit scrambled out of his cot at the shouts of the officers. Still dazed from sleep, he fumbled for his uniform, his weapon, and the ammunition he didn't yet have, while the Germans landed around them. For the smallest moment he was mesmerized by the sight of the parachutes floating down – beautiful in a way, with the sky brightening behind them.

The heavy drone of low-flying transport planes woke people all over Fortress Holland, and they rushed into the streets in their nightclothes to see German troops drop from the gaping hatches of planes. Billowing white parachutes filled the sky over The Hague's three airfields, over Rotterdam and the Moerdijk bridges south of Gerrit's station. Yet more paratroopers landed throughout Dordrecht Island, and in the city of Dordrecht itself, at the Zwijndrecht bridges that led to Rotterdam. Dordrecht's garrison commander was Lieutenant-Colonel Josephus Mussert, whose brother Anton headed the pro-Nazi NSB party. For reasons unexplained, Mussert arrived late to his post on this crucial day, and so no organized defence could be made until mid-morning. After a series of skirmishes, the Germans captured the Zwijndrecht bridges.

At the artillery headquarters in the village of Amstelwijck, less than three kilometres from Gerrit's location across the river Kil at 's-Gravendeel, confusion reigned. The communication lines to Mussert had been severed, and the soldiers, holding a position in a small wood surrounding their command post, were still without ammunition. The officer in charge, Major van Hoek, sent a party to retrieve it from the basement of the headquarters' villa, and dodging enemy fire, the men returned with the goods. Van Hoek sent an urgent message to Group Kil's commander, Major D.P. Ravelli in Strijen, that two hundred German parachutists were closing in from all directions, and Ravelli assured him reinforcements would come. But he warned van Hoek that parachutists had landed in Dutch uniforms and farmers' clothes. When in doubt about a soldier's identity, Ravelli instructed, shoot.

No reinforcements arrived, and van Hoek's losses that morning were significant. The Germans surrounded the Amstelwijck command post, and slipped two hand grenades through the periscope hole of the concrete shelter. The explosion filled the room with smoke and knocked the lights out. Men dove for cover and the telephone switchboard crashed to the floor. Van Hoek and his men stumbled to the exit, but the first ones through the door were shot. The rest put their hands in the air, and became prisoners of war.

As van Hoek surrendered in Amstelwijck, Gerrit's company waited on the other side of the river Kil for the trucks that would take them to the ferry. Throughout the early morning they'd watched transport planes drop human cargo in the distance, and heard the report of guns and artillery. Hands more at ease gripping hoes or the handles of a barrow now gripped rifles, and the men sat quietly. Gerrit noticed the many things that made the day seem ordinary as it came to life around him – the smell of spring, the sun rising – but other details had the surreal quality of dreams. A priest arrived on a bicycle, Bible strapped to the back rack. "Could the Catholics gather for a moment?" he called to the troops in a clear voice at odds with his ashen face and tangled hair. "Pray for repentance," he told them as they kneeled on the grass around him, "and I will give you the Holy Absolution." Gerrit watched the ritual, but turned away when he saw some of the men sobbing as they crossed themselves. The priest climbed back on his bicycle, called "God bless" to the soldiers, and wheeled off to find more of his own. And so the day passed.

When Gerrit's company eventually crossed the river that afternoon, the men formed a bridgehead at Wieldrecht, not far from Amstelwijck, but the expected reinforcements – the same ones Ravelli had promised van Hoek – were delayed by enemy fire from occupied farms along the riverbanks, and the wait grew long. When the supporting troops finally arrived, they brought with them two sections of heavy machine guns, and as the sun tilted in the evening sky, Group Kil opened fire on Amstelwijck, believing the Germans still there. By radio, the watchtower on Hoekse Waard reported success: a farm building in flames. Gerrit thought of the animals that might have been in the barns; he remembered the sheep grazing each morning before this one, a constant sight. With his fellow soldiers, he proceeded slowly through the ditches to Amstelwijck, expecting the enemy with every step.

Instead, they found the villa headquarters eerily quiet, its windows blown out and debris scattered over its grounds. In the nearby wood the command post stood empty. The Germans were long gone, and only casualties remained. Gerrit's legs trembled. He could see one Dutch soldier on his back, an arm thrown forward; another slumped beside the doorway, his head hanging to the side. Others lay farther off, under the trees, where the leaves rustled in the breeze. The setting sun shone through the branches and made a pattern on their still bodies. Someone would snap off one end of the metal tags that hung around the soldiers' necks to gather the identification of the fallen, and Gerrit thought of his own against his skin – HARTOG, DEN, GERRIT – and his regiment number below. Names would be entered in a log, and the few soldiers who remained behind as a defence screen when Group Kil moved on would dig their graves and lay wildflowers on top of them. He did not want to stay to bury the bodies, he thought shamefully. Nor did he want to go forward.

He was relieved when Major Ravelli said they'd stay at Amstelwijck for a hot meal and a night's rest. It was wiser, thought the major, to wait for daylight to begin the march north than to cross canals in the pitch dark. But Ravelli's superior disagreed: at sunrise, the men would be easy targets for German planes. Thus Ravelli was ordered to advance immediately and retake the Zwijndrecht bridges at Dordrecht city. At eleven o'clock at night, they started north, but soon Ravelli changed the route, choosing one he presumed would meet less resistance. He bicycled at the head of the battalion in the crisp, clear night, and Gerrit's company travelled just fifty metres behind the vanguard.

As the first troops passed the Zeehaven harbour, machine-gun fire erupted in the blackness. The men of the vanguard took what cover they could, and the shooting stopped. Again Ravelli decided to await daylight, and leaving the column in its vulnerable position, went on foot with his adjutant to inform the others of his decision. In the small space between the vanguard and Gerrit's company, a stray shot was fired, and it killed the adjutant instantly. Major Ravelli repeated his order to stay put.

Gerrit's company had found better shelter behind a café and a villa on the Glazenstraat, parallel to the main road. He lay with his rifle beside him, moving his head from side to side to stretch the stiff muscles in his neck. His back throbbed on the hard ground. By moonlight he could see the signs on the café's brick wall that advertised coffee and tea and cookies, and that made him think of his brother-in-law, Jacques, who worked for a company that made biscuits, and who'd been just over the age limit for fighting a war. "Really it's my blue blood," he'd cracked months earlier. Gerrit closed his eyes, thinking he wouldn't be able to sleep, but he drifted off almost immediately. He dreamed of Jacques beside him, stretched long on the grass, his giant feet next to Gerrit's smaller ones. The dream felt good until his vantage point changed and he spun upwards, then looked down on himself and his brother-in-law, two corpses with grey skin against green uniforms. He started awake to a burst of gunfire, and light-markers streaking the sky, and then again the night fell quiet. An owl hooted from a branch high above him, and he slept in fits and starts.

Just before first light, intense machine-gun fire shattered the stillness. Trained though he was as a sharpshooter, Gerrit's finger shook on his trigger as he and his unit returned fire. In the semi-dark he could barely see where to shoot. Then the lieutenant was shouting, and from the main road, the vanguard troops came running towards them. A man cried, "Go back, go back!" and Gerrit crouched at the base of a tree, thinking, *Go back where?* and again heard the rattle of machine-gun fire, saw someone fall near him. He turned and ran with the others, not stopping until he found cover in the woods near the Zeehaven harbour. He peered through the trees and could just make out the river glistening. On his knees alongside some of the other men from his company, his pulse slowed, and the breath came less raggedly from his lungs. Incredibly, his hand still clutched his rifle. Behind him, twenty-one Dutchmen lay dead, sprawled along the roadway; later the Germans would record their triumph with a camera.

Overnight, during the ambush on Gerrit's regiment, a battalion of the bicycled Light Division had crossed the Merwede River east of Dordrecht and reported to Lieutenant-Colonel Mussert, who'd ordered them to take Amstelwijck. But when they arrived at the village they'd found it already in Dutch hands – the rear guard left by Ravelli to bury the dead and hold the area. Mussert's next command sent them to Zeehaven with orders to clear it of the enemy, with no warning that Ravelli's troops were already there, although Ravelli had reported his position. In the meantime, Ravelli gathered his haggard battalions together and at Zeehaven formed a defensive screen against the pursuing Germans. Not expecting the Light Division troops – who in turn didn't expect his – each group fired on the other, until, through binoculars, Ravelli spotted the Dutch uniforms. On Ravelli's orders, a soldier nervously lifted his bugle to his lips to blow the Dutch national anthem. The tentative notes of "*Wilhelmus*" sounded out amid gunfire, and the stunned troops stopped shooting. After further contact with Mussert, the men of the Light Division cycled east, and Ravelli charged north to attack the Germans at the Zwijndrecht bridges.

Shortly after noon on this second day of fighting, with almost no sleep and little food, the deaths of their comrades a fresh horror, Gerrit and the rest of his company marched towards the bridges. Gerrit by now was tired, hungry, and, most of all, scared. He thought he might sleep standing up, lulled by the marching rhythm, and kept imagining he'd seen the priest cycling ahead, in the vulnerable open road. Before long, the space for daydreams vanished, and his group came under an attack so sudden and so fierce that, amid heavy gunfire and screaming, men broke rank in droves. As they retreated into the terrain near the Zeehaven harbour, Ravelli's shouts for them to hold their positions faded behind them. In vain, Ravelli tried to stop other sections from withdrawing, and with his officers just managed to organize a thin line of resistance.

As he stood with his remaining soldiers, an odd sight appeared on the dike road, marching from the enemy's direction: a column of Dutch soldiers waving white flags and calling out "Don't shoot!" and *Oranje boven!*" Orange above all! Assuming Mussert had sent reinforcements, Ravelli led his officers towards the men, not pausing to question why the new arrivals were unarmed, or why they made no further movement forward on the raised roadway. Major Ravelli only recognized the treachery when the Germans clambered up from behind the grassy bank with weapons levelled. The flag-bearers were no more than decoys – the very men captured from the earlier attack on the villa at Amstelwijck – forced along the dike road by the Germans travelling out of sight below them. Using human bait, the Germans took another cache of prisoners.

If Gerrit had already fled by the time Ravelli and his officers were captured, he'd have made it to the crossing at Wieldrecht, and been ferried to relative safety on the other side of the Kil. But not all of the company's soldiers went south straightaway. Others rejoined the remnants of their group near the Zeehaven harbour, where the most senior officer, Captain J.A. Schouten, assumed command and eventually led them south, back to Wieldrecht where the first group had gone. By now, however, it was late afternoon, and the men waited nervously while Schouten crossed the river Kil in a small boat to request that the large ferry come to transport the company. But the captain returned with bad news: the ferry wouldn't sail, and the men had to hold their weak position, backs to the water, in anticipation of Mussert's Light Division capturing Dordrecht. If and when that happened, the ferry would become an important possession. Support should arrive in the morning, Captain Schouten told the men, but his tone was not convincing.

Then, as Schouten moved his small force into position, heavy fire flew from the farms and houses nearby, which unbeknownst to the men had been taken over by German soldiers before they'd arrived. The situation quickly turned chaotic, as some of the Dutch artillery fire lobbed across the Kil fell perilously close to the men. The German troops had confidence enough to advance, and their commander called to Schouten's group to surrender. Instead, the captain shot and killed three German soldiers, then was shot in the head himself.

Only a handful of men managed to get away. They dove into the cold river and swam across the Kil to safety, ducking underwater to avoid enemy bullets, and weighed down by their boots and uniforms. Most likely, Gerrit was not among them; he never swam a stroke in his life, before or after that day, and the Kil was and is a wide river with a strong current. So here again Gerrit's true fate breaks into possibilities.

Back at Dordrecht, the Light Division faltered, and the island was lost to the Germans. Lieutenant-Colonel Mussert looked suspect for making not just poor, but shady decisions that might have been influenced by his brother Anton. As an army officer, Josephus Mussert couldn't belong to a political party, but people in the Dordrecht area knew who his brother was, and that his wife handed out the NSB paper *Volk en Vaderland*. They thought his sympathies were obvious, and several officers took it upon themselves to accuse Mussert of treason. In a bungled arrest in which Mussert appeared to reach for his gun, he was shot four times by a fellow Dutch soldier, and later died in hospital before his many puzzling actions could be defended.

But one vengeful death couldn't stop the wave of misfortune. The Dutch air force made a desperate attempt to destroy the German-held Moerdijk bridges with one of the few bombers left, but the first bomb

hit the water, and the second fell beside a bridge-pillar without exploding. A German Messerschmidt intercepted, forcing down the Dutch
plane. Similar bad luck plagued the Dutch forces at 's-Gravendeel,
where the soldiers trained their three ancient cannons on the rapidly
advancing Germans. The first didn't fire at all, the second dropped its
ball from the cannon's mouth, and the third veered harmlessly to one
side. The road to Rotterdam stretched open.

The Germans captured Overschie early in the invasion, and held an
important road linking Rotterdam to The Hague. To retake Overschie,
Dutch troops marched towards it from Delft, one of the many towns
that surrounded The Hague, seizing stray Germans, weapons, and supplies as they went. But despite their encouraging progress, the men were
ordered back to Delft just before they reached their target. With the fall
of Dordrecht, The Hague had to shore up its defence. Overschie's
rescue was left to whatever troops Rotterdam could spare, and a ragtag
band of soldiers tried to organize themselves for the mission.

Near the Schiekanaal, and the garden where Jacques grew vegetables for his family, German gunfire rang out from windows hung with lace
curtains. The driver of a Dutch armoured car was told to push through to
the heart of the assault, leading the infantrymen, but found himself par-
alyzed by fear. His commander held a gun to his head and ordered the
man forward. But when German fire intensified, the driver frantically
shifted his car into reverse, killing a Dutch soldier behind him and
wounding others. The Dutch troops withdrew, shaken by the incident.

On the opposite side of town – with Cor's family sandwiched
between – Dutch units advanced more smoothly. They crossed the
canal and moved into the streets against a backdrop of houses taken
over by the invaders. Later it would be said that outrage was their most
reliable weapon, but although they took many prisoners and fought
like they had years of experience, their commander ordered a full

retreat at sundown, having learned of the failed mission on the other side of Overschie.

By morning on May 14 – the day after Wilhelmina left for England – Fortress Holland had organized a large-scale assault on the Germans at Overschie. More than two thousand men moved in from three directions. But as they prepared for a unified attack, superiors in Rotterdam learned that an aerial bombardment of that city was imminent. Negotiations with the other side began, but while messages floated back and forth between commanders, the bombers approached anyway – the German command's order to suspend the attack wasn't received by all of the pilots heading for Rotterdam, and within minutes, they dropped their load, and the city was in flames. The smoke and ash quickly spread to Overschie, but the Dutch troops proceeded with their mission. They were on the verge of retaking the village when the final word came: General Winkelman, with the authority of the government now in England, ordered his men to stop fighting "to spare further bloodshed and complete destruction of the country." Reeling with shock, the Netherlands surrendered.

The devastation of Rotterdam was visible from Gerrit's vantage point, and from Cor's too. Separately, each of them stared at the billowing clouds of smoke. Rige, their eldest, stood on the Tedingerstraat, watching the smoke lift and roll out into the sky, staining the blue day black. Rige's pulse sped and slowed again with dread and shame. She thought of an old wives' tale that said picking the *koekoeksbloem* brought thunderstorms, and wondered if she, then, was the culprit. She'd never seen such black clouds.

Within three hours, Rotterdam was in ruins. Neighbouring Schiedam, too, suffered massive destruction. Cor's cousin Cornelia, who helped in the bookstore, stood with her mother and sister in the doorway of their house, watching bombs explode in the schoolyard while

air raid sirens screamed and people fled. Their rucksacks were strapped
to their backs in case they, too, needed to run. The destruction multiplied when a margarine warehouse erupted, and a strong spring wind
spread the shooting flames. The intense heat spun into a whirlwind that
lifted roofs off houses, shattered glass, and bent young trees to the
ground. The blazing streets grew thick with people fleeing for their lives,
but the small details seemed to happen in slow motion – a pot of flowers
tumbling from a windowsill, an old man falling. For three days, the core
of Rotterdam was black with smoke, and its buildings continued to
smoulder; debris rained down on Overschie and beyond. When houses
were unlivable but the inhabitants had survived, people left messages for
loved ones in the rubble, and walked to a safer place: *We are all right*,
they wrote, and scribbled an alternative address.

The Posts in Overschie had been spared by just a few kilometres, but
for several days Cor had no news of them or of her brother Gerry and his
family, who were living right in Rotterdam. When word finally did filter
through that all had survived unharmed, Cor learned that the offices of
the shipping company that employed Gerry had been totally destroyed,
but that Gerry had set sail just days before the invasion. She was glad that
at least he had escaped, but worried for Gerrit as she watched the disciplined band of Wehrmacht soldiers march through the main street. The
staccato sound of their boots on the pavement echoed in her mind at
night, magnifying her fear that Gerrit had not survived.

Two days after the capitulation, Cor listened as the radio
announced that at various points in the Netherlands, German troops
would be entering en masse, and that civilian traffic was to be halted
between 5:45 a.m. and 12:30 p.m. to make way for them. Among the
terms of occupation: German "credit certificates" were to be accepted
as cash, beer was to be reserved for German officers and soldiers, the
air raid blackout would be strictly maintained, and all carrier pigeons
would have to be registered, and were forbidden to fly free. Cor remembered the radio reports describing the release of pigeons at the Berlin
Olympics, and the announcer saying they'd carried a message of peace

to the world. The irony was already astounding – but within two years, the Germans would go further, and order the birds slaughtered, requiring the ringed, severed legs as proof of the deed.

In Rotterdam, there was little time for licking wounds. The bodies, once counted, would number between eight hundred and nine hundred, though the international press estimated much greater figures, reaching as high as one hundred thousand. The *New York Times* reported that Nazi film footage of the destruction had been shown to correspondents in Berlin, and that the images gave the impression "not a single house . . . was left untouched by fire or some other instrument of destruction." The voice-over accompanying the footage maintained, "The responsibility for this rests on a government that criminally did England's bidding and afterward cowardly left their people to their fate."

Within Rotterdam, the devastation was great, if overstated. Firefighters were called in from other towns and cities, including Leidschendam and Voorburg. People with automobiles were urged to go to the city with food and bandages, and anything that might help with the cleanup of mountains of rubble and charred wood. Meanwhile, the newly homeless flooded out of Rotterdam to surrounding areas like Overschie, and farther on to Leidschendam. Next door to the den Hartogs, the rooms Bep and Henny had vacated were taken over by a family whose house had been swallowed by fire. The couple arrived with a train of little boys behind them. The children looked strangely calm, but the parents' faces were white with shock, even days after the bedlam faded. Cor, too, was stunned. Almost overnight, familiar surroundings had changed profoundly: Vader den Hartog had seen a German plane in the Tedingerbroekpolder beyond the *tuin*, its broken fuselage embedded in the soft earth. And she and Moeder had seen hundreds of dead and wounded trucked to the Saint Antonius Hospital in Voorburg – mostly Dutch soldiers but Germans too, and apparently also an English pilot and crew whose plane had crashed in the area. It was said that corpses were stacked in the mortuary, and surgery went on in the hallways. Cor ached to think of what might have happened to her own soldier.

For days she kept the radio turned loud, hushing her children so that she could hear every scrap of news. Dutch soldiers must surrender their weapons, the reports said, though the officers, for now, could keep them. Every member of the Dutch army must consider himself a prisoner of war, and troops were ordered to stay where they'd been at the time of capitulation. Later, lying awake in the half-empty bed, she recited psalms to block out what the radio had told her, but the reality was all too raw. If alive, Gerrit was probably a prisoner – but where, and under what conditions? She pulled Rokus, the baby, into bed with her, and curled herself around him, praying for patience and strength and Gerrit's safe return. But for the first time in her life, prayer was insufficient. Even with Rokus there, Gerrit's space in the bed yawned wide beside her, and when sleep wouldn't come, she wrapped herself in a blanket and went out onto the balcony. The crisp night air was soothing, and staring out at the blackness, recalling the sound of Gerrit's voice, the warmth of his hands, and the strength she drew from him, she made a decision.

In the morning, she told Moeder and Vader that she couldn't sit waiting any longer. There were rumours that the Germans would order the men back to their original posts, so she was going to find Gerrit, and Strijen was the logical place to start looking. What she'd do when she got there, she didn't know, but she needed to go. Strijen was four hours by bicycle; it would likely take hours more because of barricades and destruction, but she was used to long bike rides – as a girl she'd gone as far as Oosterbeek, near Arnhem, to visit her Tante Ester, and this was closer than that. Gerrit's parents tried to dissuade her – there was no telling what she'd encounter, they said, or which roads had been destroyed in the fighting. "Then I will find other roads," she answered, her expression determined.

The next day she hugged each child too hard and left them in their grandparents' care, pedalling fast right from the start of the journey, though Vader had warned her to pace herself. Moeder had filled her rucksack with food and water, sensible things Cor might have forgone, notwithstanding her pragmatic nature. As she passed the chars of Rotterdam and Overschie, tears streamed from her eyes, but she fought the urge to check on Truus, Tom, Maria, and their parents. Foremost in her mind was the necessity of finding Gerrit – getting to him, wherever he was. She wished she'd told him about the baby. She was almost three months pregnant, and though her condition sometimes made her queasy and tired, it gave her an underlying strength that might have vitalized Gerrit, too, in this last while, rather than causing him worry. These were the things that busied her mind as she raced through South Holland, past the cherry trees in full bloom and the pungent lilac and the sun climbing up in the sky. The meadows laden with marguerite daisies, the yellow iris at the water's edge, were no more than peripheral blurs of colour as she followed the seemingly endless dike roads hemmed by rows of poplar. Today it was the new scars on the land that held her attention, and the Wehrmacht trucks she passed on the narrow roadways, bristling with German soldiers and heaps of absconded weapons. En masse, the men were ominous, with their metal helmets and jackboots, but when she dared to look at their faces – one with a moustache, another with a pug-nose – they seemed much like those of men she knew. *How can this be happening?* she asked herself. She felt strangely fearless, but angry.

She didn't know whether she could find Gerrit and make it home again that night, or at least back to Overschie, but it was spring, so the days were longer, if chilly and windy. As she passed a tram-post ringed in white paint she remembered that the blackout was in full effect now, the white paint an effort to reduce collisions in the dark. If night fell while she was still riding, she'd be enveloped in darkness, and a white ring might not save her. She pictured herself tumbling headlong into the murky water of an unfenced canal, with no one to hear the splash. She'd be no help to anyone – not to Gerrit or the children at home or the baby inside her – if she drowned.

Thinking of the unborn child brought on a well of nausea, and she stopped her bicycle and sat for a while in the sunshine, eating the bread and cheese Moeder had packed, and reminding herself that absolutely everything was part of God's plan. This was a peaceful spot, with birds twittering in the poplars, but in the flat distance she could see smoke and uprooted trees and a cluster of army vehicles, one turned on its side. The devastation of the countryside shocked her as she continued on, despite what she'd already seen close to home: buildings with shattered windows, impassable streets filled with rubble, the downed plane in the polder. The ruin went on and on, and Cor saw the shredded stumps of trees that had been dynamited for makeshift roadblocks, barricades made from old buses and trucks left to slow the panzers, pulverized fields littered with dead livestock and useless field artillery. The towns and villages were the worst – whole sides of buildings torn open, revealing broken, overturned furniture, doors hanging from their frames, floors littered with smashed roof tiles. The smell of burnt timber hung in an acrid fog. She passed the crumbled wall of a bookstore where a man in an apron picked through bricks and shredded wood, stacking what books he found in neat piles. She thought of her family's little bookshop, and felt sorry she hadn't stopped in Overschie. But for now, the rumour that her family was fine would have to do – until she found him, her priority was Gerrit.

She stopped again near a roadblock and watched a German motorcolumn churn through the mud of a polder, and she couldn't help but wonder if these very soldiers had shot at Gerrit, and if he'd survived the storming. Another soldier was rerouting traffic, blowing his whistle and holding up his hand. She stared hard at the back of his head, as if her gaze could bore through the metal and into his skull. But when he whistled again and turned and met her eyes with a look that was oddly kind, her courage was replaced by a cold stab of terror. He motioned her forward, smiling and nodding as she passed. "Sorry for the wait, *Mevrouw*," he said in competent Dutch. And to her amazement, Cor found herself nodding back, afraid of his reaction to any lesser response. She pedalled on, stunned by the way lives resumed after disaster – or even within disaster. Women like her cycled along the dike roads, hair covered from the wind, wicker baskets holding sustenance for the trip. She spoke to a few of them, and learned that, like her, they were looking for husbands, fathers, brothers, and sons. Some would be luckier than others. When the farmer who had billeted Gerrit's group opened the door to Captain Schouten's wife, he saw that her white face held a look of hopefulness. It was up to him to tell her, "Things are not so good," and to recount the captain's last brave act on the shore of the river Kil.

Cor's husband survived, though the details of their reunion have been lost. At the end of May he was released with the other Dutch soldiers – a gesture of goodwill, Hitler claimed. Gerrit returned home to his garden and his family, seemingly none the worse for wear, except that a quiet man was quieter still, and now and again he cried real tears in his sleep, shouting out and then gasping for breath.

THREE

The Quiet Knocking
1940–1941

WHILE WILHELMINA HAD BEEN QUEEN for almost half a century and had garnered respect and admiration from her people, it couldn't be said, by wartime, that they loved her. However esteemed, she was a figurehead, a patriotic symbol – a familiar face only when seen on a coin or a postage stamp. Certainly few of her nine million subjects would have recognized the tired and forlorn woman who stepped off the boat in England, metal helmet askew.

From Harwich, a train carried her to London, and when she disembarked at Liverpool Street Station, Juliana, Bernhard, and the children greeted her, guarded by four Secret Service men. King George, clad in his admiral's uniform, shook her hand and kissed her cheeks, and she became his guest at Buckingham Palace, joined shortly by Norway's King Haakon, George's brother-in-law. In the tangled branches of her family tree, Wilhelmina was also related to these kings and queens of Europe, a cluster of distant cousins fleeing German bombs. But Bernhard, the true German among them, turned back. Against his mother-in-law's wishes, he reappeared in the wings of the battle-stage, remembering the talks he'd had with Willem Röell, and their plan to stay and fight if the country was invaded.

Bernhard had suffered relentless poor health since babyhood, but it seemed to have made him more virile. Plagued by throat infections and finally pleurisy, as a young man he'd had six pieces of rib removed, and the surgery had left heavy scarring and a hollow where the bone used to be. In Germany, he'd joined the so-called League of Air Sports because he wanted to learn to fly. The league had no direct political implications, but was initiated by the Nazi regime, and offered a way for the party to train war pilots without seeming to be doing so. But Bernhard's plane had crashed, and thereafter he'd turned his interests to racing fast cars. Drawn to jeopardy – or at least to a spot close by – he now sneaked back into Dutch territory, and popped up on May 17 in Zeeland, where the fight had continued for several days after Dutch capitulation. But the tiny province's defeat was imminent. The beautiful centre of Middelburg – Bep's hometown, and seemingly of no strategic interest to the Germans – was razed. Commanders told Bernhard the situation was near hopeless. He continued to France, but the Germans kept coming, and soon enough, Bernhard returned to England to be with Juliana and the queen.

Wilhelmina was relieved that they were all together, but distressed by France's fall: the enemy now occupied a great swath of land across from England's shores. Already, London warehouses were packed with cardboard coffins, pits had been dug for expected mass burials, and city children had been evacuated to the country in anticipation of Germany's attacks. There were reports that spies in Berlin had seen the names of Wilhelmina and her family on the Gestapo's blacklist. Within weeks of her arrival in England, the queen decided Juliana and the children had to be sent farther from danger. Luckily, the queen's connections were widespread. Princess Alice, granddaughter of the late Queen Victoria, and Wilhelmina's cousin on her mother's side, was married to Lord Athlone, who was Canada's new governor general and Wilhelmina's cousin on her father's side, thereby doubling the appropriateness of Canada as a haven for Dutch royalty. On June 2, Wilhelmina waved to Juliana and her girls as Bernhard took them to the ship that would carry them across the ocean. The nanny, as well as Martine Röell and her daughter, accompanied the princess to Canada, where she'd settle in Ottawa's wealthiest neighbourhood, Rockcliffe Park.

Far as it was from the war, Juliana's placement was key: Canada was an Allied country, but its land had not come under attack. If the queen herself died, the line to the throne would remain intact through Juliana. Her arrival created a stir in Canada, but in her first radio address, the princess played down her royal image, and introduced herself simply, setting the tone for her stay: "My name is Juliana. . . . Please, do not regard me as too much of a stranger." She stressed the Nazi blacklist as the reason for the family's arrival, and insisted that neither the queen nor Prince Bernhard intended to leave London. "My only great fear," she admitted, "is that my husband is exposing himself too much to danger, for he is by nature reckless, with no regard for his own safety."

But war was good for Bernhard's shaky image. In the Netherlands, on his twenty-ninth birthday, vendors sold cartloads of white carnations, and people wore them in their buttonholes as reminders of the prince's ever-present boutonnieres. A defiant crowd moved towards Noordeinde Palace and laid flowers at the statue of Willem of Orange. Displays like this showed the Germans what they were up against: an allegiance stronger than they'd expected, and one that would have to be broken if they were to achieve Hitler's goal of winning over the Dutch population. The Hague blazed with orange flags, ribbons, skirts, and kerchiefs, and a profusion of orange flowers sprouted in gardens and window boxes – all vibrant symbols of the exiled royal family and a freedom that would slowly slip away.

In the turbulent days of the invasion, a few hundred Dutch Jews had rushed south to France or Spain, or had tried crossing to England in boats not made for the journey; most drowned. Among those who remained in the occupied country, a ripple of family suicides took place, which at first seemed a tragic overreaction to the occupation, because so little immediately changed with Nazi presence. Hitler had a long-term plan of moulding the Netherlands into a national socialist state that would be part of Germany once the war was won. On their best behaviour, the uniformed German soldiers who called themselves "cousins" moved freely through the occupied towns and cities, chatting amiably with street vendors as they bought flowers and souvenirs. They always seemed to be carrying boxes of pastry, and quickly earned a reputation as *geweldige snoepers* for having a wicked sweet tooth. Often polite and helpful to the conquered – as Cor's traffic director had been – their actions contrasted with the news of atrocities perpetrated in Poland, where it was said that even children were lined up and shot in the market squares. In the Netherlands, it sometimes appeared that a partnership was forming: early on, the Dutch railway company made a deal with the occupiers that they'd be able to keep their own operation running as long as they handled transport for the Germans.

Lured by the attractive posters advertising work in Germany's factories, a number of Dutch citizens took jobs that would further the Nazi cause. Others enlisted voluntarily in the German army, and would go on to receive German medals for bravery. Still others formed covert resistance groups, and began the work of thwarting the enemy. From the earliest days, Cor's brother-in-law Jacques was part of the organized resistance, meeting with colleagues in the garden he kept at the edge of town. Dick Zandbergen, husband of Cor's friend Marie, was also involved. And in Voorburg, Henny, with his drafting and photographic skills, doctored passports for the Jewish community, working with a civil servant at city hall who had stayed in his job to undermine the Germans. The bulk of the population settled somewhere between resistance and collaboration, anxious about the invaders now living in their midst, chilled by the calm after the storm.

When Hitler appointed Arthur Seyss-Inquart his Reich commissioner in the Netherlands, the Austrian Nazi quipped to his wife that the führer wanted him to plant tulips, but to the Dutch people he said apologetically that Germany had to invade Holland to prevent it becoming an Allied base, and that now, thanks to the führer's magnanimity, Dutch territory would be protected. The Dutch soldiers had fought valiantly, he told them in his proclamation, and civilians had duly tolerated the presence of German soldiers. "Nothing should prevent us from treating each other respectfully." He eased into his task as head of a civilian rather than a military government, keeping the secretaries general Wilhelmina had left behind, and emphasizing that the Dutch were kin, and that Germany's actions had been compelled by its enemies. His moderate tone was exactly the reason Hitler had chosen him, a meticulous lawyer who had facilitated the German takeover of his own country two years before. Now, Hitler expected that through Seyss-Inquart, the Dutch – who, unlike the Poles, had Germanic blood – could be brought around to Nazi ideals. Other prominent Nazis doubted Seyss-Inquart's abilities. "When all is said and done," wrote Joseph Goebbels in his diary, "the fellow is only an Austrian." Though, of course, so was Hitler.

In the Netherlands, news travelled quickly that Seyss-Inquart's quiet demeanour masked a formidable man: an open anti-Semite and former soldier in the Great War, where he'd been wounded and decorated three times for bravery. Jokes circulated about his leg – mangled in a mountaineering accident that had left him with a pronounced limp – and people called him *manke poot*, or lame paw. But the ridicule barely masked the fear seeping through the population when Seyss-Inquart moved with his wife, Gertrud, their twelve-year-old daughter, Dorli, and their Irish setter into Clingendael, one of The Hague's finest mansions, and had himself sworn in at the Binnenhof's medieval Ridderzaal, the place reserved for the throne speech every September. Since 1904, thousands had gathered for the tradition of watching Wilhelmina ride to the hall in her gilded carriage. She should have been seated on her flowery throne, reading from spectacles she held on a long stem, but Seyss-Inquart had supplanted her, and replaced the throne with a podium. An aficionado of classical music, he chose a Wagner overture to be played at the event. With musicians arranged among the potted ferns, Wilhelmina's absence was as sharply felt as the new German presence.

Even Anton Mussert, the fleshy faced leader of the NSB whose brother Josephus had been shot by a Dutch officer, was miffed by Seyss-Inquart's appointment. He'd hoped Hitler would make *him* leader of a new and improved Netherlands, not ruled by but partnered with Germany, and had even formally suggested to Seyss-Inquart that he himself take on a prime ministerial position. Instead, the naive man with big dreams found he was little more than a minion, snubbed by a regime that didn't bother to invite him to the swearing-in ceremony. The Dutch had long poked fun at Mussert, but now the international press ridiculed him too, and called him a tiny traitor more famous for marrying his wealthy old auntie than for any major political achievement.

Of course the average Dutch were strangers to the Seyss-Inquarts, who insulated themselves on the Clingendael estate, of which Gertrud had overseen the refurbishing. A select few high-ranking members of the NSB began to visit them there, but Anton Mussert would never be a favourite, since Seyss-Inquart disdained him as a man of lesser intelligence. Most mornings, Arthur strolled the grounds, enjoying the Japanese gardens planted by Lady Daisy van Brienen, the Dutch owner of the estate who'd died the year before, conveniently making way for him. He spent his days in his office, and in the evening continued to work in his main-floor study with its view of the ponds and grounds, and the ever-present guards that filled the spaces between the trees. On occasion, soloists performed on the terrace, and in his free time he studied music and played the piano. A man of some restraint, he didn't overindulge in food or drink, and insisted that house staff be served the same meals as he and his family and the guests who came to Clingendael.

His police leader, Hanns Albin Rauter, was perhaps his polar opposite: an aggressive, impulsive man appointed by Berlin, and not of Seyss-Inquart's choosing. Like Seyss-Inquart, he was Austrian, but there the similarities ended. Rauter is an overgrown child, the Reich commissioner told his wife, with a child's penchant for cruelty. His presence would complicate Seyss-Inquart's mission from Hitler, to seemingly befriend the Dutch people.

In all their variety, the most prominent invaders took grand homes and headquarters throughout the country, and some members of the German High Command set up house in Het Loo near Apeldoorn, Wilhelmina's summer retreat and the place dearest to her. Officers settled into the larger houses and farms, and spent their leisure time sightseeing in groups with cameras at hand. In Leidschendam, inspectors from the town hall visited the neighbourhoods to determine who had room to house soldiers. The den Hartog house was fortunately full, but several families on the Tedingerstraat were appointed hosts to their invaders, and were paid handsomely for the job. The van Kampens at number 86, whose picture window mirrored the den Hartogs', took in two men. One, Richard Kaan, was a career soldier, and thus a watch-guard for his younger mate, Helmut Kube, who'd been drafted and was sorry to be there at all – his superiors knew his kind was less likely to follow Nazi rules. They were given a small bedroom upstairs, and asked to adhere to Mevrouw van Kampen's rules of decency: wipe your boots, don't come into the house drunk, and never use foul language. Few would challenge a short-tempered *huisvrouw* like Mevrouw van Kampen, thus Richard followed the rules as diligently as Helmut, but their presence – and that of others up and down the row of houses – changed the mood of this otherwise undistinguished street, and made Cor pleased to comply with the blackout regulations and pull her blinds closed against them as each day ended.

In other streets, more than the mood changed with the arrival of the Germans. Seyss-Inquart began to erase all reminders of the Dutch royal family, which meant that in Leidschendam, Prinses Julianaweg became Provinciale Weg, and in Voorburg, on the street where Bep and Henny lived, KoninginWilhelminalaan became Admiral de Ruijterlaan. (For Bep, this affirmed an eventual victory, since she was descended from Admiral de Ruijter, who fought in the first Anglo-Dutch wars, and remained a Dutch hero if there ever was one.) Emmaschool, which Rige attended and Gerrit's brother Nico cleaned, kept its name; so did Emmastraat, where Nico lived with his family – but then Wilhelmina's mother Emma had been German, and the Nazis liked examples of Dutch and German histories connecting.

The links were easy to find. The Dutch had always felt closer to their German neighbours than they had to the English with whom they now found themselves allied. With the arrival of an Austrian overlord, Cor thought of the young Austrian girl who'd come to stay with the Posts in 1918 when Cor was nine years old. After the Great War, many Dutch people had opened their homes to the underprivileged children of Germany and Austria who needed good food and a rest away from the setting of defeat. The girl had stayed for several months, and had been included in a family portrait like a sister: a fat bow in her hair, her hand resting on Cor's father's shoulder. Cor wondered what had become of her.

At the time of invasion, the Netherlands was flecked through with German sympathizers thanks to this intertwined history and geography, and the country had its own share of anti-Semites. Now that Nazis were in charge, national socialist beliefs were bolstered, and enrolment in Mussert's NSB grew. Some joined because of what might be gained by siding with the powerful: choice jobs and houses, and the daily necessities that would become more and more scarce for the average person. Others were impressed by simple things: the marching and singing, and a sense of camaraderie. Some people felt the rise of communism was a threat, and national socialism the best way to counter it. On the left side of the spectrum, their opponents sneered at the mention of Queen Wilhelmina with her undeniably German roots. They said her flight to England made her nothing more than a traitor, or a coward at best. Cor's "red" uncle, Simon de Korte, was one of these, though communism was shunned by the Gereformeerde Church. Since Cor still made her biweekly rail trips to Overschie to visit her family, she heard first-hand from her mother Neeltje about the day Oom Simon came to hang Neeltje's new wallpaper. As he stood on his ladder and handed the portrait of Queen Wilhelmina to his sister, he snickered, "Here, take Gretchen," a derogatory reference to the queen's ancestry. Neeltje, with her religious and patriotic reverence for the House of Orange, had flown into a rage and ordered red Oom Simon out the door, putting loyalty above blood relations and the state of her walls. But Simon's sentiment wasn't rare. Many these days felt not only that the queen had deserted them, but that she'd planned her departure rather than been forced to make it.

With her sisters Truus and Maria, Cor couldn't help laughing at her mother's indignation, obvious still in the retelling, and also at Jacques, who'd been stuck with the messy wallpaper job when Simon was ousted. She watched him reach with his roller to the ceiling, and groan when the paper creased under his careful stroke. Truus shouted out playful instructions, and he barked back at her, and Cor marvelled at how lighthearted they could be – for Truus had already told her, on this visit, that Jacques had linked up with the resistance, a whispered word that sounded menacing to Cor. She wasn't sure what the resistance would do, or if it was even necessary at this point, for she couldn't conceive of things getting worse under God's watch. Jacques's eagerness was admirable, she supposed, but she wondered if it stemmed from the fact that he'd been too old to join the soldiers who'd fought in May. If he'd seen what Gerrit had seen, he might have felt differently.

Riding home on the train, she saw Gerrit in the *tuin* from the car's window, and thought of the nights he cried out in his sleep. He didn't like to talk about the things he'd seen and done as a soldier, and she didn't press him, but Cor knew that twenty-nine of his battalion had died in five days of fighting, and scores more had been injured. The battles had ended, but she'd heard that soldiers sought each other out – not to talk, really, but just to be in one another's company. And she wondered if Gerrit felt that need. Jacques couldn't know what his experience was like any more than she could, and she hoped he never had to.

As the train pulled into the station, Cor used her last few minutes alone to pray for Jacques, and some of her other relations with far left leanings and a penchant for speaking their minds. Most of them descended from Oma Kee, she realized, and in spite of herself she smiled at the thought of her grandmother, a sprite disguised in an old woman's clothing. But the concerns were real. In their late-night discussions in Overschie, when Truus's girls were tucked into bed, Truus had passed on family worries about their cousin Dirk de Korte, who openly despised the Nazi ideology and the German presence on the streets of Zaandam where he lived. Apparently, Truus said between sips of tea, he aired his views to any who'd listen, unconcerned that the wrong ears would hear. And in July, when the Germans outlawed listening to foreign news, Dirk had defiantly turned up the volume of his radio, tuned to the BBC. "If anything happens to me," he'd boasted, "be assured I will take several of the enemy with me."

She was glad that Gerrit's convictions were not so militant. Since his return from Strijen, business was better than ever. Gone were the *doorgedraaid* days of unsold produce. The occupiers had hearty appetites, and requisitioned the best of his yield. He had no choice but to sell to them if he wanted to stay in business at all, but it was a strange and uncomfortable feeling, for both him and Cor, to know that his labour nourished the enemy, and that putting money aside, as they had always tried to do, was just a little easier now. As her train had rushed past the garden, she'd waited for him to look up and find her in the window, but he was deep in concentration, hands on his aching back, thinking of the earwigs that invaded the *tuin* from every angle, and of the cutworms that ate through the stems of his youngest plants, leaving the tops to fall useless on the ground. The insects were enemies he knew and understood, but the hatred at the heart of the Nazi philosophy baffled him.

Lately he was further confounded by the "good" side, since the first Royal Air Force bombs had begun to fall in the occupied territory. Den Helder, at the tip of North Holland's peninsula, had undergone a two-night raid, with terrified inhabitants running over ground that rose and shifted beneath them. Windows bowed inwards before exploding and walls fell in pieces to the floor. It was the Luftwaffe, people thought – the German air force engaging in scare tactics to push the Dutch into submission – but they were shocked when the truth came out. The bombs that had killed and wounded and ripped up the city had come from Allied planes aiming for targets precious to the Nazis. Here and elsewhere, the bombers often missed. Gerrit knew first-hand what happened when bombs screamed down: how the ground vibrated, how solid, dependable objects like lampposts and street signs could twirl up into the air. He knew, too, what happened to people. Whenever he heard planes pass in the night, he braced himself, wondering if the bombs would land here, on top of his own family. And each time the sound diminished, he felt a brief euphoria for having been spared.

By late July, the peas in Gerrit's garden were finished, and the long vines of *suikermeloenen* twisted over the black soil. The fruit that extended out of the star-shaped yellow bloom would be fat by summer's end. Underground, the beets swelled, and sent their rich red juice up through the veins of the glossy leaves. In the sunshine, Gerrit kneeled by the ditch and rinsed the bundled summer carrots in the stream, packing ten bunches into each wooden crate. Coffee, tea, bread, and flour had already been rationed, and he felt a level of satisfaction in producing something as basic and necessary as food, even if only a portion of it went to the Dutch people.

Father of three, he no longer ate lunch with Cor in the garden, but returned home for a warm meal with his growing family: potatoes, another vegetable, porridge for dessert. Little Rokus was a year old now, and already had Cor's keen gaze and the dark eyebrows of Truus and her brother Tom. Gerrit noticed that she seemed to feel more comfortable cuddling Rokus than she did the others, stroking his hair forward and whispering words of endearment: *"Onze lieve Rokus."* Happy and healthy, the boy seemed to thrive on her embrace, whereas Koos, nearly two and a half, barely needed it, and squirmed if she tried to snuggle with him. Cor had told Gerrit she found that streak of independence troublesome, but he hushed her fears and said it was harmless.

She fussed too much about all of them, even Rige, who was a serious child with a strong intuition, and at heart a good girl. He appreciated Cor's vigilance, though, and liked to lie beside her as she rested her Christian mother's manual on her pregnant stomach. Precise, succinct, unrelenting, these pages reassured her that there were indeed answers to everything, and he knew that was just what she needed to believe. Beside her, Gerrit devoured Jules Verne's *Five Weeks in a Balloon*, and imagined being high above the earth, sailing through the clouds to Africa. Cor resisted this sort of evasion, despite the mood of the times. Sometimes she recited a passage to him – a strict rule she thought they should enforce – and he put his book on his chest and listened. They discussed each rule or punishment at length, but it was Cor who brought the children in line when they strayed. He rarely raised his voice, unless they interfered when he listened to the news.

Each day, Gerrit tuned in to the BBC's Dutch-language broadcast at a low volume, and leaned close to the speaker while Cor kept watch in case anyone came to the door. Unlike Cor's cousin Dirk, his was not an act of defiance. It unnerved him to disobey the occupiers' commands, but he needed to know what was happening, and had trouble discerning the truth without news from abroad. Nazi propaganda oozed from the Dutch stations, interspersed with German orchestral music too grand and cheerful for the times. The English broadcasts were difficult for Gerrit, but he listened anyway, and clung to every word of the Dutch ones. And as though being rewarded for his perseverance, on July 28, he heard Queen Wilhelmina speak. Gerrit's mouth fell open as her voice travelled all the way from London into his humble living room.

"My compatriots," she told him in this first broadcast on what would be known as Radio Oranje. "Because the voice of the Netherlands could and should not remain silent, I, at the last moment, made the decision to take myself and the government, as symbols of our nation, to a place where we can continue to work as a living power and make our voice heard." She almost shouted the words, as though straining to push them across the waterway and into the homes of her subjects. The *"Wilhelmus"* anthem followed, and Gerrit remembered Major Ravelli and the attack stopped by a bugle – how the soldier's fingers had trembled over the keys, just as his own had on his rifle's trigger. He blinked the grim memories away, and marvelled at the queen's timing: only the day before, Seyss-Inquart had said demonstrations for the House of Orange would no longer be permitted, and forbade mention of Queen Wilhelmina at political gatherings. But here she was, speaking straight into Gerrit's ear.

In Rotterdam, Arthur Seyss-Inquart was photographed for the newspapers in distinguished fedora and overcoat, smiling and clasping hands with seemingly happy children who leaned out of a train window and waved small swastika flags. Some six thousand Dutch boys and girls were being sent to summer in Austria, in gratitude, said Seyss-Inquart, for the hospitality Dutch families showed Austrian children after the Great War. What didn't show up in the photographs was the telling work happening in Dutch schools that summer: libraries painstakingly reorganized, their books "edited" for anti-German passages or anything written by a Jew. Gerrit's brother Nico must have witnessed the business at Emmaschool. Each summer he gave the school a thorough spit and polish, waxing the floors and washing the windows with a crew that included Moeder den Hartog. By the time classes started again, the school would be gleaming, and there would be new texts that emphasized the Germanic roots of the Netherlands. Even the much-loved boys' book *Zoon van Dik Trom* would go underground. One in a series of popular fiction written long before the current conflicts, it was condemned for its depiction of a vigorous snowball fight that saw a group of boys divide into Dutch and German adversaries.

The feeling of us versus them was impossible to ignore, as evidenced one Sunday that summer, when the den Hartogs received visitors. It was unusual for them to entertain out-of-town guests other than the Post clan or Gerrit's pretty nieces by his sister Mar, but this couple and their children had come from Tuindorp, and had billeted Gerrit during his mobilization before his regiment was posted to Strijen. Kids, parents, and grandparents strolled along the Broekweg, past the *tuin*, towards the polder, where the family often walked on Sundays. The ground there still bore the imprint of the downed Luftwaffe plane, but the spot had grown over with grass and weeds. The little ones raced ahead, and Moeder den Hartog pushed Rokus in the pram that would soon be needed for the new baby, due in December.

Lagging behind was the visitors' eldest son, a lanky boy named David, whom Rige turned to peer at now and then. No longer a child, not yet an adult, he would no doubt rather have been with boys his own age, instead of ambling at a dull pace with a family he barely knew. Under the warm summer sun, he began to yawn, and his shoulders drooped. As the group passed the toll house at the crossroads, where several Germans were posted, a soldier pointed at him while his mouth stretched open. David pulled his jaw closed and stood straighter. His eyes watered from the yawn, and he stepped briskly to catch up with the others, but the soldier smirked and nudged the man beside him, who nudged a third.

"You! Over here."

The words were in German, but the command was plain and everyone stopped, though Vader den Hartog ran to slow Koos, who had ignored the soldiers and toddled ahead. Now, they looked on as the soldier beckoned to David. He stepped towards them. His mother made a move to go after him, but her husband stopped her. The soles of David's shoes crunched over the gravel. As he approached, he was motioned closer, and closer still. His parents remained absolutely silent, even when one of the soldiers pulled a handkerchief from his pocket – wrinkled and used – and tied it around David's head as a blindfold, tugging the knot tight. Another waved his pistol in the boy's face, pressing it into his cheek so he could feel what he couldn't see. David stumbled as all three of them spoke at once, and his mother clamped her hand over her mouth. Rige felt sick to her stomach. She looked at her father and mother, but no one said anything at all. Gerrit caught her eye and gave a barely perceptible shake of his head. And as quickly as the ordeal began, it ended, and the blindfold was ripped from David's face. Rige saw in his eyes a fear that mirrored hers. One soldier held the rag to his nose and blew, staring at David, then he stuffed it into David's pocket. The soldiers laughed, and one shoved him off towards his family. David's mother began to sob and his father's face was white with rage, but Rokus in his stroller gurgled at a leaf that had blown into his lap. Moeder den Hartog turned and pushed the stroller homeward, and the rest followed her in silence. That afternoon, David and his family went home to Tuindorp, and never visited again.

The Germans by now had discovered they weren't welcome, and Seyss-Inquart said as much in a lengthy report to Hitler. Among the Dutch, the opinion that the Netherlands had been wrongly attacked was close to unanimous, he told the führer, adding that few understood or believed the Netherlands had violated its neutral status, and that therefore the invasion was necessary. However, he claimed, some did concur that the Dutch media and emigrants from the Reich had tainted the people's impression of Nazi Germany over the last seven years.

Deeper into his report, he laid out his priority to "reduce consumption" within the Dutch population in order to acquire supplies for Germany. The Netherlands was rich with goods, he wrote. He assured Hitler that the old government's secretaries general had been kept in their positions only in order to achieve these kinds of goals smoothly, for the Dutch were a difficult bunch, and devoted – out of habit, he said – to their exiled queen. In fact it was she who had asked them to stay at their posts, before fleeing herself. But Seyss-Inquart stressed that these employees understood that the parameters of the job had changed, and that they would now accept orders only from the Reich commissioner himself. With a certain pride, Seyss-Inquart noted that the co-operation of the secretaries general had enabled him to seize an abundance of supplies and send them to Germany, leaving a paper-trail of Dutch signatures that made each act look voluntary. Over time, he felt sure the Dutch could be won, though their allegiance to the queen who'd abandoned them rankled. He stressed to Hitler that the population had been told the queen was nothing less than an enemy of the state for allying herself so firmly with the other side, and failing to contest air raids on her own country.

Though of course they had not read the Reich commissioner's report, most people agreed on the real enemy, and recognized the weapon of propaganda when they saw it. But farther off, beneath the ocean's black waters, a quieter foe lurked in the form of German U-boats, travelling in predatory "wolf packs." The Posts and the den Hartogs knew about the constant battles in the Atlantic, but from Cor's brother Gerry, who was an engineer on board the *Zuiderburgh*, they'd still heard nothing. Originally Cor had thought he was lucky to be away when the

Germans invaded. Now, though, she knew that if he was still alive, he was in a most perilous place. He'd most surely been folded into the war effort, put to work with other sailors on one of the vessels travelling to the East Indies, where Cor's Oom Marinus was, or transporting food, supplies, and people back and forth between Britain and North America and points beyond. The U-boats made life for Allied merchant-ship sailors as dangerous as it was for seamen on naval ships.

Late in the summer, a convoy of evacuation ships left England for Canada, among them a Dutch liner called the *Volendam*, which would figure in the den Hartogs' future. Unbeknownst to the six hundred passengers – more than half were British children – two German U-boats stalked the convoy. Sometime after midnight, in choppy seas five hundred kilometres off the coast of Northern Ireland, torpedoes struck the starboard side of the *Volendam*, rending a huge gash in the ship's hull. Despite the rough water, all eighteen lifeboats were launched successfully, and the only life lost was that of a Dutch seaman hit in the head by a swinging pulley. Ships from the convoy rescued the survivors, and the *Volendam*, almost miraculously, remained afloat, and was towed to port for repairs.

In the outside world, Rotterdam made the news again in July, when the *New York Times* reported that the Germans had inflicted "the greatest mass destruction the world has so far known" in its bombing of that city. The estimated death toll had dropped from one hundred thousand to thirty thousand, a figure still wildly off the mark, but horrifying none-theless to Dutch people abroad, the queen included. Throughout the summer, as the Luftwaffe bombed British airfields, the frequent explosions reminded Wilhelmina of those frightening days in May. But the sirens and the subsequent eruptions were such a constant sound over the city that eventually they became background noise, and the queen often needed reminding to leave her desk and descend with all her papers into the dark room that served as a shelter in her home at Eaton Square. On one occasion, she was walking in Hyde Park when the warnings came, and took refuge in a public shelter as the birds disappeared into the leafy trees. Wherever she was, she referred to the siren and the movement it inspired as "musical chairs."

In September, the Luftwaffe slowed its raids on British airfields and began, instead, to bomb cities, hoping to break English morale. Britain defended itself with a sky full of Hawker Hurricanes and Spitfires. RAF pilots devoured carrots, thinking they'd improve their vision, but the night bombings overwhelmed them. When in turn they bombed German cities, more Allied aircrews died than did German civilians, because RAF bombers, unescorted by fighter planes, lacked the speed, range, and power necessary for the job.

It was after one of these sorties that an RAF plane, crewed by six Czech flyers, crash-landed in a polder on the outskirts of Leidschendam. Gerrit was at work in his *tuin* that morning, the heavy mist soaking through the cloth of his coat, but he didn't see the aircraft with its RAF bull's-eye belly-flop onto the spongy ground four kilometres away. By lunchtime, word had already spread that the crew had slipped into the forest, escaping detection. Over the backyard fence Mevrouw Blom told Cor how a farmer on the other side of town had been milking his cows when the plane came down in the field across the railroad tracks from his farm. Through the fog he'd watched the men scatter into the woods, but later, when the Germans questioned him, he pretended not to understand them. Frustrated, they gestured to the heavy aircraft beyond the tracks, and he gaped as if seeing it for the first time, although, Mevrouw Blom chuckled, how could anyone miss a bomber embedded in the polder? The next day, a local newspaper pictured the aircraft surrounded by German guards, and posted an offer of reward for information on the missing men, but the townspeople remained silent.

Cor wondered what would become of the crew, and before the week was out she had her answer. By splitting into two groups, the airmen had hoped to get away altogether, but one man in the first group cut himself badly on barbed wire, and when a doctor was summoned to tend him, the Germans followed and arrested the trio. The second group evaded capture longer, stealing a farmer's overalls from a clothesline to hide their conspicuous flyer's uniforms, and receiving food and shelter from several people. But eventually, after making it to nearby Wassenaar, someone betrayed them. Cowards and turncoats were just as dangerous as the Nazis, Cor thought. One of the crew had had previous experience with the Germans in Czechoslovakia, and turned his pistol on himself.

The Wellington bomber, which the crew had set aflame before abandoning, was saved when the mist extinguished the fire, and in a few short months would be in service with the Luftwaffe, another loss on a long RAF list that revealed the air force required major expansion. Queen Wilhelmina stepped in as the single largest sponsor of Spitfires, giving enough for the purchase of an entire squadron of these sleek planes with their Rolls-Royce engines. But Goebbels scoffed in his diary that the donation was perverse, since RAF planes were incessantly bombing Dutch cities. His ministry was quick, he wrote, to make the most of such absurdity.

While Wilhelmina's gift bolstered RAF numbers, it did little to rein in the Luftwaffe, and by autumn, conditions in England had turned hazardous. Prince Bernhard, very nearly trapped in a blaze caused by bombs that fell near the prestigious Lincoln's Inn, emerged unscathed, but stayed in the thick of it, helping fight the flames that threatened to destroy the grand building. Already the historic clock tower had been sliced in two by the bombing. Once the fury ended, Bernhard – who rivalled Henny in his enthusiasm for the camera – snapped a shot of the razed room he'd been in when the sirens sounded, and sent it to Juliana with an inscription that hinted at his lust for danger: *Tom's flat in Lincoln's Inn where we were almost written off.*

Perhaps the near miss was invigorating for a prince in the doldrums – he was unhappy these days without his wife and children, and frustrated by his inability to take an active role in battle – but his mother-in-law decided the risk had become too great in London.

Worsened by the constant threat of shock during a raid, the environment was not conducive to the calm she needed for her decisions, so the queen and Bernhard moved to Stubbings, a country-house near Maidenhead, just an hour's drive from London. From there, she could still see the bombings in the distance, but her immediate surroundings – the garden, the fruit trees, and a meadow that reminded her of home – gave her the peace and space to contemplate. In spite of her safe haven, she knew the Nazis could well succeed in taking England, and in that event, she'd made a plan to escape to Canada. Should she fail to do so, she'd ordered her aide to shoot her.

In the meantime, though the country had surrendered, its leaders had not, so with the ministers who had also fled to England, Wilhelmina had formed a government-in-exile. She was a full and vigorous partner, ruling her remaining colonies and attempting some influence on the country now under enemy control. News began to trickle in from the Netherlands, welcome after the initial months of silence and brought by escapees termed *Engelandvaarders*, each of whom Wilhelmina met to hear his story. She grasped their hands in a firm shake, and as the birds chirped in the surrounding fruit trees, these men sipped tea with the queen, delivering a picture of life under Nazi rule. They told Wilhelmina her people showed stalwart allegiance to the House of Orange, and that resistance groups were forming. They brought copies of the underground newspapers that spread "real" news – one would even take the name *Je Maintiendrai*, the motto of the royal family. Heartened, Wilhelmina became the catalyst for Dutch resistance on a larger scale, refusing the advice of Prime Minister Dirk Jan de Geer, who felt the war could never be won and advocated collaborating with the occupiers, as France had done. Wilhelmina knew the emotional effect that would have on her country, but she was also an astute businesswoman and strategist, and understood collaboration would allow the Germans access to the Dutch East Indies and its wealth of oil (in 1940 it was the world's third largest producer). She fired de Geer, a domineering move in the absence of a ratifying parliament, and appointed

Pieter Sjoerds Gerbrandy prime minister. These were the kinds of decisions that caused Winston Churchill to proclaim her "the only man in the
Dutch government."

Gerbrandy was an intense fellow with a small voice and feet that
barely reached the floor when he sat in conference with his queen. He
leaned towards her as he spoke, and his thick moustache hid his lips.
He and Wilhelmina, with her stout peasant's body, her fur stoles, and
her pearl necklaces, made a comical pair, but their views jibed. Never
doubting victory, they agreed on the kinds of reform that would come
with liberation, and on the fact that the post-war government would
necessarily comprise only people who had lived through the war in the
Netherlands – with the exception, of course, of the monarchy. A trusted
accomplice, Gerbrandy cast an eye over the resistance speeches
Wilhelmina wrote for broadcast on Radio Oranje.

Queen and prime minister were united in their optimism, but on
December 5, Saint Nicolaas Eve, Gerbrandy holed up in his modest,
paper-strewn apartment and Wilhelmina sat homesick and heartsick at
Stubbings. She celebrated with Bernhard, but English sweets were a poor
substitute for the spicy, hard *pepernoten* thrown into the room to herald
the arrival of Saint Nicolaas's aide-de-camp, Zwarte Piet. The English
candies were "a doubtful kind of product" that soured in her mouth and
underscored her separation from country, daughter, and grandchildren.

It was a cold Saint Nicolaas Eve in Leidschendam. At Tedingerstraat
86, Mevrouw van Kampen felt it only decent that she invite the billeted soldiers, Helmut and Richard, downstairs in the evenings, where
they could be warm by the stove. The visits were awkward at first, but
as time went on, they became more comfortable. The men spoke of
home. One had brown eyes and fine features, a cap of dark curly hair.
He was older, and more introspective than his partner, who had a confident manner and looks the Nazis idealized: blond hair, square jaw,

blue eyes. Both of them liked the van Kampens' daughter Jeanne, a friendly little eight-year-old. Helmut taught her to mend socks, pulling his own over his hand as an example and meticulously darning. Richard brought her trinkets and sweets – at Saint Nicolaas Eve, the *pepernoten* the queen missed, and *taai-taai* dolls made of corn syrup, honey, anise, and buttermilk.

These were the same treats traditionally enjoyed at the den Hartog house, along with the almond spice-cake *speculaas*, and marzipan modelled into animals, vegetables, and fruits. All of it was carefully crafted and intricately decorated, but gone with a swallow of warm chocolate milk. Friends and relatives would gather and stay late, talking and laughing, and the house would fill with pungent cigarette smoke. A loud knocking would signal Gerrit to pull open the front door and discover a basin of parcels left anonymously on the step. He'd turn to the children, his mouth wide with mock astonishment. The basin was the same zinc tub the children bathed in, but none of them would question that as they hovered over the gifts from Saint Nicolaas, each one handmade, of special significance to the recipient. Following tradition, gifts were accompanied by a rhyme read aloud to tease or lecture or simply chronicle an event that had happened that year: Tante Bep's dustballs, or the time Cor's aging panties fell to her ankles as she ran for the train to Overschie.

But December 5, 1940, was different. Six months into the occupation, candy could still be had, but meat, clothing, and blankets had been rationed since September, and natural gas and electricity since November, so the new baby born this day was tightly swaddled, a gift and a worry all at once. His name was Gerrit, or Gert, for Cor's brother Gerry, following the proper order of naming. After the baby arrived, Gerrit had sat by Cor's bedside holding him, and Cor had been reminded of the time on the balcony before Rige was born, when they'd expressed their misgivings about bringing a child into a troubled era. Then, the war had been hypothetical; now they were living through it. That difference had been palpable through the last term of her pregnancy – with the first three babies, she couldn't wait for their arrival, and to feel like herself again, but with this last, the birth was like giving him up, for how much could you protect someone who was physically separate from you?

Though she chided herself for doubting God's plan, she often agonized over the fact that the conditions were all wrong for raising a family. The tiny bathroom under the stairs doubled as an air raid shelter, and German soldiers lived in the street and the surrounding neighbourhood. Dutch police still dealt with ordinary breeches of law, but there was no doubt about the true enforcers. Wearing crisp uniforms and tall shiny boots, German Grüne Polizei patrolled the area, and under Seyss-Inquart, penalties had been introduced for crimes that may well have been unintended, as when a crack of light filtered through curtains only partially closed. There was enough to contend with without worrying about curtains. At first, Cor had accepted the notion that Seyss-Inquart was a soft Nazi – wishful thinking, she saw now.

The Reich commissioner was frank in his belief that Jews were a threat to Nazi Germany, and any Jews employed as civil servants or professors had by now been fired. At nearby Delft College and Leiden University, the students had held a strike in protest, and Seyss-Inquart had responded by closing both institutions indefinitely, saying the schools fostered anti-German activities. Cor was appalled by these actions, and also, at times, by those of her own people. Increasingly, shops, cafés, and other public places displayed signs that read JODEN NIET GEWENST or VOOR JODEN VERBODEN – Jews not welcome, and even forbidden. She wondered what she would do if the bakery or the butcher shop were her and Gerrit's establishment, and such a request was made of her. Or if they, like the van Kampens, had been selected to host German soldiers. She felt shame heat her face, thinking of Henny in Voorburg. But he frustrated her too. He was an intelligent man – why he and Bep refused the Church confounded her, since it could save them in more ways than one. Regardless, she wished they were still living next door.

The Meulenbroeks had moved in with their brood of boys after their home in Rotterdam collapsed on that infamous May day. It must have been terrifying, she knew, to lose the roof over your family – to very nearly lose life itself – and then to be sent to a new place with little more than twenty rolls of wallpaper to start over. Those had been strange days. She was unsure who had compensated the family, but she remembered the wallpaper being brought in, and the small boys who all looked so alike. And the hope she'd had, once again, for neighbours who were like her and Gerrit. But the Meulenbroeks, it turned out, were Catholic, like the van Kampens. When the weather was warm, they brought out a table and chairs from the kitchen and played cards in the backyard – even if it was Sunday. In her own house, she followed her Church's guidelines and ruled cards unacceptable any day of the week.

Troubled, she lay back to rest, calming herself with the thought that this was the Christmas season, and she had been given the gift of a son. She felt the gentle tug of him at her breast as he learned to suckle, and breathed in his newborn smell. Moeder den Hartog had changed the sheets on the bed, and a heavy blanket kept the winter chill at bay. She could hear the noises of family close by: eighteen-month-old Rokus banging a pot with a wooden spoon; Rige reciting a rhyme she'd learned in school; Gerrit ordering Koos down from the chair-back before it toppled over. She smiled at the sound of his stern voice, rarely used but so effective. Moeder den Hartog was cooking something that smelled terrible, and likely revelling in feeding everyone while Cor was unable. Vader den Hartog would be lost in a book, placidly chewing the stem of his pipe, and she knew he would not look up until his wife whacked his shoulder with a dishtowel and said he'd been called for dinner seventeen times – which was only a mild exaggeration.

Last Sunday, still swollen with pregnancy, Cor had sat in the brown-brick Gereformeerde Kerk on the Damlaan and listened to Reverend Boukema ask the congregation to resist the occupiers and open their hearts to the Jews – *Refuse co-operation wherever such action does not threaten your life*. Such peaceful, passive resistance was just what Queen Wilhelmina asked for on Radio Oranje, urging them not to be daunted by the signs of German rule growing steadily stronger. When the sermon ended, the minister led the people in singing Luther's hymn, and Jaap Quartel played the organ even more beautifully than usual. Enclosed in the small church with fellow believers, uplifted by the music, Cor had felt certain that God would protect every one of them if they let him. She wished Bep and Henny could have heard that sermon – they would have been moved. The church had newcomers every week, and Moeder and Vader said the same was true at the Hervormde Kerk. People were hungry for the hope that came with God's message. Now, as Cor lulled her baby, she repeated Luther's hymn, tentatively at first, and anxious for the line that said "*a mighty fortress is our God.*" Her voice travelled high and quavering, slightly off-key, but swelling with enthusiasm by song's end.

Days later, when Henny and Bep arrived from Voorburg to see baby Gert, Henny brought out his camera, and took pictures of Cor resting in bed with her braids uncoiled and messy. Little Rokus had climbed up to see her, and she held him close like a shield, laughing because the camera seemed odd to her and she was uncomfortable being viewed through its lens. Henny took one picture after another, and as the shutter opened and closed, she wondered how she looked, and briefly – sinfully – thought of herself as pretty. It never occurred to her to turn the mysterious contraption around and capture this unexpected friend who would disappear from their lives so completely, but who, today, seemed as vibrant as ever – in spite of the sins against his fellow Jews. The finished prints flattered, and made her think she might actually be happier than she felt. She kept them on the dresser for some time, stealing a glance each morning and night as she brushed her thin hair, and finally tucking them away with the modest collection of photos she had already – herself at the bookstore, a favourite of Gerrit in his Sunday suit holding Rige, the *tuin* behind them. These new pictures were smaller than the others, and square – the same size as the photographs Henny shot and printed for doctored passports, a line of work that flourished underground.

Wilhelmina's speech on Radio Oranje that Christmas, lamenting her subjects' lost freedom, came amid intensified night raids on England by the Luftwaffe. In mid-November, the medieval city of Coventry, with its grand cathedral and heavy concentration of armaments factories, had met with a fate similar to Rotterdam's: its centre flattened, hundreds of people killed, more wounded. During these days, Goebbels wrote of London trembling, but also of the simple pleasure of waking his wife with flowers.

On December 29, with many previously evacuated children home in the city for Christmas, London suffered one of its heaviest attacks so far. Yet again, Bernhard photographed the devastation, awed by the black smoke ringing the dome of Saint Paul's Cathedral as the fires burned around it. At Stubbings, in the country, Wilhelmina was grateful that Juliana and the princesses were far away in Ottawa; though she missed them, their absence from this front-row seat to the carnage was reassuring. She read about Juliana's recent visit to Washington, skipping the reporter's silly accounts of her daughter's attire – mink coat over a black dress and an off-the-face, veiled hat – and noting that Juliana seemed to have made an impression on the American people, and on President Roosevelt in particular. U.S. support was vital, but Wilhelmina had also read about protest marches in America's streets. No one wanted to go to war.

In the waning days of 1940, word came from Overschie that Cor's father was ailing, the asthma that had plagued him for years now finally suffocating him. Cor brought Rige for a final visit, leaving the smaller children at home to keep the meeting serene and meaningful. She urged Rige to sit by her opa's bed and sing a song she'd learned in school, and while the girl seemed timid at first, the sound of her own high, clear voice put her at ease.

> *Blessed is he who dares to believe,*
> *Even when the eye does not see.*
> *Look – I do not ask You why,*
> *Though Your ways are a mystery.*

Cor watched Rige's face, and saw how she loved singing, like Gerrit. But Cor worried that Rige overlooked the meaning of her song – perhaps even the meaning of this visit – and was too caught up in the sounds she could make. Nevertheless, her voice brought a smile to the thin, almost lipless mouth of Jacobus Post, who at sixty-one years old looked ancient, with sunken eyes and grey skin stretched over the bones of his face. Much the way Vader den Hartog was stooped from his fishing days, Vader Post was stooped from wheezing. His chest concave, he sat up in his bed with pillows around him. Rige sang louder through his raspy inhalations, and Neeltje wept in the doorway. Cor had never witnessed her mother behave this way. Before Rige finished her song, Cor took Neeltje's arm and escorted her out of the room. She understood that the grief was layers deep – that Neeltje was sobbing for her husband, her missing son Gerry, and her baby brother Marinus in the East Indies. But it was unfitting, Cor thought, to display such emotion in the presence of a dying man and a little girl.

Back home in Leidschendam, she and Gerrit solemnly brought in the new year. With the children tucked in bed, Gerrit read, as he did each year, Psalm 90, a lengthy passage that he always timed perfectly, finishing just before the clock struck twelve. Cor bowed her head and let the words she knew well spill over her. *"All our days are passed away in thy wrath: we spend our years as a tale that is told. . . . So teach us to number our days, that we may apply our hearts to wisdom."* She smiled at the thought that, no matter how familiar the passage, the Bible held some vital message for her each time she read or listened, as long as she did so carefully. It would never let her down.

Jacobus Post succumbed on January 2. Cor travelled back to Overschie and stood over her father's coffin in the Post living room, where, until the funeral, he would rest among the potted plants and the lace-draped tables. He'd always been a serious man, but his smiling eyes had made him seem less severe. Now, with eyes closed, he looked unlike himself in his pyjamas, the traditional clothes for burial. Though she'd been given time in the room alone with him, she kept her composure just as she had when he was alive, and just as he would have were the situation reversed. She prided herself on that ability, but deeper down feared the scope of a release should she ever let it happen, and she was no longer sure which was easier: to cry or to keep from crying. These were private philosophies, shared not even with Gerrit, who understood her better than anyone. He hadn't dwelled on the pain of her loss when she told him the news, but instead had moved into action alongside her, as they packed a few things for themselves and the children and caught the train to Overschie.

Moving forward, in Cor's opinion, was the best way to deal with tragedy, which after all was God's will. So as she looked in on her father, she let go at the same time, and transferred any worries she'd had for the old man to others – Koos came first to mind, both because he looked so much like his opa, and because she knew his eczema was a precursor to asthma, no matter what Gerrit said. She thought, too, about her black-sheep brother Gerry, and wondered if he would die as their father had, struggling for breath, and if he'd be alone, far from home when it happened. Such concerns didn't seem irrational – and Cor wasn't the type to worry without reason. But lately it seemed the reasons kept multiplying. More than ever, she felt the need to keep her family close and strong. Seated between her sisters Truus and Maria at the funeral in Overschie, she listened to her own steady breathing, and wondered how it felt when the breath didn't come.

As she coped with her new baby's constant demands, a bleak January rolled on. Each day flowed into the next, so it seemed as if only one long day had passed by the time Cor's oma, Kee, followed her son-in-law to the grave, dressed, as always, in black. Before she died, she gave a tarnished brooch to Truus; in it, a photograph of Marinus, the son lost, in her mind, to the East Indies. The only two bright spots in that dark winter were the announcement that Cor's newly wed brother Tom and his wife Jeanne were expecting a child; and Koos's third birthday, for which Gerrit made him a hand-carved truck, red, with wooden wheels.

Gerrit had more time for fatherly indulgences in the winter months, and he liked using his hands. After the children had gone to bed, he worked up in the attic, carving, sanding, and fitting the pieces together. His own childhood had ended at age twelve, when he'd gone to work in Willem Quartel's market garden, but nevertheless it seemed to him that his youth had been more carefree than his children's; that he was somehow letting them down. He remembered how he had flown red paper kites in open meadows, and the confidence he'd had letting the string out at just the right moment. The kite had dipped and soared and seemed like an extension of himself up there, nearer the clouds. His fascination for the sky had perhaps begun back then, or even before. For Cor, the sky was a symbol of heaven, but for Gerrit it was so much more. He'd thought of his kite-flying days often throughout his engagement to Cor, riding between Leidschendam and Overschie, where there were so many fields suited for that activity. But now that he had his own children, kites had been relegated to the past, disallowed by the Nazis, who wanted one less distraction in the sky.

Koos adored his truck, crude as it was. Watching him roll it across the bumpy, hard weave of the carpet, Gerrit remembered that Princess Beatrix had also turned three. He'd heard about photos dropped from English planes – none had landed in the *tuin*, in spite of all the planes that crossed as he worked. Meant to boost morale, the pictures apparently showed "Trix" laughing and dancing, and sent the message that she was a sunny child unaffected by war or separation from her country and father. He didn't know how the prince kept in touch with his family, but his own step quickened at the end of each workday as he hurried home. Even in the busy months, when he worked well past the children's bedtime, he couldn't wait to get home and look in at them sleeping. What would he have done had the choice been available to him to send his family so far away? He couldn't begin to conceive of a life so different from his own, but he had no doubt he existed for the sake of his children, and would have made the choice that seemed best for them. That was the difference between being born into privilege and not: the ability to choose.

He wondered what it was like in Canada, where there were countless acres of uninhabited land and extremes of hot and cold. Other than that, he knew little about it, and more about places like Australia and its Dirk Hartog Island that he liked to think was named for an ancestor, and South Africa, which already had a large Dutch population. Before the war, he and Cor had discussed emigrating to one of those countries – somewhere that afforded a drier climate and relief from the chronic pain that burned in his lower back; somewhere far enough to stimulate their shared sense of adventure. Wherever it was, emigration would plunge them into the unknown. It was still relatively rare for Dutch people to leave the Netherlands for places other than the colonies, and neither Cor nor Gerrit could visualize life worlds away from their families. Unlike Juliana, they believed their departure, if it happened, would be permanent: that there would be no chance of returning, no visits from or to the people they'd left behind. At first, lack of money had quieted their dreams of emigrating, though they lived even more frugally than was necessary and put aside what they could towards that end. But no matter what they saved, war pushed the possibility further out of reach.

The drama of war revealed itself in microcosm everywhere. In the Leidschendam town hall, Mayor Hendrik Banning had privately resolved to hold on to his position so he could undermine the Germans from the inside, but the enthusiastic NSB supporter G. De Regt worked down the hall from him, studying his every move. De Regt was in charge of civil defence, and led the Air Protection Service. A man who followed rules well, he'd done a fine job organizing the service when it was put in place before the invasion, but it wasn't until the occupiers arrived that De Regt declared himself a German sympathizer, and thus a service that had once functioned against the Nazis now worked for them under his direction. Throughout the occupation, "protection" would consist largely of sounding the air raid sirens when Allied planes approached, and ensuring that the blackout regulations were followed. Participation in the service, though voluntary, was a plum job, since it came with an exemption certificate that allowed its men to be out after curfew. Like other collaborative bodies, it was quickly infiltrated by the resistance – which in turn, here and there, had been infiltrated by collaborators. For the occupier and the occupied, it was difficult to know, at times, which side a person was on.

On Bernhard's birthday, carnations and exuberant celebrations enlivened Leidschendam, just as in The Hague, and among the revellers there may well have been collaborators hooting and hollering and keeping their ears open. Still, De Regt was irritated by the display, and spoke to the appropriate officials when locally posted soldiers didn't make much of the incident. Banning was asked if he had seen any evidence of a celebration, but the mayor played blind and claimed he'd seen nothing of the kind. De Regt, with a statuette of Hitler on his desk and Nazi propaganda posters decorating his office walls, was determined to oust Banning, and scribbled reports about the mayor's suspicious activities. But none, for the time being, prompted German action. There were still pockets the occupiers preferred to leave alone.

In the big picture, however, civil unrest mounted, fuelled by the restrictions put upon Dutch Jews and the threat of forced labour for the unemployed. Approved by Seyss-Inquart's regime, Mussert's NSB troops paraded through Amsterdam in their black uniforms. Supporters gathered to watch, giving the Nazi salute as they passed, and proving the NSB and the Nazis still had their allies here. Eager to show off their newfound muscle, the troops began stirring up trouble in Jewish neighbourhoods, where eventually a particularly brutal fight broke out, with smashed windows and ruined market stalls, as on Germany's infamous Kristallnacht. One of Mussert's men was injured and later died of his wounds, and a day after the battle, German and Dutch police surrounded the area with barbed wire and checkpoints. Almost overnight, a vibrant Jewish neighbourhood known for its delicatessens and flea markets changed profoundly, and was closed to non-Jews.

The unrest continued. Joseph Goebbels fretted in his diary that Seyss-Inquart hadn't the stomach to deal with the trouble properly. "He is no real Nazi!" he wrote. Thus, late in February, as Cor helped Gerrit sort seeds for the *tuin*, SS Chief Heinrich Himmler ordered Police Leader Rauter to conduct a mass arrest. The Grüne Polizei, assisted by bloodhounds and their black-suited Dutch underlings, kicked down doors and eventually took hundreds of Jewish hostages – young men between twenty and thirty-five years old, whom Rauter would ship to "work camps" at Buchenwald, Germany, and Mauthausen, Austria.

In response to the widespread culling, the outlawed Dutch Communist Party organized a strike in Amsterdam, and municipal employees shut down transportation systems. Over the course of that Tuesday, February 25, office workers and labourers joined in, longshoreman closed the ports, and the strike spread to six more cities. It was a brave but futile protest against persecution – the first of its kind in all of occupied Europe, and a shock for the occupiers – but it continued for just two days until the effort collapsed under Rauter's force. The Germans fired at the strikers, killing nine on the spot and arresting hundreds. With Seyss-Inquart visiting Vienna, an aide followed Goebbels' advice to aim for Dutch pocketbooks, and fined three cities a total of eighteen million guilders for the uprising.

A couple of weeks later, eighteen of the people arrested were executed. People were stunned by the news, which, combined with the fines, brought about what Goebbels called "absolute peace." But it was no thanks, he added, to Seyss-Inquart, who thought too much before making decisions.

Perhaps due to Goebbels' disparagement, Seyss-Inquart delivered a speech in Amsterdam's cavernous Concert Hall, sending a clear message to the Nazi crowd and the party at large: "The Jews, for us, are not Dutch. They are those enemies with whom we can come to neither an armistice nor to peace. . . . We will beat the Jews wherever we meet them, and those who join them must bear the consequences. The führer has declared that the Jews have played their final act in Europe, and therefore they have played their final act."

When Reinhardt Heydrich, chief of the Gestapo, suggested Jews in Holland should be interned to protect the occupiers, Seyss-Inquart followed through. Ever efficient, the Reich commissioner had the entire Jewish population – some 140,000 people at the time of the capitulation – register themselves in a central database, promising that compliance would ensure their safety, when in fact the record of who they were and where they could be found would facilitate their undoing. Most complied with the new rule, since five years' imprisonment was the punishment for ignoring it. Later, in his matter-of-fact style, Seyss-Inquart would testify, "And then things went on, step by step." He ordered the formation of the Jewish Council, composed of prominent Dutch Jews given special privileges and the power to run their own community. But at its core the organization was a means for further manipulation of the Jewish people. And in the weeks hence, the young Jews who'd been rounded up slaved in the armament factories of Buchenwald; they carried huge rocks from the deep quarries in Mauthausen, and were beaten if they stumbled under the load.

Unbeknownst to Gerrit, he and Arthur Seyss-Inquart had things in common. The Reich commissioner had a fondness for potted plants, and made it his business to oversee the purchase of seeds and bulbs, and the design of the beautiful flower beds at Clingendael. The glassed-in terrace, warm and bright on sunny days, held exotic plants that needed protection from the cold. Arthur's wife Gertrud – he called her Trude – had initially kept busy setting up the house the way they wanted it, but life was slower now, and somewhat lonely far from home. Lady of the manor, she arranged and rearranged cut flowers from the gardens Arthur loved, and from her own autographed copy of Hitler's *Mein Kampf* she read reassuring passages about the superiority of the Aryan race, the inferiority of everyone else, and the glory of war. With her movie camera she filmed Arthur and Dorli on horseback, or swimming in a nearby pond, or rowing a small boat. Played back, the footage made the family look typically happy, and was at odds with the official shots of Arthur in uniform, his cold eyes expressionless behind thick glasses, and the photographs of Gertrud at his side, untouchable in white gloves and smart hat. Through the lens of her camera at Clingendael, Gertrud captured Dorli splashing her dad with water, making him laugh and hurry off in his swimming trunks, dragging his bad leg along. Arthur liked his exercise, and played tennis with a Dutch pro brought in to volley the ball to his strong side. Occasionally he had other partners. Among Gertrud's home movies was a match between Arthur and Heinrich Himmler, sending the ball back and forth in the sunlight, the brutish Police Leader Rauter looking on in uniform.

Unlike Seyss-Inquart, Gerrit had little time for leisure, but took his few breaks inside the *tuin*'s shed, seated on a rickety chair. A small table was nailed to the wall, and the tools of his trade hung beside it. Behind him were the stacked rolls of reed mats used to cover the heavy windows of the hotbeds. He would plant lettuce soon, and the ruffled leaves would thrive under his meticulous guidance. At auction, the other gardeners admired his uncanny knack for judging the prices and cutting the plants at just the right moment. If the price was low, he gauged the risks of waiting another day; if he waited too long, the plants would shoot into seed. He liked his work, and the jovial title of Lettuce King, but he would have been thankful for any job these days, since the Germans had finally tired of trying to woo Dutchmen over the border. The strike had shown them that soft attempts were pointless. From now on, work in German factories was compulsory for those without jobs, and even those with jobs were threatened. The Stalen-Ramen-Koop factory at the end of the Tedingerstraat agreed to start producing automobile and bicycle parts for Germany in exchange for keeping their workers at home. Gerrit wondered what he'd do if the Germans were still here next winter, when snow covered the *tuin* and rendered him briefly unemployed. Dutch winters were short, and for the most part, he could keep busy repairing fences, tools, and the like, but he couldn't say how convincing that sort of work would be to the occupiers, who wanted capable men in Germany. From his pocket he pulled a copy of an underground newspaper. He'd begun to rely on forbidden sources because German pressure had made the established ones questionable. As he read in the safety of his shed, it occurred to him that he was breaking what stood for the law these days – something he'd never done in the past – and it felt both good and necessary.

He was as much of a criminal, he supposed, when he leaned close to the radio, listening for encouragement and information, and occasionally finding a novel, disruptive idea, like the one sent out by the BBC from exiled Belgian broadcaster Victor de Laveleye. The letter *V* for victory, de Laveleye declared, should stand as a rallying symbol, a passive weapon to be employed all across occupied Europe. Soon *V*s could be seen everywhere – chalked on walls and roads, on the Dutch trains speeding by, bringing precious resources to Germany. Instead of waving, people held up two fingers to greet each other, heartened by de Laveleye's prediction that the occupiers would be weakened by the recurring presence of this sign, and the perseverance of a population eager for Germany's failure.

In Leidschendam, the optimism was infectious. The town was fast gaining a reputation to rival Oss, a city in Noord Brabant known for its petty thieves and black-marketeers. Just last week, someone had broken into a garage and stolen a truck full of wheat, crashing through the big double doors to make their exit. The truck reappeared a week later, minus the wheat – the culprits had no doubt made a hefty sum selling it underground. The thievery and sabotage made life difficult for Mayor Banning, who risked losing his job if Leidschendammers went too far while he was in office. So-called "good" mayors walked a thin line, hounded by colleagues ready to push them off when opportunities arose. In the Leidschendam town hall, the battle between Mayor Banning and De Regt continued, but as De Regt entered his office one morning and readied himself for a day's duties in service of the occupiers, he noticed his statuette of Hitler must have taken a tumble and been placed back in the same spot on his desk. A piece of the führer's ear was missing and gave him a helpless look – surely to De Regt's snickering co-workers a sign of things to come, but in De Regt's mind, likely more akin to blasphemy.

As Juliana prepared breakfast for her daughters in their Rockcliffe home one morning in June, Bernhard stepped through the doorway. He'd made the surprise journey in somewhat humble fashion – seated on the floor of an RAF bomber for the fifteen-hour trip – only to discover his daughters didn't remember him. He tried wooing them back as best he could over the short visit, but found wooing reporters was easier. The role of dashing pilot suited Bernhard, who was physically fit and reputedly a natural flyer. Both England and Canada laid claim to him, and the press called him both "a typical young Englishman" and a man resembling "any young Canadian airman in appearance and manner." In fact he was far from ordinary, with his polka-dot ascots and his sports cars. When reporters asked him about his fatherland, he responded that he felt only bitterness for Germany and its people. "I think they are going to have to take what is coming to them when Germany is defeated" – an attitude Goebbels called nothing less than high treason. "A prince," he sneered in his diary, "and he is more devious and contemptible than any worker could ever be."

Bernhard's exciting new life was unlike the lives his girls had been leading: lunching on stools at the Woolworths counter, taking in matinees at the cinema. Juliana did her own grocery shopping, and now and again babysat for the neighbours. Though she attended lavish dinner parties with Prime Minister William Lyon Mackenzie King and the like, she also knitted socks for soldiers, donated her own royal blood, and volunteered at a second-hand clothing store that raised money for the war effort. In the winter, Bernhard discovered, the girls had built snow forts, and learned to skate by pushing chairs across the ice. Come September, Juliana would enrol Beatrix in the nearby public school, like any regular girl.

A visit of several weeks was all the indefatigable prince could spare. He returned to London and resumed his training as a pilot, and after months of practice earned his wings and was named honorary commander with the RAF. The title was tinged with irony, as when he'd arrived in England with Wilhelmina at the beginning of the war, the War Ministry had turned down his services because he was German and they'd felt he couldn't be trusted. Not even King George had managed to secure a position for him. But to Wilhelmina, Bernhard had become a right hand. She'd appointed him liaison officer between Dutch and British forces, a role that would grow as the Allies gained ground.

Dutch forces in exile had continued to play a part in the war since the Netherlands' capitulation. Many soldiers had gotten out of the country when the battle was lost, racing south to France and taking part in the desperate struggle at Dunkirk. From there, the survivors had been evacuated to England, and since then, had been joined by Dutch expatriates from all over the world. Fitted in British khakis that sported the Dutch lion on their sleeves, the group was officially named the Princess Irene Brigade, after Juliana's second daughter.

Like Juliana, Wilhelmina had shed much of the formality that permeated her life in Holland, but hard as she tried to seem ordinary, her regal bearing blared through. When she met with the *Engelandvaarders* under the fruit trees at her country house, Stubbings, she felt like a man of the people, head to head with the heroes of the underground movement, a queen with well-worn galoshes. Wilhelmina could barely contain her glee when she heard that Hitler had double-crossed the Russians and invaded, tearing up the non-aggression treaty that had served him so well as he concentrated his attack in the west. The Americans, still not officially a part of the ever-growing war, dispatched their navy to Iceland, seeing Germany's latest move on Russia as an encroachment on the pathways to the Western Hemisphere. Wilhelmina was thrilled. Now that the United States had moved closer to the position of active ally, she predicted "the beginning of the end." In her next address to the Dutch people, she prodded, "Those who act at the right moment, hit the Nazis on the head."

Gerrit heard the speech, and another that came by summer's end, when Wilhelmina turned sixty-one. Radio Oranje broadcast birthday greetings to the queen, and he and Cor were among thousands who gathered privately with the volume turned low and two illicit treasures next to the radio: the queen's portrait and a miniature Dutch flag at half-mast. They heard Prince Bernhard wax poetic from England – "Already our eyes see in the far distance the rays of a light heralding victory" – and listened as Princess Juliana in Canada added the wish that her mother's next birthday would be celebrated in a liberated homeland. But after the broadcast ended, Cor and Gerrit decided that the most realistic words had come from Prime Minister Gerbrandy: "We stand here in dark times while the war goes on, and nobody knows how long it will last. But . . . we know that the powers of evil will not ultimately be victorious."

"Nothing so terrible can last forever," said Cor as she folded the flag.

Gerrit agreed. But he realized that some of the things that had happened over the last year had been beyond his comprehension before the invasion. Here they were, listening to the radio illegally and hiding the queen's portrait. Last month there'd been sweeping arrests of politicians, and political parties had been disbanded, with the exception of the NSB. That, and the presence of the soldiers across the street, told him more unbelievable things could yet occur.

Rige was in her second year at Emmaschool by this time, and could puzzle through a few words in the papers her father liked to read. The school was a new building, and even had a gymnasium, unusual at the time, but Rige was more impressed by the light slanting through the stained-glass windows, the gleam of the wooden floors kept polished by her Oom Nico, and the painting of Jesus surrounded by children of all races. Not yet five, she already had a shadow of awareness that the colours and the composition moved her more than Jesus himself.

It took twenty minutes for children's legs to walk from the house on the Tedingerstraat to the elementary school in Voorburg, and Koos would not attend until September, so Rige followed her mother's strict admonishment not to dawdle or change her route and made the trip four times a day, following older children past flowers sprouting in the cracks of brick roads. She crossed the rail-bridge that spanned the Vliet, and passed a willow-treed park carpeted with mauve and white crocuses. The park was named Vreugd en Rust, or Joy and Rest, something Rige felt when she escaped her brothers. School provided that kind of reprieve, but it was also lonely until a girl new to the neighbourhood appeared both there and at church and aimed her wide smile at Rige. Her name was Ineke Batelaan, and she was just Rige's age. She had straight hair cut squarely above her earlobes, set off by a huge bow. Rige was only allowed a bow on Sundays, for church, but Ineke's was always present, coordinated with her outfit. Rige watched it bobbing along with her as she trailed home behind Ineke one day, under the railway bridge and past the flower shop. The smell of cut flowers lingered in her nostrils as she worked up the nerve to ask Ineke to be her friend. Once she did so, they made the trip back and forth together, Ineke a plump, outgoing girl and Rige a shy, thin one. They were unaware of how the arrangement satisfied their mothers – Rie Batelaan had approached Cor to urge such a union if it didn't happen on its own, since both houses were overrun with brothers, and the women were determined to see friendships form within the Gereformeerde faith. But for Rige and Ineke, the friendship had nothing to do with church – though it made Sundays more fun.

In the spot Gerrit gave them in his *tuin*, the girls turned the soil and pulled wriggling earthworms free. As they watched Gerrit working, Rige felt a surge of pride when he carried the yoke hung with watering cans on his shoulders; she was sure he must be the strongest man in the world. She and Ineke planted *slaapmutsje*, or nightcap poppies, and paid no attention to the trains passing the *tuin*, carrying stolen butter, beans, sugar, rice, tobacco, oil, textiles, and arms. The poppies had a habit of self-seeding, and occasionally Gerrit found their wispy greens sneaking up among his vegetables.

Rige became a regular visitor to the Batelaans' house beside Leidschendam's coal gas plant, where Ineke's father Henk, an elder in their church, had an important job as general manager. He and his family had come to Leidschendam from Rijssen, in the eastern part of the country not far from the German border, where they'd lived at the time of the invasion. As a perk of Henk's job, they were ensconced in a house much bigger than the den Hartogs', and Rige wished she could be enveloped in this loud, affectionate family – hers seemed wan and reserved by contrast. Her mother, so strict and serious, was nothing like Ineke's mother, Rie, who hugged and kissed her children easily, which maybe meant she loved them more. The Batelaans lived in the whole house, not just the upper half with an oma and opa below, as at 61 – theirs was four stories including the ground-floor offices of the gas factory, and had a large balcony, and multiple bedrooms and washrooms, while at the Tedingerstraat a zinc tub got pulled out on bath days. *There's plenty of room for me at Ineke's*, thought Rige, but guilt followed, and as she passed the park, she muttered an apology to God, having been told by Cor that he – *He* – knew what she thought, what she did, every moment of the day. Like the bogeyman, or the one who made the curtains move when the lights went out.

Close to home, she studied an important-looking sign pasted on the community centre's wall, but to her great disappointment, the clumps of letters made no sense to her, and she carried on, adding frustration to her load of guilt and uneasiness. She considered asking her parents about the sign and what it said, for such notices had begun to appear everywhere in Leidschendam – but she knew she would be told not to look, not to ask, not to wonder, and she tried to obey these rules. And already in her mind before she had even arrived home, she was upstairs in her nightdress, on her knees preparing for prayer while her mother sat on the bed waiting. The shoe on the jute carpet tapped impatiently, and Rige began: "The bad things that I have done, O Lord, do not make account of them. Even though my sins are many, for Jesus's sake, make me pure."

Ineke's mother, Rie, paused in front of the same sign on her way to church, and wrote about it in a secret journal begun that summer. The notice – German, without a Dutch translation – warned the population against helping pilots whose planes had been gunned down on their way to Germany, like the Czech men who'd landed in Leidschendam last year and disguised themselves in farmers' overalls. *You will be shot*, it said to those who could read the warning. Most couldn't, and so Rie's husband Henk wrote an official request to the mayor that, in future, announcements to the Dutch people be written in Dutch. That letter was not the only one he slipped into the post around this time: another travelled back to Rijssen, to a Jewish shoemaker Henk had befriended there. If need be, Henk wrote, the Batelaan home was open to the man and his family. The shoemaker and his wife refused the offer, expressing gratitude but saying it would be too difficult to follow a Jewish lifestyle in a Christian home, and forwarding the letter to their grown son, Max, in Amsterdam, in case the need arose.

It took courage to refuse the offer, but also to extend it, for by now, an increasing number of people suspected of subversive activities were being held in a prison in Scheveningen at the edge of The Hague, where high walls overlooked the wind-whipped dunes. The Dutch called the prison the Oranjehotel because of its patriotic inhabitants, and the thought of ending up there didn't deter men like Henk Batelaan or Cor's cousin Dirk. In Zaandam, near Amsterdam, where he worked as a carpenter, Dirk had joined a resistance group, and delivered copies of the illegal communist newspaper, *De Waarheid*, hiding them in the seat of his bicycle. But the stakes of such daring rose along with the necessity for it. By now, the Germans had demanded all copper, lead, tin, and nickel possessions be handed over for weapon production, so the Batelaans, the den Hartogs, the Bloms, and the Quartels all found hiding spaces for their treasures, set on keeping what was rightfully theirs and also thwarting the occupiers in any way they could.

Throughout the Netherlands, the *V* symbol had expanded into Morse code, and the BBC used its sound, three short beats and a long, tapped out on drums, as station identification throughout its European service. Announcers had explained how the *V* sound could be made using anything as an instrument, so that children clapped the *V* with their hands, and trains called it with their horns. The "quiet knocking" rebellion had an effect, so much so that on July 14, at the stroke of midnight, the Germans began their own *V* campaign. By morning, the occupied territories were covered with posters that read, v = VICTORY, BECAUSE GERMANY IS WINNING FOR EUROPE ON ALL FRONTS.

For the people living through the occupation, it often felt that way. Jews were being rounded up around the country and grouped in specific areas, and Bep and Henny, living in The Hague now, had finally married, solely because the Germans had said that Jews with non-Jewish spouses would be given special consideration where the growing list of rules was concerned. But Nazi promises, they knew, were shifting things, and within the year, Germany's racial Nuremberg laws would be in full effect in the Netherlands, making it illegal for Jews and non-Jews to marry, or engage in sexual intercourse. Already Jewish businesses had been closed or taken over, ostensibly to protect national security. Dutch Jews continued to pour into the allotted districts in Amsterdam, while German Jews were taken from Dutch cities and towns and sent to Camp Westerbork, where a relentless wind lifted sand and coal dust and covered everything with a fine black powder. In this remote, barren place of dazzling sunsets, barracks were constructed, each designed to hold three hundred people.

On *Prinsjesdag*, what should have been Wilhelmina's ceremonial opening of parliament, Seyss-Inquart announced the confiscation of royal "enemy" property, which he claimed was a valid response to the queen's recent lashing of Hitler at the onset of the fighting with Russia. While the buildings of Noordeinde and Huis ten Bosch officially remained in the hands of the Dutch government, their contents were ransacked. Private archives were looted, vintage bottles were pulled from the wine cellar, and silver, crystal, china, furniture, tapestries, and paintings – the kinds of finery that made up a queen's household – were shipped to Germany, or to privileged residences within the Dutch borders. The audacity stung, but Wilhelmina knew that many of her own and the country's treasured belongings had been hidden before the invaders arrived: at the Koninklijk Palace in Amsterdam, art treasures had been bricked up in the cellar; closer to Leidschendam, the famed Oranjezaal paintings had been removed from the walls of Huis ten Bosch and stored in the dunes in a top-secret location. Rembrandt's masterpiece *The Night Watch* had been rolled for storage and heavily crated, and other national treasures hidden in vaults and even on barges. There'd been a sudden rush to build proper storage places to house vulnerable pieces, but not all safe holds had been ready by the time of the invasion, so the Germans took it upon themselves to finish the job, and in turn protect the work from an Allied invasion, as though it was theirs to guard. In similar manner, the Germans had requisitioned the Queen's Office in The Hague, and set up a casino amid the gilt-framed mirrors and opulent chandeliers. Soon Anton Mussert would refurbish the space for his headquarters, removing the gaming tables and adding a French garden between wings. Seyss-Inquart's Clingendael home was not far from here; nor was Bep and Henny's small apartment on the Rhenenstraat. And Leidschendam was situated at the edge of Seyss-Inquart's self-proclaimed seat of government, where some of the most appalling decisions became law, stamped with the seal of The Hague's Court of Justice.

Under editors judged suitable by the Propaganda Ministry, newspapers like *Het Nationale Dagblad* did their best to put a positive spin on alarming news. They reported that Dutch people could attend concerts, frequent public baths, and sip drinks at a café without the presence of Jews sullying those places. Rie Batelaan wrote mockingly in her journal: "What excellent care for our people! But – we barely show our appreciation." Once again, under Police Leader Rauter, Jews had been selected for deportation. Almost no one went willingly; most were forced from their homes during night raids. Henny's cousin was among the twenty taken from his hometown of Hengelo and sent to the Mauthausen quarries to join those deported around the time of the February strike. By coincidence, Bep's cousin was married to a Hengelo Jew, and he, too, was sent to Austria. Henny's relative, a strong butcher, wrote to reassure his family that although the work was heavy, "I shall try to keep up." Yet within weeks they received news of his death, and by year's end, Bep's cousin had also perished. The BBC revealed that the men at Mauthausen were dying by the hundreds, and the illegal paper *Het Parool* concurred. "In spite of all the rumours doing the rounds," the paper reported, "no one knows with certainty how these unaccused young men were murdered by the German beasts."

What often struck Cor was how quickly her own family and others around them adjusted to the forced changes. Even Gerrit's parents surprised her: sometimes, when a rush of planes passed, Moeder sang hymns, hoping to distract the children until it was quiet again. An old woman shouldn't have such worries, Cor thought to herself, but there was little to be done. In a sense, they were all prisoners now. They carried their mandatory identity cards wherever they went, showing them when asked. Cards that belonged to Jews were stamped with a red J that stood out like a branding. Cor's ID, kept in a pouch hung from her neck, showed a smiling image of her that suggested happiness, and yet she followed the routine of her days with jaw clenched, heartache compounding inside her – four days earlier, a small light had flickered to life when her brother Tom became father to twin girls, but by morning, one of the babies had died, and the second would follow within weeks of her sister. Cor, upon hearing the news, got to her knees and began scrubbing the mats and floors of the house on the Tedingerstraat, work enough for several days and a substitute for tears. Three months gone, her fifth child barely showed beneath her apron.

Winter slid in, and on Saint Nicolaas Eve – Gert's first birthday – all non-Dutch Jews were ordered to register for "voluntary emigration." With the news from Mauthausen fresh in their minds, many opted for a different route, passing through the lowlands to France and beyond, skittish as deer in a wood full of hunters. Others believed their odds better in the camps, and waited to be taken. Everyone grew cautious and nervous, and even the tall poplars that lined the dike roads seemed to hold themselves stiff and alert.

Cor's mother, around the time Cor's father died, had pressed two coins into Cor's palm, each with a pin soldered to its back, so that whatever might happen to her between Leidschendam and Overschie, she'd have King Willem from 1875 and Queen Wilhelmina from 1912 to buy her safety, or just luck – which of course Cor equated with God. She had no doubt that God was watching the day Rige walked homeward and saw six German soldiers moving two by two along the canal path, their

greatcoats swinging. Rige was familiar with the sight of German soldiers, since several lived in the Tedingerstraat, but these six together,
stepping in unison and moving with a purpose, made her hold her
breath. They were nearing the Tedingerstraat, but she flew ahead to
keep them from finding her father, not stopping to consider why she
was worried for him, or what he might have done to incur the soldiers'
wrath. She pushed open the door, ran past her oma to the second floor
and stood breathless, looking at her mother.

"There are soldiers," she said. "Six of them coming this –"

She suddenly felt silly for suggesting they were coming for
her father, of all people, but before she could finish her sentence, her
mother grabbed her arm and hurried her through to the kitchen. Hands
shaking, Rige stood at the table as ordered, peeling potatoes as on any
day. From the corner of her eye she saw Koos tearing Rokus's picture
book, Gert taking two wobbly steps, and also what she was not supposed
to see: her father, pulling on his coat, scarf, and hat, and hastening
up to the attic.

Gerrit kept his radio hidden in the bedroom closet these days, since the
broadcasts he listened to had been banned, and now he hid his own
person, too, a floor above, seated on trusses in a cold gap between the
inner and outer walls of his house. He waited for the soldiers to knock,
and his mind raced. Were they taking men at random, or had the two
soldiers at the van Kampens' been watching him? Had he been overheard listening to Radio Oranje? They said the penalty was fifteen
years' imprisonment, or death for repeating whatever he'd heard on
foreign broadcasts. Maybe someone else had turned him in for something as simple as bartering carrots for shoes last week when Cor said
Koos had outgrown his. Gerrit put his faith in Cor, knowing she would
tell them whatever she could to keep them from searching the house.
He only hoped the children would say nothing. Rige's terrified face, or

a forthright question from Koos – "*Where did Daddy go?*" – could easily give him away. Squatting in the dark, he imagined the German factories, and the sound of Allied planes overhead, aiming to bomb them. Cold as he was, he sweated, remembering the ratcheting noise of machine-gun fire coming out of the darkness on the Glazenstraat, and the panic in the voice that shouted "Go back!" He closed his eyes. What he needed to do was trust and stay quiet, so he pulled his scarf up over his nose and breathed deeply. Already his back had begun to throb, but he let an hour pass, and another, his mind returning of its own accord to worrisome thoughts: a fifth child coming, the second in wartime; the house full already with his parents downstairs. He was supposed to be head of this household – three generations under his care – but here he was between the walls, terrified to come out.

At last he opened the panel in the wainscotting and peered into the room. Cor hadn't come to tap on the wall – their agreed signal that all was clear – but Gerrit knew she would only do that if she could be sure the children wouldn't see her, even if the soldiers had moved on. The smell of potatoes wafted up from the kitchen, and he heard the faint sounds of children playing. Surely the soldiers were gone. Backwards he went down the steep attic stairs to the second floor, where he stood for a moment in the bedroom he shared with Cor, blowing on his hands to warm them. He removed his coat and hat and laid them on the bed where the white coverlet fell in neat folds at the corners. As he turned to go back to the main room he caught sight of his own reflection in the dresser's oval mirror. Watching himself, he tried to assume his most ordinary expression. Whatever the children had seen may have puzzled them, but he and Cor had agreed: the less they knew, the better.

FOUR

Kalm, Kalm, Kalm
1942–1943

AS THE WINDMILLS in the Driemanspolder turned in the lightly falling snow, American ships exploded in the Hawaiian Islands, and a place once brimming with pearls changed the already menacing course of history. After Japan's attack on Pearl Harbor, the United States joined the conflict that spread across the globe and continued to exceed its own brutality. Looking to protect the oil-rich Dutch East Indies, Wilhelmina and her government-in-exile quickly declared war on Japan, but East Indies forces, a motley mix of regular soldiers, militia, and volunteers, were no match for the Japanese fleet and army, just as nearly two years earlier, the Dutch had been no match for the Germans. Cor's Oom Marinus – the son Oma Kee had so missed – was an officer

with the Dutch forces stationed there, and a recipient of the Golden
Medal for Loyal Service. Years before the war, in 1924, he'd married an
Indonesian woman and settled down on the island of Java, in a big
stone house complete with maids to sweep the verandas, a gardener to
tend the flower beds, and a chauffeur to shuttle the family where they
wanted to go, which sounded grand to his relatives in the Netherlands.
However far away, he'd stayed in contact with his family back home,
and in 1926 had brought his wife for a visit. His older sister Neeltje,
Cor's mother, had tried to convince her favourite brother to move home
permanently, but he'd told her that the Indies was where he belonged.
Neeltje had settled for his promise that they'd see each other again, and
kept his photograph in her living room. Another sister went further,
maintaining a bedroom for him, as though any day – braving the conflict
– the darling youngest might walk through the door.

With the approach of spring, the underground papers reported
heavy losses in the Netherlands' controversial crown jewel, and
Wilhelmina broadcast her encouragement to the East Indies soldiers,
Marinus among them, and the Allied forces who'd joined the troops.
Another of Cor's relatives was also defending the territory – Teun de
Korte, Cor's cousin and a nephew of Marinus. When the Japanese sank
Dutch ships and the Allied auxiliary fleet, the queen insisted on Radio
Oranje, "We are not beaten, and the battle is not over for us." But
Joseph Goebbels, who devoured international news, ridiculed her
optimism in his diary. "This Wilhelmina is surely a sad sight," he
wrote. "One can see what happens if women have a decisive word to
say in politics." The battle ended quickly, and under the new regime,
homage to the royal family was not tolerated, as in the Netherlands:
in Bandung, the occupiers executed three radio employees for broad-
casting the "Wilhelmus."

As Gerrit leaned into his bedroom closet, listening to the radio, he
wondered if the Japanese would be harsher masters than the Germans.
He didn't know of Teun's posting, but wondered what would become of
Cor's Oom Marinus with the fall of the Indies. In fact, Marinus had

already been captured, taken from his home while a tropical breeze stirred the curtains against the shutters and nudged the wicker rocking chair on the veranda. He was placed in a camp at Bandung, though no news of his years of internment would reach the family in the Netherlands until after the war. As a young man, Gerrit had borrowed books about the Indies from Cor's family library, and read about the steamy jungle and an ocean as blue as a jewel. He asked himself which would be worse: a war fought in the fetid heat of a tropical island, or one waged in the bitter cold of a northern winter. In Russia, the war between the Germans and the Soviets had reached unprecedented ferocity, and to Gerrit's dismay, volunteer Dutch troops who sympathized with the Nazi cause fought beside German soldiers on the Eastern Front. Captured Soviets weren't protected by The Hague Convention, which Russia hadn't signed, so were regularly massacred by their adversaries. But because Russian soldiers knew their chances of surviving were small, they were more willing to fight to the death than be taken. Generals who retreated from battle were executed under Russian leader Joseph Stalin's orders, and special troops were deployed to shoot deserters. Desperate to win, both sides suffered huge losses throughout a merciless winter. Even with the mittens and socks knitted for them by NSB ladies' groups and Nazi wives like Gertrud Seyss-Inquart, many German soldiers lacked proper winter attire, and froze to death at their posts. Weapons jammed and engines failed to start. By March 1942, Germany had lost nine hundred thousand men on the Eastern Front, and pulled back to replenish its forces.

It occurred to Gerrit that war was like gambling. He thought of his fellow soldiers during mobilization, and how they had pushed money into the centre of the table only to have it pulled away from them when they laid out their cards. The more money they'd lost, the more they wagered. In war, men played the same game with lives. There were thousands, millions of people dying everywhere, which meant that every day the war at all angles required more foot soldiers, sailors, officers, and fighter pilots, as well as factory workers who churned out the parts of planes, ships, and tanks, and even made boots and helmets – all the things that got blown apart whether the battle was lost or won. As Germany reached its long fingers into the occupied territories, taking whatever it needed, and Japan plundered the South Pacific for its oil and rubber, Gerrit wondered if there was a person anywhere who remained untouched by war.

The fighting kept redrawing the map of the world, but Gerrit's garden stayed the same, two and a half acres of land that determined the shape of his days. The *tuin* had iced over early this year. Gerrit had pulled Rige on a wooden sled to the Brussels sprouts that clung to their leafy, vertical stems at the back of the garden, and she'd picked them and put them in a pail while he worked nearby. Sprouts were perfect when touched by the smallest amount of frost, but any more and he would have lost that crop altogether. Throughout the winter, he'd prayed for an early spring – if being busy was no guarantee of avoiding deportation, it was still his best chance. Around Christmastime, all the Gereformeerde churches had protested Seyss-Inquart's labour conscription for the unemployed, but it had done no good, and now that spring was upon them, new fears arose amid speculations of what the occupiers would and wouldn't do to get workers. It was not clear what the rules were and whether or not they'd be enforced, and Gerrit worried a labourer working rented land would be considered expendable. But he couldn't go underground and continue to run the garden, so if they wanted him in Germany, they'd take him. Since Dordrecht, he'd dreamed that soldiers chased him, a nightmare that now stayed with him in the daytime, when a simple breeze became breath on his ear.

Soon Cor would have their fifth child, and the idea of never meeting this baby spurred Gerrit on: in April, after long discussions with Cor, and years of frugality that had given them some savings, he approached the *tuin*'s owner and made an offer for the land. The owner was more agreeable than he might have been, understanding Gerrit's predicament, and the men quickly came to terms that made Gerrit a landowner, albeit in an occupied country. If his new status protected him from deportation, then so did German money, for much of his earnings still came from the occupiers, who hoarded the best of what his garden produced. Cor's eyes brightened as she looked at the deed, and she grinned at the thought of all those Post jaws dropping in Overschie. She could hear Jacques now, teasing the *boerenjongen* for aristocratic aspirations. But neither she nor Gerrit cared for status: the purchase was strategic – to keep Gerrit at home – and also speculative – when the war ended, which it had to someday, the sale of the land might buy their passage overseas. It was an exciting thought, but for now they put it aside, doing their best to proceed as an ordinary family living through extraordinary times.

Their eldest son, Koos, was of an age to go to school now, though attendance there had become sporadic. Jewish children were no longer allowed in public schools, but even in Christian Bible schools like Koos and Rige's, fewer children showed up. Family life was disrupted by absent fathers sent to work in German factories or hiding to avoid going, and mothers struggled with ration coupons and the hard choices necessitated by too little money and too few goods to spend it on. When they did attend classes, the children got vitamin supplements supplied by the municipal health service, but in the winter, rationing of electricity and fuel for heat forced the schools to minimize the days of operation, and so only in dribs and drabs were the children students, following a Nazi-implemented curriculum that now emphasized German language lessons and history.

Teachers who didn't comply with the new learning standards put their jobs in jeopardy. Yet signs of defiance flashed in the classrooms: one teacher kept an orange hanky tucked in the cuff of her blouse; another allowed spelling competitions with words that started with *W*, for Wilhelmina – risky games that could result in deportation. The teachers realized the ramifications extended beyond the personal, for if they lost their jobs, German sympathizers would fill the positions and do their best to influence children in a pro-Nazi way. As the years of occupation passed, children took on the burden of a war they didn't understand. Kids whose parents had joined the NSB were teased and beaten at school, and these same "good" teachers turned a blind eye to the cruelty. More than ever, war games were enacted on the playground, with each side taking its cache of prisoners. Grey-haired, grey-suited, the principal of Emmaschool oversaw it all, standing at the door each morning before the children filed in, and in the background, Gerrit's brother Nico in his coveralls swept the long hallways.

Koos – an intelligent but mischievous little boy – found the classrooms too small and quiet, but not as unpleasant as church. He had his dead opa's name and deep-set eyes, and in the spring of 1942, when he was four years old, the same raspy wheeze of asthma tightened his chest, as Cor had predicted. Several times a week – and always, strangely, on Sundays – Koos's asthma flared up, and Cor and Rige fashioned a makeshift steam room upstairs. Cor thought of her still-missing brother Gerry, and the way he sat, back straight and arms wide to open his lungs and make breathing easier. Unlike her father's sunken chest, Gerry's bowed out in front of him, as though the bones had stretched with his constant heaving.

Lately Cor's ribs felt just as stretched with the baby inside, and one day the familiar pangs of labour woke her in the chill early morning. She rose and, still in her nightclothes, prepared a hurried meal for the children, not pausing to comb and braid her hair or raise the blackout blinds in the front window. The clenching of her womb caused Cor to skip the Bible reading that morning and shorten the prayer, and she almost pushed Rige and Koos through the door to school. By the time they arrived back home for lunch, Dr. van der Stam had come and gone and a nurse was there. The drops from Gerrit's ritual nosebleed had been washed from the sink, and a brother, Nicolaas, had been born.

In the weeks following baby Niek's arrival, Henny didn't come to photograph the newest den Hartog. Bep arrived at the Tedingerstraat alone, and barely smiled, which made her seem to the children like a different person – a Tante Bep impostor. Koos tugged repeatedly on Bep's skirt before she noticed and got to her knees to be the elephant to his wheezy mouse. But the play was weak, and didn't last long. Koos lost interest and wandered elsewhere, and Bep sat at the table looking down at the tea Cor had made from dried rose leaves and spices. She let Cor do most of the talking. When Rige saw her mother's hand cup Bep's, the unexpected tenderness embarrassed her, so she sneaked away to find Ineke.

For months now, from every corner of the Netherlands, Jews had been steadily rounded up and taken to one of three areas in Amsterdam. By Seyss-Inquart's decree, they'd been ordered to relinquish all rights to property, and had to turn in gold, silver, platinum, precious stones, and pearls. Only wedding rings could be kept, and four-piece sets of silver utensils, and the fillings in their teeth. When Jews were moved, police took their house keys, and a special registry recorded meticulous, room-by-room lists of their belongings – 4 *lace curtains, 2 bed throws, tea trolley, toy box*. The intimate items amounted to an exhaustive theft of goods that were then made available to the resident Germans or their Dutch cohorts, or else shipped to Germany and distributed as charity among those displaced by Allied bombs. Jews were now barred from restaurants, cafés, pools, public gardens, libraries, concert halls, zoos, parks, and more. They could only ride transit if there was room in the rearmost car and they had the required permit. Over their hearts was the now-infamous yellow star – *de Davidster* – which had prompted a smattering of non-Jews countrywide to sport yellow flower boutonnieres, or to wear the star in protest. The star wasn't free; it had to be purchased for four cents and one textile coupon, and the word JOOD was stamped across it in black letters, marring everyday clothes and also wedding gowns, morning suits, and flower-girls' dresses.

Henny Cahn was what the Germans termed a "full Jew," but married to a non-Jew, a detail he and Bep hoped would afford him certain privileges. Just as Gerrit puzzled over the employment rules, Henny debated wearing the badge. Some of his friends felt they'd be safer without it – less likely to be grabbed off the street by Rauter's men, or hassled by NSB thugs. Others disagreed. Their identity cards, if they had them, were stamped with a J, and if they were stopped and asked for their papers, those without the badge might well be deported. Henny wavered. His contact at Voorburg city hall, for whom he falsified passports, had offered Henny and Bep refuge if the situation grew precarious, but at this point Henny wouldn't consider going into hiding.

Sitting opposite Cor, Bep put her head in her hands as she recounted Henny's predicament. "He loves to be outside," she said. "You know him – it's one of his favourite things, getting up early and walking in the Zuiderpark. He wouldn't survive being cooped up anywhere." So now he was wearing the star, she continued, but neither of them knew what would come of that. He'd only donned it, Bep said, for the sake of a friend – a woman married to a non-Jew, like him, but with two small children, and Henny had decided for a jumble of reasons that it would be safer for her to wear the star than not. "He wanted to show her," Bep said, "that it was not so bad." Reprehensible as the thing was to him, he'd sewn the star to his coat and gone to convince her. "He's so cocky," she went on, seeming both proud and frustrated. "He stayed out past the curfew, and happened upon a group of NSB men on his way home." As they approached him, he'd searched their faces and locked eyes with the one who looked almost decent. "He just stared and stared at that man, until suddenly he waved Henny away and told the others to let him go. Lucky." She pushed her tea away and grimaced. "If you can call it that."

Cor poured hot tea over the portion that had cooled in Bep's cup. She doubted luck had much to do with Henny's experience, and wanted to tell Bep it was God's work. Instead she slid the cup back to Bep and said, "I know it doesn't taste as good as real tea, but drink it up – you'll feel better."

"But now that he's been seen with the star," Bep continued, "it's just too risky for him to go without it."

Cor nodded, unsure of what to say. She knew that Jews were frequently being sent to Amsterdam, and that many had died in Mauthausen. She worried for Bep's safety too, for it seemed plausible that if Bep and Henny's marriage could protect Henny, it could as easily endanger Bep. They were linked now, for better or for worse. Gently, she suggested, "God will guide you – if you put your trust and faith –"

"Please," said Bep. "Not now."

But Cor prayed anyway, silently, and then later on her knees with Gerrit. She prayed specifically for everyone she could think of, and generally for everyone else – the good and the bad – trusting that God's plan was without flaw. The idea required enormous faith: lately, the ruthless Police Leader Rauter had begun ramping up his disciplinary tactics, executing resistance prisoners or transporting them to one of a growing number of camps in occupied Europe. Cor's cousin Dirk de Korte was entangled in the surge of retribution. In Rotterdam to visit his mother, he was overheard deriding the Nazis on a street corner. Another Dutchman turned him in, and he was taken to the Oranjehotel, where the stone walls of the cells bore the scratchings of prisoners gone before: *Kalm, kalm, kalm*, read one, and *Je maintiendrai*, echoing the queen's motto. Another cautioned, *Weet wat je zecht, zeg nooit wat je weet* – Know what you say, but don't say what you know – advice Dirk must have taken to heart. After several days of torture, he died of his wounds. His demise was not at all what he'd boasted it would be, and he took no enemies with him. His family never saw his body, and identified only his belongings. Dirk was returned to them for burial in a sealed casket, but when they pressed for information, a pitying German official told the family about Dirk's violent end: that he'd given away nothing in spite of his pain.

In Leidschendam, Ineke Batelaan's teenage brothers reported the murder of Dirk, "Mevrouw den Hartog's cousin," in the underground newsletter they'd begun, and while it must have been Cor who gave the boys their information, she never mentioned Dirk – a young man just her age – to her own children, either then or in the years ahead.

On Fridays, Moeder den Hartog walked to the auction house to collect the week's earnings. The job had been hers since her husband first became a gardener, and until this spring day she'd fulfilled it without incident. But a rapid knock on the door startled her when she'd just returned home, and she stuffed the money into the cold wood-stove before answering. Outside, the sky was black with a gathering spring storm, and Moeder took it as God's warning. She turned the doorknob with a shaking hand, but it was only the nurse, come to check on Cor and baby Niek.

Later, when Moeder lit the stove to cook dinner, Cor heard her scream, and rushed downstairs with the baby in her arms. Cor looked into Moeder's crumpled face, pink with humiliation, and felt a rush of pity. She'd burned the money. The old woman was fading – losing the sharp edge that had so often clashed with Cor's. She had red rheumy eyes and frequently a vacant expression that broke Cor's heart if she looked too long. It was wrong for the elderly to finish out their lives in fear, and she questioned the decision the old couple had come to: to move out of Tedingerstraat 61 and make way for their grandchildren. There was no room for the couple in Voorburg with Gerrit's brother Nico, who lived in a small place with his son and wife Gerda. Sister Mar's in Rijswijk was just as crowded, and Cor knew Vader would miss helping in the *tuin* if he moved too far away. So Moeder and Vader had obtained permission from the housing authority to move one street over from Cor and Gerrit, to Broekweg 14. The extra rental was more afford-able now that Gerrit owned his land. Even the most meagre profits were theirs to keep – when they didn't go up in smoke – so they would make do financially. And Cor reminded herself that the two streets were a sort of community unto themselves, where neighbours looked out for each other. Moeder and Vader would be close enough that the children could visit often, for although Cor found her mother-in-law trying, Rige and the boys loved her.

When the move came, any residual guilt fell away under the new arrangement, and Cor at last felt that she was the woman of the house.

She asked Gerrit to move the rounded, velvet-lined cabinet that displayed her cups and saucers to a prominent spot on the main floor, and placed the bookcase in the front room. Behind its leaded-glass door were translated copies of works by Charles Dickens and Jules Verne, an encyclopedia, bound Christian magazines, and the books Cor's brother Tom gave the children each birthday and Saint Nicolaas Eve from the shop in Overschie. Upstairs, the main room no longer had to double as living room and bedroom, and in these warmer months there was usable space in the attic, so sleeping arrangements changed with the seasons.

The extra room meant that when the newly arrived Gereformeerde minister, Boudewijn Rietveld, urged the congregation to help the resistance movement, Cor and Gerrit could comply. The energetic reverend was a passionate speaker, evangelizing from the pulpit and on the street, preaching against the Nazis and inviting people – even daring them – to be brave. His conviction both intimidated and inspired, and showed itself in his strong gaze, framed by dark-rimmed glasses. As he spoke to the congregation, he wore his black robe and gestured dramatically, lifting his arms high so the loose sleeves of the robe expanded like wings. He wasn't a tall man but he exuded a strong energy. He opened his home and his mind to anyone with questions, and when some in the congregation approached him with the conundrum that the Bible taught the need for obedience to those in authority – in this case Nazis – Reverend Rietveld answered them in word and in deed, giving assistance to people seeking to go underground. With the German headquarters not far from the church and Rietveld's home on the Damlaan, his flagrant opposition to the Nazis was all the more impressive.

Cor and Gerrit knew, though details were not openly discussed, that others had begun to take in *onderduikers*, or "divers," and while the idea was frightening, Reverend Rietveld's preaching, "Do not fear the things thou shalt suffer," motivated them. Their house was too full and too small to hide anyone for long, but periodically over the course of the occupation, young men arrived, slipping through the den Hartog home like ghosts. They stayed only a handful of nights, quiet visitors who left no trace. One young man was bearded, tall, slender, and studious looking. Rige saw the dark shape of him standing beside Gerrit's chair in the living room downstairs, his spectacles glinting. Another spoke a foreign language, but had he been Dutch it would have made no difference to Rige. There was no introduction, no explanation for the men's presence or sudden absence, and as with the unreadable posters, Rige tucked the awareness of these fleeting guests into the place that held other things not asked about or explained.

Thick threads of worry and fear had woven themselves into the fabric of everyday life, but they existed alongside the ordinary and the mundane, and now and then, the joyful. Such was the case when Cor's sister Truus and her family visited from Overschie to see the baby Niek and to bring good news: Cor and Truus's brother Gerry, the long-missing mariner, had sent greetings from England. By coincidence, word that he was alive and well and still aboard the *Zuiderburgh* arrived in Cor's mother's postbox on Mother's Day. Cor thought of Gerry's wife and daughter, and their certain relief at knowing they hadn't lost a husband and a father. But she questioned what could have kept Gerry quiet for two years.

As the children scampered in and out of the house with their cousins, tall Jacques got in on the fun by scooping Koos onto his shoulders and parading around, eliciting shrieking giggles as he ducked through the doorways. Cor watched him, and wondered about his resistance activities in Overschie. She knew he worked with Dick Zandbergen, husband of her old friend Marie, and that if she asked for details of the kinds of things he'd been doing, both Jacques and Truus would tell her. But cousin Dirk's awful fate had reinforced the need for silence. The consensus in the family was that Dirk would still be with them if he'd been more careful. Though they understood his motivations and were proud of his strong will, they believed his group's communist leanings were dangerous, and felt nervous even discussing his death. When Jacques sent Koos to join the other children outside, the adults took the opportunity to talk about the most recent news – some three hundred houses close to the beach and harbour in Scheveningen had been "temporarily" evacuated to fortify the coastline, and the Strandweg, the boulevard that curved along the beach, was off-limits to those without a special pass. The people living just outside this area sighed with relief, but Jacques said more evacuations were likely in the near future, and Gerrit agreed.

Neither of the men knew that some families had moved back into the evacuated area and were trying to live there in secret. Tenacity was a Dutch trait that the occupying Germans had noticed, though they used other words for it. Seyss-Inquart reported to Goebbels that the Dutchman's "pigheadedness" was relentless. But he criticized his own men too. While he rode in a shiny black Mercedes with a personalized "RK1" licence plate and a column of SS guards following, he thought of himself as a modest man, and was time and again put off by the gluttony of the Germans serving under him in Holland, as they snatched up not just necessities, but toys, cosmetics, perfumes, sweets, and trinkets, and shipped them home to Germany. He complained to Goebbels of the wild, unseemly purchases that did nothing for the occupiers' shoddy reputation in the Netherlands, and fuelled both resentment and the growing black market. But he insisted there was still hope for a shift in sentiment, and Goebbels – apparently warming to the Reich commissioner – agreed. "Seyss-Inquart," he wrote, "is pursuing a policy of restraint which, though not altogether National Socialistic, is nevertheless purposeful."

By 1942, several thousand Dutchmen assisted the Allies abroad. Like Gerry on his ship and Teun and Marinus in the East Indies, many had been working away from home when the war began. Other expatriates had arrived in London from North America and Australia, looking to offer what support they could for their mother country, while still more had escaped the Netherlands, lucky enough to slip the Nazi yoke. Now they served as pilots and infantrymen in the Princess Irene Brigade, or as spies who travelled back to the occupied zones. Their increasing numbers prompted the June opening in London of a home and community centre somewhat wistfully named by its residents Oranjehaven.

Queen Wilhelmina presided at the official opening wearing a white marguerite corsage. Hardy and prolific plants, the flowers grew abundantly in the meadows near Wilhelmina's home in the Netherlands, faces turned to the sun. Here in England, too, they speckled the fields. Wilhelmina thought they symbolized sorrow and hope, and proposed to her audience that the simple blossom would become an emblem for the displaced Dutch. Soon after, buttonholes sported marguerites in a show of solidarity, and in the fields, the flowers nodded as Wilhelmina flew overhead on her first journey to North America.

From Canada's Maritimes to Ottawa, she travelled in a bomber refitted with comfortable seats. Canada's prime minister, Mackenzie King, was there with her family to greet her. Standing beneath a wide, blue sky while waiting for the queen's plane, he attempted to shake hands with Beatrix and Irene, but only Irene complied, after first presenting him with a marguerite for his lapel taken from the posy she held for her oma. At 12:45, a plane appeared, and he watched Juliana and the children run into the field, waving up at the queen who was smiling from a window. She stepped off the plane in a suit of brown and purple mottled tweed, every inch the portly mother and grandmother. Mackenzie King noticed that she was steady on her feet after the long ride – her first time in a plane – and later he wrote in his diary that she was obviously "a woman of real character and strength; no affectation but great determination."

Her first few days in North America were tranquil and informal, spent in quiet company with Juliana in the garden, and playing with her granddaughters. Soon they moved by train to Lee, Massachusetts, where Juliana had rented a cottage for the summer, and though the queen tried to keep a low profile, her shopping trips made the pages of *Time* magazine, which reported that an armoured car took her around town to buy laundry soap, cheap linoleum, and a sponge for bathing.

One of her visitors at Lee was Franklin Roosevelt, the American president with the Dutch pedigree. Wilhelmina admired his man-of-the-people image – less convincing to real men of the people – and she thoroughly enjoyed his intermittent "fireside chats" on the radio, though in England the broadcast hour was three in the morning. He spoke eloquently of ending tyranny and the subjugation of men, and Wilhelmina applauded this view, at least as it applied to the Hitlers and Mussolinis and Tojos of the world. To her, the Netherlands was no tyrant, and must include its colonies, with a nod to self-government. Roosevelt, on the other hand, was contemptuous of imperialism, and expected that when the war ended, England and other European countries would give up their "archaic, medieval empire ideas."

Whether or not such expectations were discussed, no hint of discord showed in the photographs taken that summer, either in Lee or at Roosevelt's Hyde Park mansion. In one snapshot, Roosevelt and his tall wife Eleanor flank Wilhelmina, and the trio beams widely. In another, Wilhelmina and Roosevelt stand slightly apart, chins jutting regally, she short and round, her feet encased in sensible walking shoes, he in white suit and cane. Both exuded confidence and fortitude, each a fun-house mirror of the other, and when Wilhelmina wrote of Roosevelt's "strong personality, his will-power and perseverance," the passage could easily have been about her. Her visit, during which Roosevelt presented her with a destroyer for the Dutch navy, culminated in a speech to American congressmen and senators. Standing behind a bank of microphones, a dark hat perched precariously atop her head, she told the suited men arrayed before her, "We want nothing that does not belong to us."

The trip appeared successful, but back in Ottawa, the strain peeked through. At Government House, at a dinner given in her honour, Wilhelmina sat beside Prime Minister Mackenzie King and tried to make conversation, and that night he wrote in his diary, "I did not find the queen easy to talk with. She was clearly a little tired. . . . When I was speaking about the condition of the people in Italy, loss of weight, etc., the average citizen being from five to fifteen pounds underweight, the queen said that was nothing compared to the loss of weight of her own people. That the Germans had been stealing everything. Her Majesty said at one stage, 'It is about time we have some victory' – as though all that it needed was obedience to her royal command." The following night, though, she redeemed herself, and in fine spirits gobbled a meal of lobster, roast duck, and Alaska pudding, joking to the prime minister that the menu cards, with their image of the Parliament Buildings, were so lovely that she'd take hers home with her.

Away from official obligations, enjoying the company of family, she felt happy, though the heat and humidity of mid-August was oppressive and unfamiliar. Juliana seemed hardly to notice, and Wilhelmina reminded herself that this was her daughter's third Canadian summer. She resisted the temptation to rest in the shade, and with Juliana, took the children swimming at a country club pool, and even ventured out in a canoe on the sparkling Ottawa River. She toured the Parliament Buildings and visited the Peace Tower, and met Dutchmen training with the Royal Canadian Air Force, then watched from the field as the students winged overhead.

Before long she was flying herself, but when the pilot touched down in Ireland, flags were at half-mast. The Duke of Kent, the English king's younger brother, had been killed in a plane crash. The world seemed weightier on this side of the ocean, and Wilhelmina returned to Stubbings, laid low with dizziness and exhaustion.

That same summer, Reverend Rietveld stood at the pulpit in Leidschendam and read aloud a telegram that had been sent to Seyss-Inquart from churches across the country. Later, Rie Batelaan copied the words into her diary: "Dutch churches, already deeply shocked by the measures taken against the Jews in the Netherlands, have to their horror become aware of the new regulation by which men, women, children, and entire families will be carried off to Germany and their occupied territories. . . . These regulations clash with the deepest moral sense of the Dutch people."

Still, days later, a thousand Dutch Jews received notice ordering them to report for transfer with specific, scant possessions in hand. Those who followed the command started the first leg of their journey, and were taken from Amsterdam to Camp Westerbork, to be housed, for now, with German Jews. The roll call continued at a steady pace, and the camp quickly grew crowded, with three-tier bunks filled and the spaces beneath crammed with belongings. During the roundups, Henny hid in the cellar of the house he shared with Bep in The Hague, sometimes spending the night there. He loved fresh air and open spaces, and wondered how he could stand being inside for an indefinite period of time. If he didn't look Jewish, according to Nazi descriptions, he might assume a false identity. Many were doing just that, but it was hugely risky, and unwise for Henny, whose handsome face was distinguished by his long hooked nose. More and more people were hiding or leaving the country if they could find a safe way out. His sister Elisabeth, working in their father's umbrella shop, had come up with a plan to leave, and wanted him to come with her, but Henny loathed the idea of escaping as much as the idea of hiding, or walking bearing the star. He'd even begun to dislike the Jewish sympathizers who fell in step beside him when he still took his early morning walks, and felt suspicious of their seemingly comforting talk. But when one of his best friends was picked up out of a tram, arrested for not wearing the star, Henny could no longer ignore the reality that, via deportation, submersion, or escape, Jews were disappearing from the Netherlands. If he had to choose, he preferred escape.

For Arthur Seyss-Inquart, the suggestion to evacuate the Jewish population had come first from Gestapo Chief Reinhardt Heydrich, who'd proposed their initial confinement in Amsterdam and at Westerbork, and now said that the "hostile" group should be removed altogether, since it would no doubt pose difficulties in the likely event of an invasion. When the Reich commissioner didn't immediately act on Heydrich's advice, Hitler issued a decree, and in order to "ascertain the fate of the Jews," as he'd later claim at his trial, Seyss-Inquart sent his aides to Auschwitz for a look around. They returned with the news that the camp had adequate space for its inhabitants, that the people were "comparatively well off," and that they had, for instance, a one-hundred-piece orchestra. Though he'd later admit, "it sounds like a mockery," Seyss-Inquart felt satisfied with the report.

The first of Camp Westerbork's deportees set out on foot along the camp's central road, the Boulevard des Misères. Carrying their few belongings, they walked five kilometres to Hooghalen, where they boarded a train to Auschwitz in Poland, having no idea of their fate. Soon after, the Dutch railroad company complied with the order to build rails into the camp so that future transports could be handled swiftly, and in large numbers – on average, a thousand "travellers" each week, waving madly towards the barracks beyond the empty platform, their last contact with the thousands more left behind. Those staying weren't allowed to see them off. They crowded together at the windows of their huts, straining for a glimpse as the train was loaded. Often the deportees left in cattle cars rather than passenger trains, fifty or sixty to a car, with a barrel for a toilet and a long journey ahead. Notes flew between the slats, with the hope that strangers would find them and mail these last messages to loved ones.

By fall, Camp Westerbork was under the smooth supervision of Albert Konrad Gemmeker, who would come to be nicknamed "the German gentleman" because of his polished demeanour and seemingly humane treatment of prisoners. With a fund at his disposal from confis-cated Jewish property, he kept the camp well equipped and efficiently run using a divide-and-conquer strategy that meant he and the other Germans were barely involved in the daily routine. SS men guarded the camp from watchtowers outside its boundaries, but inside, a desperate hierarchy of Jewish inmates kept order. Refusal to participate meant deportation, so Jewish staff drew up the weekly deportation list, and Jewish police – nicknamed the Jewish SS – patrolled the grounds under the supervision of Dutch military police. But the commandant encouraged boxing, gymnastics, and ballet, and, along with other officials, took the front row for performances of the camp's cabaret and choir, laughing and applauding for the performers, who wore the *Davidster* pinned to their costumes. The artists – many of them Holland's best – were his pets, rewarded with cognac, good accommodations, and reprieves, for now, from deportation.

Regardless of the extensive facilities Westerbork offered its inmates – a Jewish-staffed hospital, a children's school, and workshops for tailoring, bookbinding, and so on – the psychological trauma escalated when the deportations began, and inmates suffered from the cyclical anxiety of wondering who would go and what would happen to them. Every Tuesday, the tidily handsome Gemmeker rode his bicycle alongside the train to see that all was in order. He waved his hand, the whistle blew, and the train pulled away.

During this terrifying stretch, Max, the son of the Batelaans' shoemaker friend, dyed his hair red and travelled from Amsterdam to Leidschendam with a suitcase in hand. He left the case with Ineke's mother Rie, who expected him to return, as planned, and go into hiding in a matter of days with his wife Lea. But he changed his mind and decided not to leave his home after all, regardless of the roundups and the grim forecasts. Disturbed by his decision, Rie went to Amsterdam and pleaded with Max to come. Ten days later, he arrived by barge from Amsterdam, huddled with his wife Lea beneath vegetable crates. Soon Lea's mother and brother would join them at the Batelaans', which meant the house, large but not that large, bulged with inhabitants and an explosive secret. By necessity, everyone in the family, even young Ineke, knew the extent of the danger – that if they told anyone about the people living with them, they might all be killed. Stunned by her father's warning, Ineke said nothing even to Rige, her closest friend.

When Rige rang the bell at the Batelaan house one autumn day, she didn't know what a flurry she caused inside. No one answered the door, which she found odd, and though she was too shy to ring again, she stood in the sunshine on the doorstep, wondering what to do next. Suddenly a voice emerged through a homemade intercom: "Who's there?" Rige leaned towards the hole and answered, "Rige den Hartog," and was asked to wait. After a time, the door opened, and the normally warm Rie Batelaan greeted Rige somewhat stiffly, inviting her in. But Ineke was not her cheerful self. She carried herself differently these days, clenching her jaw, tensing her muscles. Something else felt strange, too, but Rige couldn't name it, or find reasons for it.

The following Sunday, Rie took Cor aside at church to suggest that, from now on, the girls should play at the den Hartog house rather than the Batelaans'. Rie's expression gave nothing away, but her lowered voice and her hand on Cor's arm said enough. To Rige, the new rule was only one of many mysteries. It didn't matter whose house she and Ineke played at, though Ineke's was bigger and had more places to avoid brothers.

When the Nazis executed Bernhard's friend, Willem Röell, it took three weeks for the news to reach his wife Martine and their daughter, with Juliana in Canada. Willem had resolved to stay in the Netherlands, but everywhere these days, people were coming and going, ending up in places they'd never imagined themselves. Boys from small German villages landed in Rome dressed in Wehrmacht uniforms. Saskatchewan kids wriggled through English mud on their bellies, learning to keep their heads down and rifles ready. Dutchmen from the East Indies found themselves in Stratford, Ontario, training to join the Royal Netherlands Army, and in both Germany and England, small children stared through train windows, shipped off to the countryside where their parents hoped they'd be safe from bombs.

When Gertrud Seyss-Inquart's Austrian parents visited Clingendael, they looked woefully out of place, the old man in his cap and his wife in traditional dirndl. They had the luxury, of course, of returning home, unlike so many other travellers. For the most part, Gertrud purposely learned little about the deportations of Jews – she described herself as "not Jew-friendly," and believed it was "fine" that Jews be segregated, barred from universities, and prevented from marrying non-Jews. "But the murdering is scandalous," she'd say after the war ended. One day at Clingendael her dentist arrived in the company of a Jewish woman, who pleaded for the release of a friend brought to Westerbork despite earlier assurances from the Reich commissioner himself that she would not be deported. Gertrud went at once to Arthur, sitting in the next room. When she told him the story, he immediately phoned Rauter and demanded the woman be freed. Gertrud could see how her husband disdained the likes of Rauter. "Angry people," he told her, "have no song." He sometimes found what he considered the necessities of war distasteful, as did she. Letters addressed to her at Clingendael begged help for the Jews, but she felt she could only be expected to do so much. When she held out a letter to show her husband, he told her, "Please. Leave it. I cannot do this."

And the exodus continued. Talk spread of further evacuations along the Dutch coast, and Seyss-Inquart was ordered to produce forty thousand workers for German camps. On one of Cor's increasingly rare visits to her sisters in Overschie, she watched an open truck pass with its cargo of men. If they came to take Gerrit, she vowed, she would protect him with her own life. She was glad of one migration: the German soldiers billeted at the van Kampens' and in other houses along the street had moved on to Russia. Helmut and Richard had left their pictures behind – posing in uniform – and one of them had penned a sweet message in the van Kampen girl's scrapbook, an album that also held childhood photos of Jeanne, Corrie Blom, and other kids in the Tedingerstraat, likely snapped by Henny Cahn.

By October, Henny, too, was on the move, having finally made the agonizing decision to flee the country with his sister Elisabeth, leaving Bep behind, and also his father, who was too frail to make the journey. The rotund and rheumatic umbrella vendor went underground with relatives – Henny's mother had died years before – but on the first night he emerged again, having forgotten his pyjamas. Later, Henny would write, "What is it that a human being gets into his head when he is in a tight spot? Amazing." His father was noticed outside after curfew, arrested, and sent to Camp Westerbork, one of scores of others rounded up in early October. Thousands arrived around the time that Henny's father did, young and old, sick and well, dressed and barefoot. But Henny's father had little time to make sense of the chaos, and the bizarre, flea-ridden place where some wore goggles to keep the black dust out of their eyes and the savviest wheeled and dealed to get themselves and their loved ones off the deportation lists. He was quickly chosen for the Tuesday train to Poland, and died in just over a month's time.

By the time the elder Cahn met his end, his children's journey was already well underway. Henny and Elisabeth had nothing more than their wits to protect them, along with strict instructions from a Frenchman, a deserter from the Great War, who now helped people sneak out of the occupied territory. "Make sure that you have cover for the night," he warned them. "Watch your appearance, how you're dressed. Always go straight for the official border crossings. Almost always there is an unguarded route around the customs house." Henny and his sister followed the advice closely, and made it safely into Belgium, where, in a darkening village, a priest turned them away and a farmer took them in. They spent the night in a hayloft, sleeping with carrier pigeons, the kind that had been slaughtered in the Netherlands.

The next day they travelled by train to the Belgian city of Charleroi, hoping to catch a tram that would take them close to the French border. As they waited for the tram, anonymous in the growing crowd, German soldiers passed in the street, and soon a man arrived and announced the tram wouldn't be coming. The crowd dispersed, leaving Henny and his sister alone, with night closing in. They linked arms and sauntered off, trying to look like an ordinary married couple rather than a brother and sister on the run. The doors that closed in their faces on nights like this were many, but eventually someone took them in, or at least led them to shelter. A young girl guided them to the home of a Dutch woman living nearby, known for being unafraid of the Germans. Henny rang the bell and hissed, "Hollanders!" when a window opened upstairs, and within moments this woman, a stranger, threw open her door and embraced them. In the morning, she surveyed Henny anew and told him his clothes wouldn't do. She took him to a second-hand store and he chose a grey-green German officer's coat and fuzzy hunter's hat. From here, the woman helped Henny and his sister purchase tickets to Paris, making certain they were seated rather than standing, because she knew seated passengers were less likely to be searched and questioned. From the window they waved to the woman, and resumed their journey, armed with the name and address of her daughter and son-in-law, whom the woman promised would help them cross the demarcation line into so-called Free France.

On board the train, Henny in his new coat attracted the attention of a chatty German soldier on leave from the Eastern Front. He told Henny that army work fattened his wallet, and had allowed him this trip with his wife, along with the beautiful fur coat draped over her shoulders. Henny kept up his end of the conversation as best he could, but knew that once the officer tired of talking about himself, he'd start asking questions of Henny. He took Elisabeth by the arm, and they disembarked in Saint-Quentin, well before Paris. The streets were deserted. Seeing little alternative, Henny knocked on the door of a house, aware of the risk of being out after curfew. When no one answered, he pushed the door open, but behind it saw nothing but crumbling walls. The house – perhaps the whole row of houses – was in shambles.

Alarmed, they walked for hours out in the country, hoping to find a farm where they could sleep, and finally meeting a boy who agreed to help them. He took them back into the dark city of Saint-Quentin and together they went from one hotel to another. Henny and Elisabeth waited outside as the boy inquired for them, but no one would accept foreigners without papers. Eventually, the boy brought them to his own home. His father offered to help them get to someone he knew in Paris, for a price, and while Elisabeth readily agreed, Henny thought to himself, *He who will save your life for money will also sell it*. He took note of a portrait hanging on the living room wall, of German collaborator General Pétain, and his distrust increased. At his sister's insistence, they paid the man, who took them to Gare du Nord station in Paris, but before the man could deliver them to the dubious connection whom he said would help them cross the demarcation line, Henny heeded his instincts and decided to give him the slip. Once again he held Elisabeth's arm and they blended with the crowd, just as the man turned to look for them. From there they made their way through the maze of Paris to the address given to them by the kind Dutch woman in Belgium, but when they arrived, they found the daughter and son-in-law were not home.

Henny pulled out his makeshift compass and they began to head south, on this bus and that, disembarking each time the compass's needle wavered. The suburbs of Paris seemed endless. On a whim, Elisabeth stopped a woman passing by on a bicycle, and told her frankly that they were refugees and needed a place to sleep for the night. The woman's husband, it turned out, was a prisoner of war in Germany, and she was moved by the thought of strangers helping him if he were to try to make his way home to her. She took them in, and Henny slept on two chairs pushed together, his sister beside the woman in her bed – "royal treatment," Henny called it with gratitude.

From there they boarded a train to Vichy, and Henny could hardly believe his eyes as he watched the passengers move furtively about, whispering, disappearing in and out of the various compartments, trying not to give themselves away to each other. There must have been thousands on the run, he thought. Tempting as it was to be shunted across the border, he knew it was dangerous to cross by train, so they got off at Dijon, and waited for the train to Dole, which deposited them at the edge of occupied Europe. As usual, they arrived at twilight, as members of a German patrol marched neatly past them. But Henny had turned his conspicuous coat inside out, and changed his hat for a beret, and he and his sister easily passed for locals hurrying home before curfew.

Once again they relied on the kindness of strangers, and were taken in at a farm not far from the river they planned to cross. The family's father warned them not to try it – the water was too deep and the current too strong. But his son interjected. "My father doesn't swim," he said shyly, "but I do. You can make it across." The next morning, the reluctant but generous farmer led Henny to the river by bicycle, to scope out the crossing point. Henny wore his beret and pedalled past SS men heading the other way. He looked casual and ordinary, but inwardly worried about his sister, back at the farm: she'd been told to stay upstairs, because German soldiers came and went at will all day. Only the sight of the river and the land across from it soothed him. He lay in the bushes with the farmer, and spotted the French flag in the distance. *"Vous êtes libre là,"* the farmer told him.

That night, Henny and Elisabeth walked in the rain through the farmers' fields towards the river. The mud sucked at their shoes, so they removed them and continued barefoot, finally reaching the woods, where the raindrops falling on the leaves sounded like footsteps approaching. In the moonlight, they took off their clothes and packed them into Henny's big coat, and as quietly as possible, Henny slipped into the water with his bundle and began to cross. Their plan stipulated that he swim first and Elisabeth follow when he reached the other side, but the great noisy splash that erupted behind him told him she'd plunged in, afraid to be alone and eager for the crossing to be over. He braced himself for the German searchlights, or for gunshots responding to the splash. But nothing came. Together, after days of travelling, they climbed to shore and entered unoccupied France.

Up until this time, the Germans had defended the western borders of the occupied zones rather lazily, knowing the RAF was too weak to be much of a threat along the coast, and that Nazi force was better used in the struggle with Russia. With Germany distracted in the east, the Allies planned a raid on the French coast, designed in part to test the feasibility of amphibious assaults. Six thousand soldiers, most of them Canadian, floated across the English Channel towards Dieppe under cover of darkness in open, bargelike landing craft. In the half-light of early morning, they encountered a small German convoy, and the short, violent sea battle that erupted alerted the troops on shore. With the element of surprise destroyed, the Allied offensive pressed forward, but the mission was doomed. Though there were small pockets of success, most of the Canadian tanks that did land couldn't manoeuvre over the pebbly beaches, many soldiers were mowed down by enemy fire, and thousands more were injured or taken prisoner.

Gerrit heard about the failed mission by radio, and read of it in the underground papers, looking up regions in his atlas and gaining a new awareness of his place in the larger world. Some speculated that the real purpose of the raid on Dieppe had been to draw Nazi attention away from the besieged Russians, and if that was true, then the Allies had succeeded. There were signs everywhere that the Germans had stepped up their construction of bunkers along the Dutch coast, and in the fall of 1942, when British-American fleets increased their attacks and a large-scale invasion seemed imminent, Hitler ordered the building of the Atlantic Wall, a four-thousand-kilometre "string of beads" that would stretch from Norway's North Cape down to the Pyrenees. Gerrit, of course, knew few details, but regretted that he had never made the time to take the children to the seaside beach at Scheveningen. He and

Cor had gone during their engagement, and strolled along the Strandweg arm in arm. He remembered how he had watched the spray of the waves on the pier that jutted out into the sea, while she had admired the ritzy Kurhaus Hotel – though she'd made it a point to add that she had no need for such luxury in her own life, which was best enriched by God.

Lying in bed beside Cor each night, he told her what he'd heard and read. She never asked for these bulletins, but always listened intently, and it seemed important to Gerrit to be able to articulate what he'd learned, as if the knowledge could somehow arm them, even a little. Her head turned towards him on the pillow one night as he told her the rumours that there would be further evacuations in Scheveningen and The Hague. He heard her snort when he added that Anton Mussert, surely grappling to stay on Seyss-Inquart's good side, had called the upheaval a humanitarian gesture on the part of the occupiers – after all, the main purpose of the move was to keep civilians away from a poten-tial battle zone. Gerrit slept fitfully that night. The rest that did come was for Cor's sake, because he knew how tired she was, and that she lay awake when he did, though she kept still and said nothing until morning.

Over time, tens of thousands were forcibly removed from areas of The Hague and Scheveningen. By 1944, the number displaced would reach 135,000. Soon only birds could be heard in the old fishing quarter, cawing from rooftops of houses with boarded windows, falling silent at night, when the neighbourhoods vanished in darkness. The homeless residents went to other Dutch towns, Leidschendam included, finding shelter where they could or having places found for them. In a small, densely populated country, such a massive shift was not easily made, despite the surprising obedience of most people, and there was little room or hope for work wherever they went. The Batelaans and their guests braced themselves when a municipal official came to measure their house to see if they could accommodate evac-uees, but they were fortuitously spared that added burden. Those who didn't obey their eviction notices were removed from their homes at gunpoint, and once they were gone, some neighbourhoods stood empty as ghost towns, while the wrecking ball crushed others. Steel and concrete structures with roofs two metres thick were gouged into the dunes and valleys, and identically outfitted with armoured doors, periscopes, bunk beds, and field telephones – everything necessary for the troops lying in wait for their enemy. For their part, the Allies saw that the coast had been evacuated, and newspaper headlines shouted evidence of Hitler's "invasion jitters," try as he might to mask them.

Since The Hague had once housed the Dutch government and its royal family, the Germans had situated many of their own dignitaries in those regal surroundings, to emphasize their power in a symbolic way. This new pressure from the Allied forces, however, made their officials extremely vulnerable. Thus all, with the exception of Seyss-Inquart and family, were moved inland to more secure locations. In fact, he wanted to go too, but Hitler decided such a move would make the occupiers look all the more nervous, and ordered him to stay put at Clingendael, near Wilhelmina's palace, Huis ten Bosch. To placate the Reich commissioner, a special bunker was built on the grounds of the Clingendael property, and served as a refuge in emergency situations. Close to the main house, the bunker was surrounded by a continuous anti-tank ditch that would have sliced through the woods of Wilhelmina's lovingly restored palace, had some intrepid hand not redrawn the lines, thereby saving the palace from destruction, though leaving it out of the protected zone. Once complete, Seyss-Inquart's bunker measured thirty by sixty metres, and rose fifteen metres high. Two towers jutting from the roof, equipped with anti-aircraft guns, were meant to pass as chimneys, and the structure was camouflaged with *trompe l'oeil* windows and doors and cottagey grey tile.

Though the queen spoke regularly on Radio Oranje, surprisingly few of her broadcasts mentioned the plight of the Jews. But in October 1942, when so many were being moved to Westerbork and then on to Poland, she expressed sorrow for her Jewish subjects, and indignation at the way they were being treated. Gerrit listened carefully, and didn't doubt the queen's sincerity, but wondered how much her words could comfort those who'd been taken away and couldn't hear them.

Another day that fall, Prince Bernhard's voice crackled over the radio, and Gerrit, huddled in the upstairs bedroom on the Tedingerstraat, pressed his ear closer. The prince was not frequently heard on Radio Oranje, and Gerrit felt an affinity for him because he was a flying man. He fiddled with the knobs, trying for better reception, and heard the prince announce that he would become a father again with the new year. Gerrit smiled. He knew the joy a baby could bring. Caution followed the good news, though: Bernhard warned people not to celebrate the prospective event and thereby trigger reprisals from the Nazis. Gerrit's smile faded. As he tucked the radio back under the closet's floorboards, he decided that for every joy there was at least one sorrow.

Still, the pending birth seemed like a promise of sorts, more so when Cor told Gerrit not long afterwards that she too was carrying a child. So soon after Niek, the little house would be overflowing. He looked at Cor and tried to read her expression, but saw only that she was trying to read his. "July?" he asked, counting the months. Cor nodded and leaned against him on the divan. "Maybe the war will have ended by then," he said, running a hand over her hair. He thought of Prince Bernhard and Juliana in Canada. This was not the best time to have a child – another body requiring food when the supply was shrinking – but instead of voicing that sentiment, he told Cor how much he liked the idea of their family growing in step with the royal one.

For all her piety, Cor sometimes wondered how she would manage in this world without Gerrit's pure faith and his optimism. It was one thing to trust that all the suffering around them had a higher purpose, and another thing to withstand it, especially when it swept through their own family, as it did that November while the leaves dropped from the trees. Cor's mother Neeltje died as Cor sat beside her, feeling the warmth go out of her hand. For a long time Cor was still, memories winging through her mind like phantoms in the silence of the room, providing a numbing distraction. She pictured her mother on the back stoop, by the Schie, making *advocaat*, the delicious liqueur that tasted like custard. Or tossing out rhymes as she dusted the bookshelves, because she loved to play with language. Cor didn't cry as she reflected; sometimes she believed herself no longer capable of that kind of relief. Eight days later her fragile sister Maria sobbed as she stood in her wedding dress, waiting to marry a fellow Truus's comical Jacques called "the little man." The evacuations around Scheveningen had triggered a housing shortage, and if Maria remained a single woman in a family home, the housing authority would order her to move out and make the house that had been in the Post family for generations available for rent. So while her fiancé Nicolaas was a little man and a hand wringer and not her first choice, he was also a talisman of sorts, and she knew she could grow to love him. But the wedding was hardly the happy occasion it should have been, overshadowed by Neeltje's death and an un-expected blow: the authorities had refused to allow her a burial in the cemetery beside her husband, saying only that its grounds were closed.

Christmas that year was sombre. As Gerrit read from the heavy family Bible, Cor smacked Koos's hands when he fidgeted under the table. She tried to concentrate on the passage, and closed her eyes to the Bible's thick stack of pages, which reminded her of the recent alarm-ing news that the Dutch Bible Society had been dissolved, its assets seized because it distributed books to Jews, hoping, in evangelical tradi-tion, to convert the Jews to Christianity. Eighteen thousand Bibles had been shredded, the thin pages rendered unusable for even the black market. This last while, the holy book had become a commodity. The black market had been buying vast numbers of Bibles, and selling them in bulk to cigarette-rollers. Now the Germans said they needed the paper, just as they needed metal to make shell casings, and men to work in factories. To meet the ridiculous quotas set out by Berlin, Seyss-Inquart would have to conscript Dutchmen, employed or unemployed, by the tens of thousands. Already, those who refused to work for the occupiers were muscled into "volunteering" when they were denied unemployment compensation as well as ration cards. Rie Batelaan wrote in her diary: "The ghost of conscription comes nearer. If they dare to do this . . . may God grant that our people will refuse as one man."

But the Atlantic Wall was a colossal undertaking, and during the time of its construction, all other building projects were disallowed. The Germans supplied the design and the equipment, but they weren't about to spare soldiers as builders, so the Dutch did the work. They took the jobs offered because there were scant others to be had, and because deportation – to a camp or to a routinely bombed German factory – was a frightening option. Within two years, twenty thousand "beads" would be erected along the Dutch coast, forming a continuous, impenetrable line. But few bought Mussert's earlier suggestion that the wall's erection was Hitler's humanitarian gesture. Still, Mussert seemed to have scored with the führer. In December, when Mussert returned with Seyss-Inquart from a meeting with Hitler in Berlin, Seyss-Inquart wryly announced the Dutchman's appointment as "leader of the Netherlands' people" – just the lofty sort of title Mussert had craved for so many years, but which in actuality meant little. For the Nazis who bestowed the title *der Leider*, it was mildly humorous. In Dutch the term meant "the leader," but in German, it translated as "the unfortunate."

Though it seemed less and less so on the surface, in his own way, Mussert was fiercely patriotic. Over the course of the war he'd visit Hitler several times, putting forth his dream of a League of Germanic Peoples – independent nations united by a common bond and overseen by Hitler. The führer always answered no, but in spite of Mussert's sinking realization that German occupation was bad for the Netherlands, he didn't break ties with the Nazis.

Gerrit kept a low profile, not wanting to be nabbed as a volunteer for the wall's construction, or for some other project that would benefit the occupiers. He listened anxiously to each broadcast from Radio Oranje, waiting for some good news. It came in January, though not in the form of military victories. A princess had been born in Canada, a healthy baby with fat cheeks and a strong constitution. Gerrit's thoughts flitted to Cor's own pregnancy, so difficult this time around. She was paler than usual, and always so tired, and still had a long way to go. He blinked, and concentrated on the happy newscast. The Canadian government had proclaimed a four-room suite at the hospital "extra-territorial," so that the baby would have only Dutch nationality. Prince Bernhard, waiting in the suite while Juliana laboured, phoned Wilhelmina immediately after the birth of Margriet. And now, Wilhelmina effused into her radio microphone: "Who does not remember the marguerites that bloom in meadow and field in the month of May, and that every year overlay the memory of all the suffering and the sorrow of those terrible days of May 1940 with their whiteness, whispering to us of a better future?" And just for an instant, Gerrit shocked himself with a small, bitter thought: it was easy for her to say, from outside the occupied zone.

FIVE

Darkness and Light
1943–1944

THE ONGOING BLACKOUT had its greatest effect during fall and winter months, when dusk settled in around four o'clock. Gas lanterns along the streets of Leidschendam remained unlit, and on Sundays, the afternoon service at the Gereformeerde church started two hours earlier than usual. Families hurried home under bleak skies, retreating into their houses and pulling their blinds closed as the town, with the rest of the country, folded into darkness. The Air Protection Service had dispensed booklets with instructions about air raids, bomb shelters, and the blackening of windows, but this last remained a source of annoyance to De Regt, in charge of the service in Leidschendam. He complained to the mayor that there were still too many infractions of the blackout rules, and he intended to crack down.

On a winter evening following the birth of Princess Margriet, Cor and Gerrit put the children to bed early. As Gerrit stoked the fire in the round belly of the stove and Cor puzzled through the week's ration coupons, Rige lay upstairs, trying to make out the rails of her green iron bed frame in the darkness. She strained so hard to see them that her imagination conjured snakes slithering up from the floor, and twining around each of the bars. Their pink tongues darted in and out as the snakes came towards her, but just as she thought they were about to wind themselves around her, three loud raps jolted her out of her imaginings, as someone knocked on the door downstairs. Rige lay still, listening, but she couldn't make sense of what was being said by the man at the door, or her father, who answered in low, apologetic mumbles. If Rige's mother said anything at all, Rige didn't hear her, try as she might to catch any fragment of the bewildering encounter. Soon she heard the door close, and a hushed exchange between her mother and father. The dim lights from the rooms below were extinguished, and she heard her parents climb the stairs to their bedroom. A long while passed before Rige finally fell asleep in the overwhelming darkness.

In the morning, when she came downstairs, Rige saw her father drilling a hole in the wall that neighboured the Blom residence, and Meneer Blom feeding a wire through.

"The electricity has been cut," said her mother, by way of explanation, "because we let light escape."

How the light got out – from which window – her mother didn't say, but Rige imagined her own curtains moving, her bright face appearing at the window to survey the street below, and a beam of light flooding out as she did so. She knew it couldn't have been her fault – that her room was always pitch dark in winter – but she still worried that somehow she was responsible. And it made her nervous to know that they weren't allowed electricity, but that they were taking it anyway, from the Bloms next door. She understood that they were breaking a rule, despite all of their lectures to her and the boys that rules were not made to be broken.

The hole made them all feel more vulnerable than they had before. When a fine was paid and the electricity restored two weeks later, the wire disappeared, but the hole remained, the only flaw on an otherwise smooth wall, subtly papered with bluish-grey flowers. Five-year-old Koos, always drawn to oddities, pressed his eye to the hole and peered through to the Bloms on the other side – Corrie and Piet and their parents, playing a game at the table and dipping into snacks in a bowl, not minding at all that it was Sunday. A piece of candy would fit nicely through the hole and into his mouth – but his mother yanked him away from the wall just as the thought occurred. And though he was scolded for spying, he returned to the hole later, wielding one of the copper rods that held the carpet runner in place and pushing it through – not knowing what that would accomplish, but just needing to do it. As soon as the rod entered, an "*Ouch!*" bounced back from the other side, and this time his father grabbed his collar and spun him around, the rod clattering to the floor. Close up, for just a moment, his father's face lost every shred of kindness. He held Koos's arms and then let him go without saying a word. That was all, but Koos, watching him walk away, felt more shattered than he ever had by his mother's smacks and scoldings. Tears swam in his eyes but before they could fall, he pushed past Rokus and toddler Gert and through the front door. There was nowhere to go in the cold without a coat, so he sat on the step with his arms folded around his knees, too stubborn to go back inside.

By rights, the copper rods should not have been within his reach. If the occupiers had got what they'd demanded, the rods would have been turned in along with the pewter decanter and the good silver, all of them melted down and rebuilt into weaponry. The greatest indignity came in February, when the bells were removed from local churches, loaded into a truck, and driven out of town. Koos was caught up in a snowball fight with the milkman's son near the Vliet, and didn't see them go. Afterwards, he was one of the few who barely noticed their absence. For what seemed an eternity, the bells had clanged on the hour and half-hour, calling people to work, to lunch, and home again, ringing at length not just for church service, but for weddings and births, and any special occasion in the royal family. Without them, the town seemed too quiet, except when the air raid sirens moaned from their various locations around town – like the Stalen-Ramen-Koop factory at the end of the Tedingerstraat – and Allied planes dropped bombs or passed on the way to Germany. In Leidschendam, the crack of the anti-aircraft weapons could be heard from The Hague, and at night, the broad beams of searchlights swept the black sky.

Reverend Rietveld refused to be disheartened by the theft of the church bells, which had taken place across Europe, and he admonished the congregation to hold fast to their convictions. But when the resistance movement assassinated NSB general Hendrik Seyffardt in Scheveningen – shooting him twice in the stomach when he answered his door – the repercussions reverberated to Leidschendam and beyond. At the university in Utrecht, professors and female students were lined up against the walls to watch as soldiers shoved male students through the hallways at gunpoint. In Leiden, at the school Ineke Batelaan's brothers attended, boys jumped the fence at the back and hid for the remainder of the day. In Leidschendam, German military vehicles crawled through the streets, and young men were dragged from their homes and schools. Next door to the den Hartogs, teenager Piet Blom climbed down a rope into a narrow space under the attic stairs. He sucked in his stomach so he'd fit between the beams, and waited and listened. Like Gerrit, he knew that if the Germans searched the house, they'd plunge their bayonets into every dark nook. By the end of the day, thousands of boys had disappeared, fifty from Leidschendam alone. Cor, seeing the grief on the mothers' faces when she passed them in the street, thanked God that her own children were too young to be taken, and her husband – for now – too old.

Age was not a factor some weeks later when the Germans ordered all former Dutch soldiers to report for transportation to POW camps in Germany. Goebbels wrote that the soldiers no longer deserved the clemency extended by the führer when he'd released the troops after the campaign had been won, and that Dutch families losing their men to this new order had the English to thank. As a gardener whose produce was in high demand, Gerrit had attained an exemption certificate that should have protected him from this decree, but these days nothing was guaranteed, even for men more privileged than he: Gerrit knew that Dutch physicians had gone on strike to protest Nazi rules forced on their profession, and that doctors had then been arrested at random and sent to a camp in Amersfoort, where their heads were shaved and even the old were forced to dig moorland. The popular mayor of Leidschendam, Hendrik Banning, had finally been pulled from office – done in, perhaps, by fanatical De Regt, and replaced by the NSB man Martinus Simonis, who was as willing as De Regt to do Nazi bidding. From this time forward, the NSB *Hou Zee* greeting would be used at the Leidschendam town hall. An equivalent of the German *Sieg Heil*, it offended the anti-Nazis still at work in the building, as did a telling occurrence at Mayor Simonis's official installation: a moment of silence for "our fallen comrades" at the Eastern Front.

In the midst of all these baffling changes, Gerrit cocooned himself with his radio. Hand cupped around his ear, he heard Radio Oranje urging the former soldiers not to obey the German order. Soon enough, an illegal manifesto made its way into his hands, and told him the same. He pored over every word, and came to the end: "There is only one answer: refuse. Absolutely refuse." As he read the message, relief took the edge from his fear.

The screws turned on the able-bodied, and Seyss-Inquart ordered a stop to all non-essential industry, funnelling skilled workers into jobs that by August would demand seventy-two hours per week of their time. Forced labour, either here or in Germany, was now a reality, so there was company for Jewish *onderduikers* living with friends or strangers, slipping into attics and beneath floorboards when there was an unexpected knock on the door. As Rie Batelaan wrote, "If all the Dutch houses could speak and would give away the secrets they hide within their walls, what surprises there would be!" The unlucky were found, and taken to the new camp at Vught in Noord Brabant, built with money confiscated from Jews and boasting crematoriums and hanging yards.

No element of society remained untouched by the Nazis. The German-instituted Kulturkammer, or Chamber of Culture, required all artists to become members, and policed their work, so that those theatre companies still operating had to submit lists for approval. Despite the Englishness of its author, Shakespeare's *Merchant of Venice* was allowed, having been deemed sufficiently anti-Semitic. No longer tolerated, however, were public caricatures of a red-faced, shouting Hitler, or Hitler in a suit of armour surrounded by gas-masked flunkies. Instead, comics like *Koenraad van den Arbeidsdienst* (Conrad of the Workforce) appeared in the censored papers, blatantly encouraging Dutch youth to collaborate with the Germans. For most, *Koenraad* really was a joke, ridiculed by the underground newspapers, where the humour printed beside the bad news was welcome. One issue contained an edict that imposed a curfew on dogs and ducks, mocking the frequent new rules of Police Leader Rauter.

But if the Dutch were covertly laughing, no one found it funny when Germany helped itself to "occupation costs" of 50 million marks per month, taken from the Dutch treasury. The demand that Gerrit had heard, that former soldiers turn themselves over as prisoners, further incensed the population, and a spontaneous strike that began in Henny's hometown of Hengelo promptly spread countrywide. This time, Seyss-Inquart acted quickly. More than two hundred strikers were executed, but instead of cowing the population, the action caused passive opposition to spiral into acts of organized sabotage, theft, arson, and assassinations. In Amsterdam, resistance workers set fire to the walls of the Rembrandt Theater while the German film *Die Goldene Stadt* – The Golden City – played to an NSB audience inside. At the civil registry on the Plantage Kerklaan, which held thousands of files used to trace Jews, resistance workers, and men for the labour camps, another resistance cell detonated explosives, destroying the top floor of the building. Nearer to Leidschendam, a group derailed a train carrying bulldozers and heavy equipment past the *tuin* to the coast, where work on the Atlantic Wall continued. But for every act of rebellion, the Germans struck back, often aided by the Dutch who had sided with them. Over the course of the war hundreds of resistance workers were walked into the dunes of Scheveningen, shot, and dumped in shallow, sandy graves. Still more met a similar fate elsewhere.

Behind the scenes, the Germans exacted quieter forms of punishment as well. "The question has been put to me," wrote Joseph Goebbels, "whether the radio sets in the Netherlands should be seized. Undoubtedly British propaganda . . . was a decisive factor in the recent strike. I therefore favour taking the radio sets away from the Dutch as quickly as possible. Anyway, we can make good use of them in our air-raid areas."

With only a shadowy awareness of the grim goings-on around them, the children played. Jeanne van Kampen from across the street often knocked on the door and asked Cor if she could take baby Niek for a stroll in his pram, like a mother, and Cor watched unseen behind a lace curtain as the girl wheeled him up and down the sidewalk. There would be slightly more than a year between Niek and the new child when it came in the summer, and Cor felt tired just thinking of it. She remembered feeling fatigued, too, when Niek was due and Gert was not yet one and a half – once Gert had escaped before his bath, and run down the Tedingerstraat naked in the brisk spring air, and she had run after him, shouting over his giggles and holding her big belly. Her mother Neeltje had always said that the more children you had, the easier raising them became, and Cor hoped that was true. All her children were close in age and so far she had managed each time. She rubbed her stomach tenderly, and already felt the fierce bond that made her so protective of the others. The frequent school closures meant the older ones were underfoot more often, but at least she could keep an eye on them, or send them to the *tuin* to play, under Gerrit's watch.

When school was open, Rige, Koos, and Rokus walked there together, and played games along the way. Near the flower shop, they cut through a yard, nicking a scrub brush from the back step and depositing it mischievously on the front. At the end of the Broekweg, where their grandparents lived, an old lampshade left outside the Café Centraal begged to be kicked and rolled along the street, and although the lampshade reappeared day after day, the giggling children never suspected that the proprietor of the shop placed it there for his amusement as much as theirs. Caught up in their play, the children took no notice of the German soldiers who regularly lounged in the café, out of sight of their superiors. Nor did it occur to them that there were *onderduikers* living upstairs in the school, or above the rafters at the church or the minister's house, or in the hospital, or in any number of houses along the well-trod route between home and school. They didn't know that the teacher they called "Stokvis," because he looked like a dried cod, was actually a member of the resistance – much more than a strict French teacher with a wrinkled, sallow complexion.

But not everything went unseen. In the early days of the occupation, Gerrit had tucked Cor's pewter goblets, tin plates, and brass candle-holders into the rolls of reed mats stacked in the *tuin*'s shed, and two years later, the contraband was still there. Four-year-old Rokus chose the shed as his hiding spot one day while playing war games with Koos and the Meulenbroek boys from next door. Crouched behind the pile of mats, heart thundering with the excitement of outwitting his "enemies," he peered through the rolls and saw the round base of one of his mother's candlesticks wedged in the folds. Outside, Koos raced past, stick sword drawn, and Rokus squeezed out of his hiding place to chase him, but the image of the hidden metal remained in his mind. He said nothing to Koos or anyone else about his discovery, instinctively knowing he'd seen something he shouldn't have seen.

Gerrit was thankful that his children were so young and knew so little. Late on a May evening in 1943, he locked the gate to the *tuin* and began his walk home. The sun was only now sinking and there would be just a few short hours of rest before it climbed again. These days were long for a *tuinder*, but in spite of his backaches, he enjoyed his work, breaking only for brief meals and the chance to listen to the radio. A few days ago all radios were ordered turned in, but Gerrit, like many in the street, had already hidden his when the Germans outlawed listening to foreign stations, so it was easy enough to pretend he didn't have one. Three days before the radio became an illegal possession, he'd heard Prince Bernhard encourage unyielding resistance. Still, as a precaution, Gerrit had moved the equipment to the attic, and next door, Theodoris Blom had nervously smuggled his out of the house and hidden it at the factory where he worked as a tool and dye maker. But before long, talk that the Germans planned to strip the place of its machinery prompted Blom to sneak it home again, and put it in Piet's hiding place beneath the attic stairs.

As Gerrit passed the Broekweg on his walk home, he noticed *de prater* in her usual spot, on the bench outside her house. The old eccentric sat in the darkness, not talking, for once, but humming a song he'd not heard since childhood, and he had a memory of himself as a boy, standing at the muddy edge of a river with his father beside him. He nodded to *de prater*, and considered continuing down the Broekweg to check on his parents at number 14. Their house sat farther down, close to the Vlietweg and the Café Centraal where the soldiers congregated. He knew his parents disliked the noise and the drunkenness. But he was tired, and continued on into the Tedingerstraat. There was nothing he could do about the presence of the soldiers anyway, much as he hated to admit it. The men at the van Kampens' were gone, but others swarmed like an infestation of potato beetles that couldn't be popped between gloved fingers. *If only*, he thought, and grinned at the idea, startling when he heard a girl giggle as if she had shared the joke. He looked around and saw her leaning against the wall of the Stalen-Ramen-Koop factory, twirling something shiny on a string. He couldn't see her clearly enough to be certain, but he supposed she was a neighbourhood girl – the daughter of someone he knew. Beside her, his shoulder to the wall in a casual pose, stood a German soldier. He brushed the girl's hair back with his hand, and stooped to kiss her cheek. Even in the relative darkness, the uniform and the confident stance didn't belie the fact that the soldier, like so many others, was only a boy.

Princess Margriet's christening was a gift for Bernhard's birthday on June 29, 1943, and Wilhelmina arrived in Ottawa a month ahead of time, flying into Uplands airport in a silver bomber. Once again, Prime Minister Mackenzie King waited in the sunshine with Juliana and the young princesses, but when the queen disembarked she told him pointedly that this was not a state visit, that the times were particularly difficult for her people right now, and the length of her stay would be determined accordingly. She made time, though, for a dinner party with an intimate collection of high-society members. Mackenzie King sat next to the queen as she expounded on the rumours of Nazis stealing her belongings. "I don't mind the loss of the silver or the possessions," Wilhelmina told him between bites of delicious food. "There are other things much more valuable in life."

Cor and Gerrit would have concurred. Sitting by their radio in the attic, they listened to snatches of Princess Margriet's christening ceremony, straining to hear the baby coo, closing their eyes to better imagine the scene. Confined though they were from the rest of the world, they knew that the princess's illustrious godparents were Queen Mary of England, Governor General Athlone, and President Roosevelt, but Martine Röell remained anonymous. Since her husband Willem had been murdered by the Nazis, the royal family worried what the occupiers would do to Martine's relatives back home if they heard she'd been named one of Margriet's godmothers, so for now she was listed only as the widow of a martyred resistance fighter.

The title of godparent was also bestowed on the entire merchant marine, including one Gerry Post, brother of Cor. Seven members had been flown in for the ceremony, and Cor pictured Gerry as one of them, strikingly handsome already, but more so in a uniform that now sported a white marguerite badge. With Margriet's ceremony in Ottawa, Irene's in London, and Beatrix's at home in the Netherlands, it occurred to Cor that each of Juliana and Bernhard's daughters had been christened in a different country, whereas ceremonies for the den Hartog children had all been held at the little church on the Damlaan – and the babies had worn a gown fashioned from Cor's wedding dress. The new one inside her would do the same when its turn came. Cor, who shunned excess but respected the royal family, wouldn't have had it differently.

As Rie Batelaan wrote in her diary, "Each Sunday is an oasis in a miserable world," and surely Cor agreed. In July, she slid into her regular pew and tucked the frayed hem of her dress out of sight. Rige sat down beside her and Cor's eyes picked out the tiny stitches that mended a tear in Rige's too-short skirt. Not church clothes by pre-occupation standards, Cor thought, glancing away, but no one had anything better. Even those with money to buy new had to apply to the distribution office for permission, which was usually denied.

These days, she and Rige came alone to the afternoon services. She knew Rige enjoyed the peacefulness of church with only her mother in the pew beside her, and Cor admitted to herself that she, too, liked the hour with her daughter in the house of God. Cor waited for the service to begin, fanning herself against the sticky heat with the church bulletin. Inside was printed the announcement that a young couple would bring a child for baptism today, and Cor felt a wave of nausea. She pressed a palm over the hard mound of her stomach and felt the child move sluggishly, scraping inside her. She wondered if the baby could sense how she felt: tired, irritable, less than motherly as the pregnancy went on, and guilt washed over her. She shifted on the hard bench, and turned her attention to the low mumble of voices and the creak of pews as people arrived in the church.

The man who climbed to the pulpit was not Reverend Rietveld, but a guest preacher named Frits Slomp, or these days Frits "*de Zwerver*," or the wanderer, for his wandering ways and his ability to evade the Germans. Neither name appeared in the church bulletin, for if the Germans knew he'd come, they'd have been quick to arrest him. In fact, he was almost detected on his way to Leidschendam from Overijssel. Slomp was a member of the Gestapo's most-wanted, and had been in hiding for more than a year, but popped up week after week at a different Gereformeerde church to deliver fiery, anti-Nazi sermons. "I saw Satan fall like lightning from heaven," he quoted with dramatic fervour. "Be not afraid." Beads of sweat dripped down his forehead in the hot, crowded church, and despite the heat, Cor shivered.

But here in Leidschendam, the sermon was only a precursor for the main event. Slomp's true purpose was revealed later, at a congregational meeting that took place that evening. The church was filled to capacity, and after the earlier sermon, most people suspected the man's identity and were curious about what would be said. Cor and Gerrit sat in their regular balcony pew, having left the children in Moeder den Hartog's care, and Cor's hand slid into Gerrit's. At great risk, a few *onderduikers* had come too, sitting in the balcony so they'd be able to escape quickly into the rafters if necessary, and aware, no doubt, of the German headquarters down the street. The group was so large that Reverend Slomp worried they'd drawn too much attention and that it would be reckless to continue, but Reverend Rietveld – an equally persuasive man – convinced him to stay and speak his mind to the congregation. The doors were locked and the crowd fell silent, all eyes on Reverend Slomp. Descended from strong-willed people herself, Cor recognized this man's power of persuasion, and felt the apprehension in the room.

Slomp began by asking the audience not to speak about what they would hear that night, not to others and not among themselves. Then, point-blank, he told them to open their homes to those who needed a place to hide, saying that he had helped hundreds find a place, but too many had been remiss, and that was why he had come: to insist they do more. He said he headed a resistance group that helped the burgeoning population of people gone underground – the Landelijke Organisatie voor Hulp aan Onderduikers, or LO, it was called – and he and others took on the exhaustive work of finding contacts and hiding places, screening those eager to get involved, arranging for counterfeit ID cards and ration coupons in order to keep the *onderduikers* safe and fed. "To keep them alive," he added, holding the gaze of one in the congregation and then another.

Those who were already sheltering people avoided meeting anyone's eye, for fear of revealing their involvement: Gerrit's friend Jaap, his sister Paulien, and their aging mother sat quietly. They had recently taken in Flora and Louis, middle-aged Jewish siblings living unseen at Tedingerstraat 9, where the excess of laundry was hung with great calculation to prevent tipping off the neighbours. Equally silent were Rie and Henk Batelaan, whose "guests" had delivered their first child in hiding a month ago. Inwardly, Rie was exhilarated by Slomp's sermon. When she got home, she wrote in her diary, "How much good it did us to be part of so large a gathering. . . . I do not know the result. It is better not to know. And even if I did know, I still wouldn't write it. But I pray that God will open many hearts and homes."

From the balcony on the Tedingerstraat, a glow sometimes appeared to the east, in the direction of Germany, and evidence of battles could be seen over the Netherlands' flat panorama. One night, Rige got out of bed to find her parents and Koos standing on the balcony, watching distant red and green balls float through the night sky, falling who knew where. They looked more beautiful than stars to Rige, who was puzzled by her mother's words – *those poor people* – and by her father's sunken expression. She reached for Koos's hand, and for once he didn't pull away. They stood like that together in their nightclothes as their parents recited a psalm, but for the children, the familiar, lyrical words of the Bible made the bewildering scene more frightening.

Cor and Gerrit found solace in prayer, and relied on that comfort late in the summer when Cor struggled through a difficult birth in the bedroom upstairs. The nurse came, and the doctor, and the children went to Broekweg 14 with Moeder and Vader, but in the end there was nothing to be done for the child, small and stillborn with the cord round its neck. Gerrit watched as the nurse took the unmoving bundle away, and felt his throat constrict. *What happens now?* he thought, and wondered if he should go after the nurse and ask. But his feet didn't move. He stood in the middle of the room, saying nothing, doing nothing, while Cor lay in silence on the bed. Her head was turned away from him, but Gerrit knew she was staring unblinking at the wall. Her hand rested on the sheet, the fingers nearly as pale as the cotton, the wedding band she wore a single dark mark. *I love you*, he wanted to say, and *I'm sorry*, but of course it was no one's fault and God's will – usually Cor's reminder to him, though it was likely herself she was convincing. He sat on the bed, took her hand, and in his low, beautiful voice, began to sing a psalm: "*. . . for he shall give his angels charge over thee, to keep thee in all thy ways.*" Cor's fingers curled around his as she closed her eyes.

Winston Churchill and the Bomber Command were thinking of a less benevolent God when they named a series of assaults on Hamburg "Operation Gomorrah." The ten-day strike left the city devastated, as night after night bombs dropped on the inner core. From a height of six thousand metres, the glow reflected on the departing planes, and across the countryside the pink flash of target-indicating pansy bombs could be seen. In all, Operation Gomorrah caused fifty thousand fatalities, most of them on one night alone. For the Allied forces, it was a huge success, and proof that the tide was turning in their favour. With the close of summer, Italy surrendered unconditionally, and over Radio Oranje, the queen insisted that liberation would come soon. Winston Churchill had promised help to the occupied countries before autumn, and even Joseph Goebbels, in his diary, admitted that an invasion attempt was most likely to happen in the Netherlands, because of weak defences and a population backing the other side. The Dutch, he believed, were unfailingly insolent, though he was pleased with Seyss-Inquart's rule these days, and seemed to have forgotten his earlier assessments. "I have the impression that the treatment of populations in the occupied areas is being handled best in the Netherlands. Seyss-Inquart is a master in the art of alternating gingerbread with whippings, and of putting severe measures through with a light touch."

Seyss-Inquart's wife Gertrud did her best not to know about any "whippings," and wished she and Arthur could spend more time swimming or riding their horses through the dunes. The sunsets were beautiful in the Netherlands – so different than at home, where the mountains obscured the view. But Arthur worked long days, and then often couldn't sleep. His mood worsened when she left to visit Austria, so Gertrud tried to keep busy at Clingendael. When later she spoke of this time, she'd unwittingly echo Queen Wilhelmina: "I felt as if I were in a golden cage."

To those facing real bars, a metaphorical cage was hardly frightening. Cor's Oom Marinus had spent more than twenty months as a prisoner of war, shunted from camp to camp on the island of Java. His internment record shows that from the time of the Indies' capitulation he spent the spring of 1942 in Bandung, in a place that had first served as the barracks for the Dutch infantry. The camp had a library, a school, and a theatre where prisoners staged plays and concerts. Despite the relative comfort of Bandung, there was no gilding here. The food was meagre: white rice with occasional bits of green vegetable and shreds of meat thrown in. Discipline was frequently illogical and vicious, ranging from humiliating, open-handed slaps to prolonged beatings and executions. Three men who tried to escape were strapped to the barbed wire fence, stabbed with bayonets, and left sagging, their bodies a deterrent to those who might try to repeat the crime.

In June, Marinus was among a group that travelled under the tropical sun in closed freight cars to the camp at Cilacap, a seaport on the southern coast of Java. Six months later he moved again, this time inland to Cimahi, high in the mountains of West Java. Here, a barbed wire cage sat in the front yard, warning all comers to defer to their Japanese captors, no matter how brutal the treatment. Prisoners were employed in hard labour, and at night fell asleep hungry and bruised, listening to the lazy drone of mosquitoes. The Japanese took a page from the German book on oppression, and by fall 1943, more than one hundred thousand Dutch men, women, and children had been interned in prison camps. All traces of Dutch rule were erased: the capital of Batavia renamed Jakarta, Radio Bandung shut down, and almost everyone connected to the former Dutch government killed. Dutch became a forbidden language, and even the calendar changed, so that 1943 was the Japanese year 2603.

One day, as Marinus stood at attention for roll call, he discovered the young man beside him, Teun de Korte, shared his last name. Marinus had been away from the Netherlands for years, but he looked at Teun's sharp profile and asked, "Are we family?" Teun told him his father's name, and his oma's — Kee, the feisty old lady who'd lost her gloves at Cor's wedding. Marinus smiled. "My mother," he said, "and my brother. Nice to see you, nephew." But soon after, they parted ways. Marinus was notified of his transfer to the camp at Batavia, but he wouldn't be there long. Batavia was known as the Cycle Camp, from which inmates were shipped elsewhere, and in September 1943, Marinus left for Singapore, Malaysia. The prisoners slept on the ship's deck, exposed to the elements, and the toilets were wooden crates strapped to the railing and hung overboard. When they made port four days later, Marinus was assigned to a bamboo barrack with thirty other men. Stories circulated that what they'd been through paled in comparison to what was to come.

Back in the Netherlands, the occupier lived off the country like a parasite, and fed its ravaged homeland as well. As 1943 drew to a close, the scars on the country were clear. By now, hundreds of thousands of hogs and cattle had disappeared into the Reich, and fruit and vegetables were scarce at the greengrocers. There were warnings of possible food shortages if the Wehrmacht didn't reduce its own demands. But a reasonable response was unlikely in such perverse times, with the resistance paper *Het Parool* reporting mass gassings at concentration camps, and Rauter overseeing the roundups of the last known Jews in Amsterdam. This time his cull included members of the Jewish Council, who were no longer of use to the Germans now that the rest of the Jews were gone. The city was declared *judenrein*, but of course there were those who remained in hiding throughout the country, or who lived under false identities. "By and by," wrote Seyss-Inquart to Nazi headquarters, "they are being seized and sent to the East; at the moment, the rate of seizures is five to six hundred a week." In church, Reverend Rietveld sent around a collection plate for what he vaguely termed "special needs because of the war," which really meant the money would be passed on to Slomp's LO, in support of the *onderduikers* and those who sheltered them. Gerrit glanced up to the church ceiling and wondered if someone huddled there in the attic as he put in his donation.

Jewish spouses in mixed marriages like Bep and Henny's were being held at Westerbork, and by December they too faced the risk of deportation, a decree that went further than Germany's own. When a raid extended to her own house, which she shared with her grown daughter, Carla, Bep simply told the police, "My husband is gone," and her answer seemed to satisfy them. Though periodically she and Carla took in other *onderduikers*, it was true enough that Henny was far away. At the den Hartog residence, a postcard arrived from Switzerland, with the Berne Cathedral on its front, and a single signature, José, on the back. Rige, turning the card over in her hands and examining the Nazi eagle that stamped all mail, didn't know Henny's middle name was Jozef, and the card seemed insignificant to her. But along with a single photograph of Henny, a head-and-shoulders shot taken straight on, the card took a permanent place among Cor and Gerrit's few belongings.

After climbing out of the river in Free France, Henny and his sister Elisabeth had eventually made it to a reception centre for refugees at Lons-le-Saunier. But even there, trouble waited. The atmosphere was tense, the people unsmiling. Henny and Elisabeth were assigned to a hotel and given food ration cards, and told to report to the police commissioner each morning. They met a fellow Dutchman at the hotel, and heard with envy that he and others had arranged a further escape across the border to neutral Switzerland. Henny asked if they had room in their car for two more, but was told no. Unwittingly, the siblings were better off, they later discovered: a man drove the group to a meadow, and pointed to some bushes.

Through there, he told them, is Switzerland. They climbed out of the car and through the trees, and into the Germans' lair. Henny's acquaintance would not survive the war.

Back in Lons-le-Saunier, thanks to a friendly woman whose name he'd been given by the doomed man, Henny learned that a raid would take place that afternoon. France Libre seemed as perilous as her occupied sister. With this woman's help, Henny obtained the papers needed to leave Lons-le-Saunier and travel to Lyon, where two men remained in the otherwise deserted Dutch consulate, helping people in flight. Here, the two dogged refugees received directions and advice: Saint-Julien nearest Geneva was the best place to cross the border, but be warned – the Swiss were turning refugees back. Once across, seek out the Dutch Consulate.

In Lyon, Henny and Elisabeth found a place to sleep on the floor of the synagogue, surrounded by other Jews fleeing Nazi persecution – Poles, Belgians, Germans, French, fellow Dutchmen. Henny listened to their stories while the organ played Yiddish songs, and in the morning, he and his sister continued towards the Swiss border, taking a train and then a bus, eyeing the armed soldiers at each station with trepidation, avoiding the blue-coated police on the street. The day was long, and fraught with tension.

When the bus finally arrived at the border town of Saint-Julien, night had fallen. The few people left on board disembarked and stood in small clusters, whispering and glancing around. Soon a man in a starched white suit approached Henny, saying he had been sent to escort them across the border. The man was insistent, but Henny trusted his instincts and declined. Choosing an avenue to the right, he and Elisabeth began to walk beneath unlit street lamps and shuttered windows. They stopped and removed their shoes and socks, the better to hear and not be heard on the cobbles, but at another turn they found themselves in a shopping street where young couples strolled hand in hand. Henny and Elisabeth hooked arms, trying to blend in, hoping that in the dark no one would notice their bare feet. When the door to a bar opened, they avoided the spill of voices and the flood of light.

Eventually, they came to a wide road that Henny recognized from his map, and they followed it, finding at the end rolls of barbed wire: the border crossing! Crawling on hands and knees, they inched through holes made by others before them, collapsing onto the Swiss soil on the other side. The crest of the hill before them glowed, and it took Henny a moment to realize that what he was seeing was Geneva, a free city where no blackout paper covered the windows, and where street lamps lit the way for any who cared to walk.

The dreary industrial borough of Slough, west of London, churned out more than airplane parts and munitions. At dusk, to screen the factories from German planes, drums filled with greasy rags and used oil were set alight. The black smoke and acrid smell polluted the sky and drifted as far as Stubbings, where Wilhelmina decided she needed a change of climate. She found cleaner air and a smaller house near South Mimms on the other side of London. From her "little country place" she occasionally saw the light show of war over the city, a view like Cor and Gerrit's, one of tracer bullets and searchlights and bomb explosions.

One night in February 1944, the danger lunged closer. As she lay in her room ready for sleep, she heard a heavy explosion in the nearby wood, and then an aircraft overhead. One bomb and then another dropped in the garden, and cracks webbed the walls and ceiling. She made her way to the door, the floor heaving beneath her feet. The bomber rumbled overhead, and she waited for the third explosion, but it didn't come. She could smell gas and smoke, and see the tips of flames moving towards her. An aide shouted, "Where is the queen?" and she called back, "I'm here – I'm all right," as the man extinguished the fire.

Her house at South Mimms was a mess of rubble and broken stairs. One of her guards had been killed, another fatally wounded, and she found herself tucked into the garden's air raid shelter until the military police deemed it safe to escort her to Stubbings. It was two o'clock in the morning as she skirted London, where the bombs continued to drop and fires from the fallout lit the night sky.

The youngest of the den Hartog children turned two in April, and though Cor did not relish celebrating anything these days, the family sang, "*Oh, how happy we are today, Niek is having his birthday. . . .*" Gerrit brought home a tiny piece of chocolate as a treat and Cor grated it so everyone could have a sliver. She didn't ask how he got it. With the shelves at the greengrocers nearly empty, Gerrit's early spring produce was in high demand, but seeds were hard to come by, and the garden's output had shrunk accordingly. Though he could sell everything he grew, he received in return only what the occupiers wanted to pay, and there were rules against selling outside the German-controlled channels. To guard against thieves – and to convince the authorities he did so – a German shepherd dog had been chained inside the *tuin*'s gate, and Cor and the children no longer went there.

Niek shared his birth month with Princess Juliana, and on the eve of her special day, Henk Batelaan announced to his family that the Dutch flag would rise over the gasworks the next morning. Everyone thought he was joking, for only last year he'd received a severe reprimand from Mayor Simonis for celebrating Italy's surrender with the employees of the utility. But Henk had an excuse this time, for renovations to the plant, which were carried out despite shortages of building materials and labourers, had reached the roof's peak, and it was tradition to raise the flag. Excuse or not, Henk's action was provocative – thumbing his nose at Nazi rules could result in a range of punishments, from the loss of his job to imprisonment or death. But Henk mustered his courage, and as the banner snapped in the stiff April wind, it was quite possibly the only Dutch flag flying in the country.

⚔ ⚔

In every town and city, street-life was changing. Gypsies, Freemasons, homosexuals, prostitutes, and other so-called asocials were being rounded up. Jehovah's Witnesses had also been incarcerated; in the early days of Hitler's rule, they refused to bear arms for Germany because of their pacifist beliefs, and since then – "on principle," Seyss-Inquart would testify – the Nazis considered the Witnesses enemies wherever they encountered them. Jews had for the most part disappeared. Leidschendam's twenty-six Jewish citizens would never return, but some thirty others had come from elsewhere, like the family who lived with the Batelaans, and the sister and brother, Flora and Louis, who lived with Gerrit's friend Jaap and his family. There were those who sheltered, but there were all too many who betrayed, receiving a reward of 7.5 guilders for each person, including babies. One man married to a Jewish woman brought his wife to the local police station himself and gave her over as though she was nothing more than an illegal possession whose presence made his own life difficult.

The sound of footsteps seemed to echo in the streets, not only because there were no church bells, but because there were few cars and trucks, other than those that belonged to the Germans. The man with the barrel organ rarely wheeled through the neighbourhood any more, bringing music to the streets and people out of their houses. Small sounds seemed louder: steps being scrubbed, carpets being shaken, someone whistling. There was the *clip-clop* of horses' hooves, and the wheels of the *schillenboer*'s wagon crunching along the gritty brick roads, trailing the sweet, rotting smell of potato peels. The usual odour of burnt milk didn't waft from the coffee house at the end of the Broekweg, because there was so little milk or coffee to sell. Other things went on as usual: the church elder still came for his yearly visit, accompanied by another elder or sometimes Reverend Rietveld himself. The two men sat opposite Cor and Gerrit, who awkwardly unloaded their most private thoughts and sins, and then, when the elders were gone, went on as before.

For Cor, the town felt smaller than it had when she'd arrived. Nowadays she rarely visited her family in Overschie, and they didn't often come to her either. The trains were filthy and overcrowded by pre-war standards, and the journeys risky and full of interruptions, since train tracks were targeted by both Allied bombs and resistance sabotage. Going by bicycle, a long-standing, practical, and economical way of travel for the Dutch, was also tempting fate, and there were humiliating security checks along the way. Women with children in tow, old men, and those who held exemption certificates, like Henk Batelaan, Gerrit, and Jaap Quartel, were forced to stand in small queues, identity cards at the ready. Even with papers in order, no one was sure he wouldn't be yanked out of the lineup and told to empty his bags or to hand over his bicycle, whether or not he had a permit for it. Once, cycling had been taken for granted by everyone from businessmen with briefcases to mothers with a child front and back. A picture taken at The Hague in 1935 shows Wilhelmina and Juliana cycling in tandem, the queen in a long white coat and matching hat, Juliana in a short fur. Another exists of Bernhard pedalling alongside his brother Aschwin at Noordeinde in 1936, each with a flower tucked into his lapel. But times had changed. In the summer of 1942, the Germans had tried to seize all the bicycles in Rotterdam and The Hague, and though they'd failed miserably, the danger of losing a vital means of transportation – to either a Dutch thief or a German soldier – was ever-present. After Cor's bike was stolen, she didn't report the theft, not wanting a paper trail of the fact that she owned a bicycle in the first place; and when the bike reappeared days later in a neighbour's yard, she quietly retrieved it.

Cor missed the visits with her sisters and brother Tom in Overschie, the small guilty pleasure of having no demands as anyone's mother or wife, the pride of being able to bring them vegetables from the *tuin*. In Overschie she was Tante Cor to Truus's three little girls, and she slept in her childhood *bedstee* on the Zestienhovensekade, a soft mattress enclosed in an alcove with wooden doors. But on those visits she'd always worried about her family left at home, and never relaxed until she returned and saw from the top of the Tedingerstraat that her house was still standing, snug between the Bloms' and the Meulenbroeks'. Even then, she hadn't been satisfied until she'd let herself in the front door and heard Gerrit's greeting. All of them seemed defenceless when she couldn't be with them – as Gerrit had after the invasion, and as brother Gerry did now. She was of course glad that they'd heard from Gerry, but it was stressful knowing he might be on board a ship in the battle-plagued Atlantic. At least she could reach Truus, Maria, and Tom by letter, and receive the same back. She learned to wait patiently for the mail to come, and to take her days one after another.

But for meals, she planned weeks in advance, often assisted by Rige and one of Mar's daughters, who took turns coming the short distance from Rijswijk and learning the role of mother's helper. These sorts of apprenticeships were an old tradition but had taken on new value during the occupation. With the girls' help, she peeled, grated, and strained potatoes, then dried the mixture on a sheet in the sun. The potato-flour that resulted would be useful to thicken porridge, so that she could extend her rations of barley and oatmeal. She used to cook horsemeat on Sundays – it was tough and chewy at the best of times, but the thought of it now made her mouth water, and she wished for just a little meat to enhance the *hutspot*, that standard Dutch dish of potato, onion, and carrot. But she reminded herself that flavour shouldn't matter. As she and Gerrit often told the children, *Je eet niet omdat het lekker is* – You don't eat because it tastes good. (Though some things, she admitted inwardly, tasted absolutely delicious, even when you hadn't tried to make that happen.) These were the kinds of guide-lines she hoped they'd remember: simple, precise rules that would steer them past a maze of temptation.

Gerrit's work ensured vegetables for their table – they could even spare some to send back to Rijswijk with Mar's daughter – but other essentials were dwindling. She'd altered her own skirts and dresses to fit her shrinking waistline, and Gerrit's worn corduroys hung on his narrow hips, cinched with a belt in which he'd bored new holes. His face was drawn, and the colour was fading from her children's cheeks. A nasty flu had worked its way through the family in spring, and all of them had taken longer than usual to recover. Koos's breathing had worsened and boils inflamed Rige's skin. But summer was on its way. The peas were flowering in the garden, ready to form their pods.

One day when Gerrit should have been tending them, she saw him through the picture window, running up the walk in his sock feet, the wooden shoes he wore in the *tuin* swinging from his hands. He burst through the door and crossed the room towards her.

"The invasion!" he called, two bright pink spots on his cheeks. "The Allies have landed in France!"

In a grand scheme of deception that opened a path to Normandy, the Germans' own intelligence agents in England were won over by the Allies, and over a period of months the turncoats convinced the Germans an invasion would happen at Pas de Calais rather than on Normandy's beaches. Fake landing craft were displayed in English ports, and captured by Luftwaffe cameras, to the misguided delight of the Nazi High Command. Phony radio traffic alerted the Wehrmacht to a possible invasion of Norway, too, so they held their troops there instead of moving them south to France to form a stronger defence. Even with the Atlantic Wall, there were strips of beach along the coast that remained vulnerable as Allied power increased, and though the Germans had attempted to fortify these areas, the "string of beads" was patchy when the Allies approached. Persistent attacks by the Allies and resistance workers on French railways had slowed the work on

Normandy's section of wall, since shipments of building materials needed for the job were either bombed en route, or had no tracks to follow. Soldier-wise, the region was full of unenthusiastic conscripts from occupied countries, or those who'd seen duty on the Eastern Front and had lost fingers and toes in the freezing winter. Many were aging and unhealthy, and jokingly referred to as the ear-and-stomach battalions because they suffered from poor hearing and ulcers. The troops had been bolstered somewhat by new units, but supply and demand was an ongoing problem of war, and soldiers couldn't be turned out on an assembly line or requisitioned from Sweden, which already supplied Germany with iron ore and high-quality ball bearings. None of the men were ready for the massive assault that would come to represent the largest amphibious invasion the war – or the world – had known. Finally, the Allies had what they'd been striving for: a foothold, however tenuous, in occupied Europe.

Wilhelmina had forbidden Prince Bernhard to take part in active combat, but by now, with the Allies making strides, his lust for adventure took over. Persuasive and cunning, he convinced a general with the RAF to sign him on to Squadron 847 under the pseudonym Wing Commander Gibbs, and after snapping a photo of the crew that would ride with him in the big Liberator bomber, he took a run as an Allied serviceman, dropping bombs on rocket sites in France.

At home, Gerrit saw news of the Allied successes in Normandy pasted on walls and signposts by stealthy resistance workers. Allied planes dropped leaflets with a message from the Allies' supreme commander, General Dwight Eisenhower, on one side, and Prime Minister Gerbrandy on the other. "People of Europe!" wrote Eisenhower. "Although the initial assault may not have been made in your own country, your hour of liberation is approaching." Gerbrandy took a solemn tone, and stressed that while special resistance groups had received their own orders from the government-in-exile, the rest of the population should engage in passive rather than violent resistance. He urged them to refrain from anything that might be directly or indirectly advantageous to the Nazis, and to ignore provocation by the enemy. "We will give you precise directions from here," he wrote. "It will be unmistakably clear when a powerful action is expected of you."

The German resistance, woven through military ranks, had a less cautious plan, and in muggy July, deep in the woods of East Prussia, a model officer turned resister planted a bomb in the map room of Hitler's "Wolf's Lair." The explosion shredded the room, killing a stenographer and three officers and injuring six more, but Hitler – trousers ragged from the knees down, hair yellowed with sulphur – stubbornly survived. With ringing ears and blackened face, he walked away from the blast as his pant legs flapped in the humid breeze. Later in the afternoon, he returned to the scene and picked his way among the splintered wood and hanging plaster with Benito Mussolini, who'd been rescued from prison and propped up as a puppet dictator in northern Italy. Hitler pointed out the heavy oak table that had shielded the bomb blast and remarked to his guest that, quite obviously, fate had protected him. In a nationwide broadcast, he announced himself "entirely unhurt, aside from some very minor scratches, bruises, and burns. I regard this as a confirmation of the task imposed on me by Providence."

Wilhelmina was no longer obligated to congratulate Hitler on surviving his brushes with death, but in the queen's absence, Arthur Seyss-Inquart sent a message of thankfulness that the führer had been spared. Still, he knew the regime was losing ground. In May, he'd sent his daughter Dorli home to Mattsee, Austria, and soon he'd tell Gertrud that she and the other German wives should be ready to move to a safer environment when the time came. Gertrud was beginning to see a change in her husband – a tension unabated by the classical music that hummed from his phonograph, or even by his playing the piano himself, leaning over the keys in absolute concentration.

Hitler remained, but little by little, his empire was being taken from him. The Netherlands' Princess Irene Brigade, peopled with well-intentioned volunteers and aging conscripts, was initially held back from the Normandy landings, since it was not considered strong enough to be part of the first or second wave of attack. But by August the brigade set foot on Juno Beach, and served under the Canadian First Army, helping to liberate the French towns of Saint-Come and Pont-Audemer. In England, Wilhelmina cheered them on, and she and her government tried to coordinate the Allied forces outside of the Netherlands and the resistance groups within. In these busy, exciting days, she read in the papers that the French resistance collective had been folded into the Allied forces. She rushed to call Gerbrandy and tell him the same status was imperative for the Dutch resistance, and that Bernhard must be their commander. General Eisenhower agreed to the proposition, shelving his earlier misgivings about the prince.

Within days, the Binnenlandse Strijdkrachten, the BS, stood for all resistance factions within the Netherlands, and like the country itself, was governed from England, joining the Allies' realm under the guidance of Prince Bernhard. *Tuinder* Gerrit might have been part of this group from the beginning, but if there were clandestine meetings after curfew, or weapons hidden in the shed, or sacks of potatoes set aside for the *onderduikers*, none of it was spoken of when the children might hear – though it happened more often that "Vader has to go out now," and he appeared with hat and coat in the kitchen, and nipped out the back door while Cor busied the children with chores and stories. Sometimes, Rige, Koos, or watchful young Gert heard the front door open moments after Gerrit had left, and saw him slink upstairs, still fully dressed – yet he was invisible later, if any of them prowled the rooms looking for him. Other times, he left through the back door and was not seen by them until morning, when he sat sipping ersatz coffee, warming his hands on the mug.

Much was made of Bernhard's involvement with the BS. Wilhelmina's glee may even have surpassed her son-in-law's; the job, she wrote, was an honourable one, and suited his status and abilities. She looked forward to the day that he would take part in liberating the Netherlands as commander of "our boys." Until then, she took comfort in the BS's welcome into the greater force. The new arrangement meant resistance fighters inside Holland were legitimate Allied soldiers. If caught by the enemy, they could not be shot or tortured, but must be treated according to the rules of war – providing the enemy, of course, played by those rules.

Wilhelmina donned her spectacles and followed the Allied progress by studying the continuous reports that arrived on her desk at Stubbings. She worked there instead of at her office in London due to the frequent V1 missiles, called buzz bombs because of the noise they made, launched across the channel from the occupied coastline. News came relentlessly over the wireless, and her assistants kept track of the army's movements on a map on the wall, so that she could see at a glance how close they were to her own border. Their advances were rapid. Many of Hitler's soldiers abandoned his order to fight or fall where they stood, and ran instead, although rearguards kept a tenuous hold on vital ports, forcing the Allies to maintain a long supply line from the invasion beaches. Still, newspapers around the world declared a rout; the headline in Canada's *Globe and Mail* read, HUNS IN FULL RETREAT ALONG 170 MILE FRONT.

Behind those lines, the uproar had begun. Leidschendam's Mayor Simonis commandeered two bicycles, prepared for a quick exit, and Seyss-Inquart, alarmed by the seeming collapse of the Nazi forces, ordered German civilians to move east, closer to the Reich. Anton Mussert gave a similar directive to his NSB members, and took his family to Twente, near Henny's hometown, where he'd be ready to cross into Germany should the need arise. But many of his underlings weren't waiting to see how things turned out. As the Allies snatched Antwerp and then Brussels, they raced to Dutch towns where no one knew them, or across the border, predicting the wrath of their fellow citizens. But Germany's cities were suffering shortages too, and ironically, most of the departees ended up in camps, more like prisoners than welcome guests.

In Leidschendam, Cor could see the exodus along the Vlietweg from Moeder den Hartog's doorstep. Fleeing civilians pedalled dilapidated bicycles and milk carts, and soldiers laden with packs and bags crammed into tired buses and cars that chugged along on makeshift fuel. Skinny horses pulled wagons that sagged with Wehrmacht soldiers, the NSB, as well as wives and children. Cor wouldn't have recognized Gertrud Seyss-Inquart if the car carrying her had passed on the Vlietweg, but the Reich commissioner's wife was among the first out of the country, filling five suitcases and heading home to Mattsee. The day after she was safely gone, her husband tried to stem the flood with a decree making it illegal to leave the Netherlands, just as Hitler's field marshal, Walter Model, called on the honour of his scattered troops and pleaded via radio that they stop running. Arthur himself abandoned his Clingendael bunker and moved farther inland to an underground command centre at Villa Spelderholt near Apeldoorn.

With Allied troops poised on the Dutch border, Queen Wilhelmina sent a message to Juliana to come immediately. Over Radio Oranje, she introduced Bernhard as leader of the collective underground army, and his smooth voice with its hardly detectable German accent sounded calm but assertive as he announced that all members of his army should carry an armband on which ORANJE had been written in clear letters. Only when he gave the signal should this armband be donned. "Keep to the instructions of your leaders," he said. "They will hear from me what you will have to do."

Gerrit, hearing the report, thought immediately of his time as a soldier. Then, too, he'd been told to trust and obey, that someone would tell him how to proceed. But men had been sent into battle without ammunition, and leaders had made horrible mistakes. Soldiers had died. He switched off his radio and the attic went dark, and he allowed himself to hope that this time, the results would be different.

At such a jubilant moment – on the brink of liberation – it was difficult to believe the newest posters plastered on the walls of cities and towns. Signed by Seyss-Inquart, the decree fell in line with Hitler's new "reign of terror," and made the death penalty mandatory for any action taken against the occupiers. Swelling the sense of fear-lessness and exhilaration was an incorrect report by the BBC that Allied troops had reached Breda, just south of the Moerdijk bridges. Rumour upon rumour distorted itself when one Leidschendammer said Dordrecht had been liberated, and another that Rotterdam was free. From the Tedingerstraat's upper windows, Cor and Gerrit watched the nearby airport Ypenburg go up in flames, and they assumed – like everyone – that the Germans expected their enemy to come from that direction. When Mar's daughter came from Rijswijk, just past Voorburg, she said she'd seen crowds thick with orange flags and flowers. People were lining the roads so they could greet the liberat-ing soldiers when they arrived. But night fell and no one came. Day after day there was no news, and bunches of withered flowers lay on the roadside, fading to brown.

Though quickly maturing, eight-year-old Rige didn't know what martial law meant, or anything about the reign of terror intended to quash a tenacious resistance. She didn't know Police Leader Rauter's latest promise, that for every Nazi killed by the resistance, three Dutchmen would die. She hadn't seen the bodies laid out in the streets with bullets through their foreheads, grisly displays meant to sap both courage and determination. But subversive acts continued, large and small. Rige smiled hello to the seamstress Paulien Quartel as she passed, unaware that the little case she carried held socks for the Batelaan family and their *onderduikers*, or that they had been mended by another *onderduiker*, Flora, who remained with her brother Louis a secret guest of the Quartels. These days, everyone carried satchels or rucksacks wherever they went. Back and forth went Paulien's suitcase, travelling through what Mayor Simonis called "a difficult town" because of the constant thefts and sabotage. The irritations of the resistance soon proved too much for Simonis, who moved on to Nieuw Beijerland. Likewise, the enthusiastic head of the Air Protection Service, De Regt, abandoned Leidschendam for Amersfoort, so it was an interim mayor who responded when someone cut a telephone cable that served the Germans – most private phone lines had been disconnected long ago. A poster spelled out the crime, and warned that, "if these actions are repeated, ten civilians will be promptly and rightfully shot to death." Only a select few knew that the perpetrators were Ineke's father, Henk Batelaan, and Gerrit's friend Jaap Quartel, church elder and church organist respectively.

Rige saw the posters, but didn't ask about them. In the quiet company of her mother she mended socks and undergarments that were almost see-through with wear; she poured dried peas into the mill clamped to the table and turned them to powder; she took the tails off beans and pulled the strings free. All of it happened almost wordlessly, but occasionally her mother chattered to entertain the boys and keep their minds off waiting for a meal that she knew would not fill their stomachs.

Rokus loved the spying game, *Ik Zie*, for which Rige felt she'd grown too old. One Saturday morning, as she sat near the window with the basket of mending, she heard her mother sing, "*I see what you don't see, and it is red.*" Rokus and Koos kept guessing wrongly, and Gert guessed only green things, but Rige didn't look up from her work, thinking how few red objects there were in this plain, dark room. She threaded a darning needle with a bit of frayed wool, her tongue stuck out to the side in concentration, but a clash of voices on the Tedingerstraat distracted her and she pricked her finger. A bead of blood appeared, and her gaze moved through the window to the street, where a group of German soldiers surrounded a black hearse pulled by a single horse. The soldiers were wearing helmets and long coats, and held their guns at the ready. One of them was shouting at the driver of the hearse as he clambered down from his seat, red-faced, scrunching his hat in his hands. Rige took in the hearse's black wheels with their black spokes, and the fancy woodwork where the paint was polished but chipped. Between the soldiers she glimpsed the long black coffin, and understood the driver was being shoved towards it, told to open it. The man's terror showed even in the scruffy back of his head, which he rubbed and rubbed with his hand. His fear slid through the air into Rige, spreading in her limbs and to the tips of her toes. In spite of it, she felt herself standing to see more – to see who and how many were inside the coffin, either dead or alive. And then her mother grabbed her arm and hissed, "Get away from the window!" In the middle of a bright morning, Rige's mother closed the curtains.

The Garden's Yield
1944–1945

LATE IN THE MORNING on September 8, 1944, William Lyon Mackenzie King stepped from his car in Princess Juliana's driveway, a flat, wrapped parcel in his hand. It had rained heavily the night before, and the pavement was still wet; the forecast called for storms again tonight. Despite the dismal weather, the princess was flying back to England today, and as she greeted the prime minister in the drawing room, he could see the ambivalence that reality caused – she kept a handkerchief at the ready, dabbing her eyes, and told Mackenzie King that Margriet, playing in a corner, would be her link to Canada. He presented Juliana with the parcel he'd brought: a picture of himself and his little dog, Pat, with the inscription, *To Her Royal Highness Princess*

Juliana of the Netherlands, to recall years in Canada in the happier days of the years to come.

In the hour of their goodbye, a mysterious rumble echoed through the streets near The Hague, and the leaves on the trees quivered. Up from the woods around Leidschendam, two enormous projectiles pierced the sky, flames bursting from their winged ends. The rockets disappeared towards the sea, leaving a trail of smoke behind them. Within five minutes, they travelled more than three hundred kilometres to England, moving faster than the speed of sound. The first landed in Chiswick, where a six-year-old boy watched a bomb fragment enter his hand. It seemed to him that the furniture crumpled in absolute silence, before he'd even heard an explosion. A huge umbrella cloud formed above the row of houses, and in an upstairs room, the boy's three-year-old sister – otherwise unwounded – died when her lungs collapsed. The British government, quick to investigate, hushed up the real reason for the tragedy, and instead released to the press that it had been caused by a burst gas main. A news blackout followed, lasting two months, so that the explosions that came fast and furious over the next while also went unreported. With no mention of the devastation in the press, the Germans wondered if the new weapons had hit their targets. The Luftwaffe had been all but obliterated by now, so the German air force wouldn't chance flying over England to witness the results for itself. The Allies more or less controlled the skies except for these deadly ballistics, V2s, and the less sophisticated V1 missiles already in action. V stood for *vergeltungswaffe*, or "vengeance weapon," a term chosen by Goebbels because the damage inflicted was meant to avenge the Allies' incessant bombing of German cities.

In case civilians weren't hearing the truth, the Germans sent V1 buzz bombs across the water, equipped with leaflets instead of artillery, and the message that fell in the English streets read, "Bombs now burst on England and nobody knows where they come from." Despite the paucity of V2 news in the papers, the people grew terrified. No one could predict when a blast would come, or know whether it would land in the deserted woods, in a quiet neighbourhood, or in the crowded city streets. After each assault, survivors spread eerie stories. A man told of how he'd been standing in his house, looking into a mirror hanging on the wall, when the wall and the mirror fell soundlessly away and his garden came into view. A woman said she'd been pocketing her change at market when she nodded to the milkman, sitting on his cart close by; after the blast, both his horse and wagon remained, but she insisted the man himself had turned to dust, for he was never seen again.

Back in the Netherlands, in Leidschendam, Rie Batelaan made note in her diary of the "devilish" flying bombs that hissed overhead, and the Allied planes that circled in their wake, searching for the hidden, mobile bases that would come to include the old woods around Huis ten Bosch, the racetrack just north of the palace, and the once tranquil Vreugd en Rust park, a short walk from the Tedingerstraat. Most of wealthy neighbouring Wassenaar had become a ghost town, its people told to find shelter elsewhere, moving their belongings with pushcarts and baby carriages. Empty streets bore scorch marks from the fired missiles, and at night the trains rushed into the region from Germany – flat railway carriages that held the rocket bodies camou-flaged with sails and reed mats; rail tankers bearing loads of liquid oxygen. On the tracks next to Gerrit's *tuin*, military transports shuttled ammunition to The Hague.

In the daytime, these same trains and vehicles took cover, as the Allies attacked Leidschendam's roads, streetcar tracks, and railway lines, aiming to choke the rockets' supply route. They were likely also aware of a German transmitting station nearby, and a string of twenty-five houses east of the tracks near the *tuin*, where five hundred SS men lived. In the Allies' view, there were multiple justifications for bombing the area. Koos and Rokus ran out to the balcony at the sound of strafing machine guns in the distance, straining to glimpse one of the RAF's glamorous planes, and Cor took the stairs two at a time after them when she heard Koos shout, "Yes! I hope they get a hit!" Once she'd hauled them back inside, her hand flew across Koos's head, and he flinched when her ring nicked his scalp. He only looked at her for an instant, but his eyes showed her he thought she was mean and unfair, and she let him believe it. He was too young to understand that he was not the source of her anger, and that she feared for his life. Later, in bed, Gerrit told her that four people in Leidschendam had died from Allied guns that day. "We're caught in the middle," he said, "like we don't matter." She heard the despair in his voice and put a reassuring hand on his shoulder, but he turned away, his back rigid.

Despite a persistent enemy and the weapon's own liabilities, the Germans continued to fire the V2s. A lumbering fourteen metres in length, they were nonetheless delicate, and during the long haul to the Netherlands from Germany – where they were made by slave labour in an underground factory – the rockets were often damaged and arrived unfit for launching towards their primary targets of London and Antwerp. Some had been sabotaged by the prisoners who'd assembled them. Chances were high that something would go wrong: a rocket might fail to take off, or come crashing back down on the launch site, killing the Germans' own; just as likely, it would race up and lose control, and hurtle down close by, killing civilians in the vicinity, as happened in Rijswijk, not far from Mar's house, when a missile fell on an orphanage. On Bep's old street in Voorburg, six houses were destroyed in similar fashion. Cor prayed for the victims, and thanked God that Bep had moved to The Hague – though conditions there were even worse, with food shortages increasing.

On the main road from The Hague, a steady exodus of people passed through Leidschendam on their way to the countryside to beg or barter food from farmers. Some townspeople, not much better off, shared a cup of broth or a piece of bread if they had it; others avoided answering the door. By now most bakeries had closed because of a shortage of coal, so even with a ration coupon, bread might be unobtainable. But at Saint Antonius Hospital in Voorburg, beggars were never turned away. After the offering had been eaten, if it was past curfew and too late to walk back safely to The Hague, people were put up on stretchers in the hallways, and the scene looked much as it had following the invasion, when the hospital was overrun with wounded soldiers and civilians.

Bep often came to Leidschendam, carrying a small leather suitcase that Gerrit would fill with vegetables. She remained a welcome guest at the den Hartog house, where the children still called her "Tante" and assumed she was related by blood, like Tante Truus or Tante Maria, never having been told otherwise. For the youngest ones, Henny had vanished from memory, but for Bep herself, reminders lingered. Old contacts from the days of Henny's passport schemes still turned up at the house she shared with her daughter, and took shelter if they needed to, though shelter of any kind seemed unstable these days, with the roar of rocket engines becoming a common sound and threats from Rauter's police growing. The latest warnings in the legal newspapers said "loafers" from sixteen-year-old boys to fifty-year-old men would be picked up in all towns and villages and sent to Germany. These were the newspapers that Cor cut into small squares for toilet paper.

Mixed in with the bad news were hints of the occupiers' desperation and the nearness of the Allied forces. American troops had already crossed the Dutch border and liberated Maastricht and parts of the province of Limburg. Preparing for an invasion, the RAF and Bernhard's BS made night flights that dropped weapons inside enemy lines in green metal canisters as tall as a man. These pre-arranged drops were aimed, with great risk, at remote areas, where there were no searchlights, inundated polders, or *Rommelspargel* – the pointed wooden posts placed to prevent Allied landings, named for both Wehrmacht general Erwin Rommel and their speared, asparagus shape. Wherever the goods landed, they had to be retrieved by brave souls who then transported them to the resistance groups expected to use them. Sometimes resistance men in stolen Wehrmacht uniforms collected the shipments and drove them across the country in German army trucks, the ultimate masquerade. Traditional family men from the church on the Damlaan had stashed such uniforms in their crawlspaces, or in the parsonage itself, and in these peculiar times, weapons travelled in milk carts and motorboats, or buried in vegetable crates packed on barges like the ones that took Gerrit's produce to auction. In Overschie, Cor and Gerrit's friend Dick Zandbergen moved five shipments this way, while others arrived by horse-drawn mail wagon and bicycle couriers. These last chanced being stopped by the Germans, who wanted the bicycles, but if the weapons made it past the enemy, many were taken to a large depot on the Zestienhovensekade, where Cor's family still owned the bookstore and the house where she grew up. Smaller caches – hand grenades, bazookas, and Sten guns – were stored throughout Overschie: at Dick Zandbergen's workplace, in the Catholic boarding school, and in a brewery. Acquiring weapons was a huge problem for the resistance, and many of the men who'd been soldiers thought back to the thousands of guns turned in after capitulation, and regretted the fact that they'd been too afraid to disobey the order and hide their weapons for later use.

Some of the packages dropped by the Allies drifted down by para-chute into polders and farmers' fields, and those who opened the baskets looked in on blinking pigeons with names like Scotch Lass and William of Orange, birds with the drive and ability to fly hundreds of kilometres back to where they'd come from, armed with information about the strength of German presence in various areas. A message gave strict instructions to the finder, whoever he may be, to answer the list of questions about German actions and whereabouts to the best of his ability, put it in the tiny canister attached to the pigeon's leg, and release the bird.

One Sunday, there were whispers after the last church service that paratroopers had landed within the occupied zones, on the banks of the river Lek near Arnhem. Cor's Tante Ester, one of Neeltje's sisters, lived near there in the village of Oosterbeek, and Cor's cousin Cornelia – the girl who helped at the bookstore – was staying with her aunt at the time because there was more food there than in Schiedam. Cor felt a surge of hope for this branch of her family when the rumours started. There were noises, too, of a countrywide railway strike, but Cor wondered if that could possibly come true. Tens of thousands of workers were employed by the railways, she knew, and she wondered where they would all go if they had to hide while striking. Just hours later, after she and Gerrit had put the children to bed, heavy bombers raided the V2 launch sites close by, rattling windows in the Tedingerstraat and in the Stalen-Ramen-Koop factory at the end of the street, where production had expanded to include stretchers for the Red Cross. Cor muttered a prayer, and Gerrit's fingers curled around the threadbare arms of his favourite chair. If they thought the war was almost over, they couldn't have been more wrong.

The "vengeance weapons" had provided further incentive for an Allied invasion, thus the talk heard at church was true. The troops landing near Arnhem belonged to the recently formed First Allied Airborne Corps, a largely American-British collaboration, which also included a Polish parachute brigade that had never seen action. Some ten thousand strong, their task was Operation Market-Garden, an unassuming name for the largest airborne offensive ever undertaken. For all its grand scope and ambition, the mission was flawed before it started: its strategists never consulted the Dutch, who of course knew the terrain better than anyone. Had they been included they might have protested exposed routes and foolhardy drop zones before the morning of September 17, when thousands of aircraft lifted into the skies over England. The noise was deafening and the sight spectacular; still more planes would follow in the coming days. Juliana and Wilhelmina, watching from the lawn at Stubbings, were among those who gaped in awe. Like Prince Bernhard and the other Dutch advisers, they didn't know details of the plan, or the fact that British Field Marshal Bernard Montgomery predicted it would end the war by Christmas, but the scene inspired just those kinds of thoughts.

"Market" referred to the airborne part of the plan, in which

American paratroopers would capture bridges at Eindhoven and Nijmegen, while the British division, known as the Red Devils, would take Arnhem. "Garden" was primarily an elite British armoured division charged with sweeping up the one-hundred-kilometre corridor opened by the paratroopers, and crossing the Rhine River, the final hurdle before advancing on Germany. In the midst of the Garden soldiers was the Princess Irene Brigade, transferred from the command of the Canadians to the British. Though eager to be among their country's liberators, they were not alone in their misgivings about Montgomery's bold plan. Meticulously synchronized, Market-Garden allowed no margin for error or bad weather, and had no backup strategy should any single part of the scheme go wrong. Worst of all, the organizers dismissed warnings from the Dutch resistance of a renewed German presence around Arnhem. British reconnaissance photos confirmed the claims, but the decision-makers preferred a two-week-old truth: that the enemy, beaten and scurrying for Germany, had all but deserted the area.

Highly motivated and filled with bravado, the Allies for the most part discounted their rivals' ability to regroup after their rout from Belgium and France. A German infantry division retreating up the coast from Belgium was left to escape across the Scheldt Estuary, and began marching towards Arnhem, where it united with two panzer tank divisions threaded through the forest. Reduced in number but still strong, the crews had been resting while the tanks were refitted. In neighbouring Oosterbeek, where Cor's relatives lived, sleek Wehrmacht staff cars appeared, pennants flapping from the fenders. Purely by coincidence, hoping for solitude and a restful setting in the wake of the Belgium debacle, Field Marshal Walter Model had chosen this placid village outside Arnhem as the new headquarters for Army Group B. Unwittingly, the Germans had congregated less than five kilometres from Market-Garden's northernmost drop zone.

Apart from a few glitches, the landings came off well for the Allies. Some aircraft and personnel were lost, but that was expected in war and Montgomery remained optimistic. The Dutch watched the skies from their rooftops, and headed into the streets as if the armoured corps' drive north was nothing more than a victory parade. But their enthusiasm was premature, and the cheering throngs hampered the progress of the Garden troops.

In Oosterbeek, Cor's cousin Cornelia was away from Tante Ester's house, plucking chickens for the butcher. From the shed where she worked, covered in feathers and chicken lice that would fall off when she shook her clothes at the end of the day, she stared through the open door as the Market troops parachuted down. She stepped outside, wiping her hands on her apron, shielding her eyes as she peered up. The neighbour who'd been beating her floor mats on her stoop paused as well. Then a shot rang out and the woman crumpled. Cornelia took three running steps towards her, panic surging, but a hail of bullets followed, so she turned and ran back to the shed, where she crouched in a corner while the fighting escalated in the narrow streets.

In Eindhoven, the American Screaming Eagles were able to secure the bridge assigned to them, as were their fellow Americans landing at Nijmegen. But the accomplishments were not smooth, and Operation Market-Garden had fallen far behind schedule. Radio communications broke down and the Garden troops, rolling up the narrow highway from Belgium without cover, were ambushed. To the north, closest to Arnhem, the British Red Devils had dropped nearly on top of the panzer tanks, and the unit fragmented. Cut off from their commander and without radio contact or reinforcements, the Red Devils held out for nine days – five more than had been asked of them in the original plan, which had already expected too much. Polish paratroopers, jumping two days late due to bad weather in England, landed to find their supplies had been dropped fifteen kilometres away, beyond the opposite bank of the Rhine, thick with Germans. The ferry had been sunk, and the Poles had no way to get to the besieged Red Devils.

Gerrit gathered news as it came, but each day it was harder to believe that the Allies would break through. At night, as he prayed with

Cor, he saw the trust on her face, and listened to her thank God for His miracle – saving the country – as though that fortuitous event had already happened.

At his post in Brussels, Prince Bernhard likewise followed the battle anxiously, and with his Dutch military advisers shook his head at parts of the Allied plan now unfolding. He sent reports as he got them to Queen Wilhelmina, who waited with Juliana for news of the Allies' success, and received from her the headstrong directive that when the Allies overtook any royal estates they burn them, sullied as they were by enemy occupants.

Bernhard knew his mother-in-law's order was an emotional over-reaction, and for now, was spared passing on such a command. On September 26, Montgomery ordered the shreds of the Market troops still holding out at Arnhem to abandon their positions and rejoin the Allied lines to the south. Some didn't have that option. Of the more than ten thousand men dropped at the farthest bridge, roughly three-quarters remained there, captured, wounded, or dead.

The railway strike Cor had heard about went hand in hand with Operation Market-Garden. Nearly thirty thousand railway workers had gone into hiding at the request of the Allies and the Dutch government-in-exile, who hoped the move would thwart transportation of German troops, supplies, and rocket paraphernalia. A day after the strike began, Seyss-Inquart insisted the newspapers print a missive that the railway-men were playing a dangerous game with the fate of the Dutch people. But the Reich commissioner was losing his edge; not only had the railway industry finally turned on him, but most of the newspapers didn't comply with his request.

With the failure of Market-Garden, the government-in-exile asked that the strike continue – no simple feat, since so many were in hiding. Furthermore, there was no transportation for ordinary citizens who still risked travel by trains, no quick route for messages from one resistance sector to another, and worst of all, no coal or food easily shipped from other areas of the country to the west, to the big cities that needed it most.

Seyss-Inquart made a second attempt to end the strike, warning that it would lead to starvation, but again the newspapers refused to print his message. At the end of the month, the presses of the un-cooperative *Haagsche Courant* were blown up with dynamite. When the Dutch secretaries general still at their posts refused to appeal to the strikers on Seyss-Inquart's behalf, the Reich commissioner made a lethal decision, forbidding all inland shipping by any means until the strike was halted. He knew what this would do to the food supply, but he reminded himself that the Dutch people were responsible for the situation, and that anyway, the military interests of the Reich were just as important. As he'd later say at his trial, "There could be no graver accusation against me than for the German people to say that I did not do everything humanly possible to help to win the struggle."

Already scarce, food grew scarcer. Allied planes shot at anything that moved – truck, boat, barge, or the trains now run by the Germans – and food that did make it through was requisitioned by the Germans or by NSB police. A horse belonging to one of Leidschendam's remaining bakers had been taken, and the milkman, heeding the warning, had put his own horse into hiding and was doing his rounds with a pushcart. He had little to sell. The milk ration was tiny, even for the children, and kept shrinking as autumn wore on.

In the middle of these indignities, yellow posters appeared through-out The Hague and area, requesting blankets, clothing, even underpants, all badly needed in Germany. The posters claimed that those who relin-quished a certain amount of this warmth for the Reich would receive a certificate that protected them against house searches. Cor paused to read one of the posters on her way home from church, shivering as a cold wind bit through her coat, and doubted that many would comply. Keenly aware of winter's steady approach – knowing how much colder it would seem with little food and light – few did, and a resistance group copied the certificates and gave them away in great numbers, though it was unlikely even the authentic ones would be honoured.

Autumn closed as a disappointment for the Allies, who'd been riding high on the successes at Normandy and had been so sure Market-Garden would be the end of the war. The Americans, who had charged west after Normandy, were stalled one hundred kilometres from the German border. Despite increasingly terse demands to Eisenhower for gasoline, supplies couldn't reach them fast enough without a major depot. The British had taken Antwerp, a plum possession as it was Europe's second-largest port after Rotterdam and had been captured with all of its forty-five kilometres of docks intact. But the heavily mined and defended Scheldt Estuary, a long, snaking body of water that connected Antwerp to the North Sea, was still held by the Germans, rendering Antwerp useless as a supply depot. The task of freeing the Scheldt went to the Canadians.

Throughout October, the Canadian soldiers fought on both sides of the waterway, in nightmare conditions: open, flooded polders, driving rain, land mines, and booby traps. One company of ninety men had only four survivors by day's end. The Germans allowed no quarter, firing on the wounded when anyone moved, so the stretcher-bearers waited until dark to make their recoveries. But there were more successes than failures. Three days after a disastrous battle in the same area, the town of Woensdrecht at the entrance to the Zuid Beveland peninsula was taken. In the south, the division charged with wresting control of the pocket around the Leopold Canal had chased the last holdout Germans into concrete bunkers, and soon silenced them altogether. On the north side of the Scheldt, the Canadians pushed to the coast and sank German vessels in the Zijpe harbour. By October 31, Zuid Beveland had been taken and the Canadians, joined by Polish and British troops, prepared to assault Walcheren, but the bowl-like island's dunes and dikes were studded with gigantic bunkers and artillery batteries, its flat lands littered with barricades and minefields too flooded for infantry but not deep enough for amphibious vehicles. The RAF solved the problem by blowing an enormous hole in the dike at Westkapelle, and seawater flooded in. Now the Allies could attack both by land and over water, but the residents became unintended victims. Those who had hidden in cellars drowned, as did the dozens in one town who flocked to a windmill to escape the swell. The seawater rose and swallowed them, and only three made it out alive.

But Walcheren's capital, Middelburg, remained relatively dry. Bep's hometown, the proud city that had had its heart bombed out in the very first days of the war, now took in refugees from the flooded countryside, and despite the devastation, few people were grumbling at the Allies' methods. The Germans were being beaten back, and the people congregating, sometimes fifty to a house, were excited and eager for liberation. When the same forces responsible for bombing their dikes and flooding their island arrived, the people rushed out to greet them. The island was close to ruined, but the strategic Scheldt had been won. Minesweepers began cleaning the channel, and by the end of the month the first Allied ships, led by the Canadian vessel *Fort Cataraqui*, docked at Antwerp, bringing the armies' long-awaited supplies.

Back near Arnhem, the failure of Operation Market-Garden was palpable. German soldiers ordered entire streets in the region emptied. Cor's Tante Ester and her family had already been evacuated from Oosterbeek when the offensive began, but her cousin Cornelia had hidden with the chicken butcher and his family, out of sight throughout the fierce fighting. One morning in October, they opened the door to find guns pointed at them, and without explanation they were forced to leave. A few among hundreds, they began walking. Eventually Cornelia's feet swelled and she had to carry her shoes, and somehow lost one on the journey. Any kind of shelter they came upon was full, and they spent their first night in a potato cellar, shoulder to shoulder with strangers. After days of travel, Cornelia and her surrogate family located a forester's shed in the Veluwe woods to the north. For weeks they lived there, sleeping on shelves, before the Germans came again and demanded they move on.

Stories like these were everywhere, and as the hardships multiplied, so did the resolve to fight back. Behind enemy lines, weapons drops for the resistance increased. New conscripts were trained in the use of Sten guns, hand grenades, and bazookas. They travelled to the training grounds blindfolded, so they wouldn't be able to give away the locations in the event that they were captured and questioned by the Germans. The transport of weapons continued under the occupiers' noses. Down the street from the Post bookstore on the Zestienhovensekade, Dick Zandbergen and a friend filled a carrier tricycle with Sten guns, covering the already heavy load with a bed and blankets. As they crossed town, they struggled at the bottom of a hill. Their hearts already raced from exertion, but thudded harder as a soldier approached. To their shock, though, the young German fell in beside them, and helped push the load up the hill. At the top, he bid them good-day, and carried on in the other direction.

For Christians like Cor and Gerrit, these moments of luck and unexpected generosity seemed God-sent. But as conditions worsened, compassion was tested. Many people were frightened and worn out and barely had the strength or the means to look after themselves and their own. Others gave what they could spare when strangers came begging. With the railwaymen still persisting in their strike, the most basic food – potatoes – had become a rarity. When word spread that a gardener still had some, the droves came straight for him – not just from The Hague, Leiden, and Delft, but from as far away as Amsterdam. Sometimes the lines at farmhouses and garden gates were hundreds of people long. And yet during this time, in Germany and Poland, where people were also starving, whole fields of potatoes were grown to make rocket fuel.

Rige knew nothing about the V2 rockets, or the Allies' gains and losses. Her father's dealings at the garden – what he sold, traded, or gave away against German orders – were also a mystery to her, and she never saw his customers. Whatever illegalities he was involved in, he had so far been careful they didn't affect his children. But one autumn day as she headed home, she saw a stream of people lining the path behind the Tedingerstraat houses. Some were familiar – *de dronkaard* and *de prater* from the Broekweg – but most she'd never seen before. She kept pace for a while, glancing up at the haggard faces until a hand grabbed her sleeve and someone told her to move to the back and wait her turn. Rige hesitated, but pulled away and continued farther, ignoring the others who called out to her to get in line, looking at the ground to avoid eye contact. Shoe after shoe was split open at the toes. One girl's feet were wrapped in dirty rags. The line curved and moved in through Rige's own back fence, and at the end of it, or the beginning, she saw her father, ears splayed beneath his old cap, tufts of straw sticking out of the clogs he wore at the *tuin*. There were crates stacked beside him and the wheelbarrow from the *tuin*, all filled with potatoes, and she watched him hand them out until the last one was gone.

The weather grew colder, with rain and hail, mornings thick with fog. Foragers looked for food and wood, frantic as squirrels before winter. Willows were lopped down and hacked into pieces, and carted home for fuel. The majestic trees that lined the Vlietweg were nearly all gone. The most determined people waited until dark to creep into forbidden places and take what they needed – anything that would burn in a stove. Wood was lifted out of railway tracks, and pried from abandoned houses. The den Hartogs' teenaged neighbour, Piet Blom, sneaked out time and again after curfew to steal a few hunks of coal from the German stockpile near the auction house. Once, as he and some friends were filling their pockets, someone shouted "Germans coming!" and

Piet's legs spun beneath him as he raced across the tracks in the darkness, past Gerrit's *tuin* and into the quiet Tedingerstraat. Just behind him, two of his friends were nabbed and disappeared into Germany.

Before the stream at the *tuin* iced over, Gerrit caught an eel as it slithered across a patch of grass to get to the canal. He brought it home, still wriggling, for dinner. Rige watched as Cor gutted and skinned the long creature, then cut it into three-inch pieces, tying a thread around each portion, and steaming them. The house filled with a rank smell that churned even the hungriest stomach. But lately they'd consumed lots of things never considered before. Sugarbeets, like cucumber and potato peelings, had been nothing more than pig fodder before the occupation, but now Cor boiled the gnarly brown tubers, and the children, Rokus especially, sniffed the sweet air in anticipation and watched the clouds of steam rising. Cor was extracting the juice, which she'd caramelize in a pan on the stove, transforming a root vegetable into dark brown candy that melted in the mouth. The pulp itself tasted foul, so she hid it in soups or porridge, hoping it wouldn't be recognized.

There was food, but not enough, and little variation. Grain, protein, and fat were almost non-existent. When seamstress Paulien Quartel visited, she followed the new custom and brought a meagre packed lunch along, leaving it with her coat near the door. She set to work measuring the children, and choosing fabric – Cor's dresses, Gerrit's shirts – that could be remade into clothes for Rige and the boys. Niek, the youngest, was measured first and then he toddled from the room unnoticed. He spied the little sack in the hallway and squatted before it, and the smell of food reached him. Settling cross-legged on the floor, he undid the string and devoured every morsel of Paulien's small lunch. Cor, moving through the hallway, saw him stuff the last bite into his mouth. "Niek!" she cried, rushing forward. She scooped up the sack and looked inside, but she knew already that it was empty. Suddenly weak, she leaned against the wall, wanting to cry. Niek got to his feet and wrapped his arms around her knees and Cor put her hand on his blond head. "I'm sorry," she whispered, words she would also say to

Paulien, but which she directed now to her boy, for the hunger she couldn't assuage.

Even after Seyss-Inquart lifted the food embargo in November, hungry children were a big concern in Leidschendam, and the Gereformeerde Church began to organize trips to the northern provinces of Friesland and Groningen so that children could stay a while with families who had more food. The children's frequent escort was a respected church elder, but also – unbeknownst to them – a member of the resistance who used the opportunity to meet with his contacts in the north. The trip was exciting for some of the kids, and terrifying for others, who wanted only to be in familiar surroundings with their parents close by. They left at night, when it was safer to travel, as they were less likely to be targeted by Allied planes. By now, the Allies assumed any vehicle was carrying something of use to the Germans.

Families from other towns were doing the same for their children, and not always with the ulterior motive of a resistance meeting. At various times, Gerrit's brother Nico's son had gone away for health reasons, and Jacques and Truus had occasionally sent each of their three girls outside Overschie. Every time, parents weighed the risks of sending children across a war zone under a sky busy with Allied planes, against those of keeping them at home where the lack of proper food meant cuts and scrapes didn't heal well, diarrhea was common, and a simple cold wouldn't go away.

During the bleak, particularly rainy November that year, the RAF's Bomber Command started a new "priority one" offensive, striking V2 launch sites and transport routes with Spitfires rather than heavy bombers. The power-diving Spitfire carried two 250-pound bombs and zoomed in to release its load at some nine hundred metres. When the pilots pulled out of their dives, they followed through by strafing the area. Ostensibly, this new plan allowed for greater precision with less damage to the civilian population, and sometimes, when the target was a railway track, the bombers did a fly-past, warning of their intended attack, and the train would screech to a halt while the conductor ran the length of it, pounding on the compartment doors and screaming "Get out! Air raid!" But ordinary people still found themselves in the line of fire – anywhere there was a train or a road. It was easy to forget that this was part of the process of liberation, as the Allies' measures were sometimes as terrifying as the Germans'.

Seyss-Inquart knew that the Dutch government had set up "an illegal army" – the BS – and that weapons were being dropped into the Netherlands, where men were encouraged to join in droves. An increase in deportees to German factories seemed the best counter-offensive, thus leaflets soon appeared in mailboxes throughout the Rotterdam area, Overschie included. All men between seventeen and forty were told to stand outside their houses and await pickup by the occupiers. Early that same morning, trucks fixed with loudspeakers crawled through the streets blaring the command, and telling everyone else to stay inside their houses. The leaflets promised that "The daily compensation consists of good fare, cigarettes, and current standard payment. Family members left behind will be cared for." But they also added, "Inhabitants of the community are forbidden to leave their dwellings. Those who try to escape or resist will be shot." Even men like Gerrit, with certificates to exempt them from forced labour, were told to be outside with the rest and to carry the document with them. Thousands of men obeyed, standing nervously in front of their houses; thousands more were pulled from their hiding places, either found during searches or betrayed by their neighbours. Mothers frightened by what might happen if their sons didn't comply sent the boys outside with the stipulated bare necessities: eating utensils, warm clothes, sturdy shoes if they had them. At each stop the column of men grew longer. By the end of the day there were fifty thousand shuffling slowly out of Rotterdam in the cold rain, hemmed in by soldiers with their rifles ready.

Soon afterwards, Cor received a carefully worded letter from her sister Maria, which told of the raid in Overschie, and that "all the men have been picked up." Cor felt her heart sink. But in a new paragraph, Maria went on to say, "Little Nicolaas, little Tom, and little Jacques are playing across the street feeding the rabbits," and Cor understood that the three grown men – Maria's and Truus's husbands, and their brother Tom – had gone underground, like rabbits, in the factory opposite the family home. She burned the letter in the stove, and took it as a clear warning that a similar raid would soon occur in Leidschendam.

On November 20, the town's electricity, already stingily rationed, was cut completely. The following day, the leaflets were delivered and the same demands for men were made. No one other than the wanted men was allowed on the streets; the roads were barricaded and the bridges pulled up. Army trucks stopped at intersections and uniformed men got out. They set up machine guns and aimed them into the neigh-bourhoods, and in some streets went door to door, barging in if a knock went unanswered. From Leidschendam, fifty men were procured that day. The rest kept themselves well-concealed – young Piet Blom next door inside the wall with his belly sucked in; Gerrit in his burrow behind the wainscotting; the Reverend Rietveld, perhaps, with the Jews above the rafters of his church. But two men were spotted – first the red-faced *dronkaard*, sober enough to run, and then another man, who kept moving casually away when a soldier hollered at him. The soldier's shot blew him forward, and he died on the brick road. Those who dared to look out their windows recognized the man immediately and knew that, stone deaf, he couldn't have heard the warning.

Cor watched the Tedingerstraat in silence, wordlessly praying that the soldiers wouldn't bang on her door and push past her and the chil-dren, tramping through the rooms until they found Gerrit crouched behind the wall in the attic. Her hands shook, so she held them tightly across her body, gripping each arm. The wait was excruciating, and had to be more so for Gerrit, who would stay in his hiding place until she gave him the signal. None of the children questioned his absence, and if she saw fear in any of their faces, she told herself she was mistaken, that it was her own fear reverberating. She forced a smile and, attempt-ing normalcy, told Rige to set the table. Without asking, Rige laid places for everyone except Gerrit.

Over the following days, the bad weather worsened. The rain changed to sleet and the temperature dropped. In another week, the last ration of gas – from five to six o'clock – was taken away, so now there was neither heat nor light. The only fuel for warmth and cooking was wood, but Leidschendam's few forested areas and parks were already almost bare. The number of hungry people turning up on doorsteps escalated, and while the main raid had come and gone, the house searches continued, flaring up now in one part of town, now in another. Gerrit's brother, Nico, had gone into hiding at Moeder and Vader's house on the Broekweg, but his nine-year-old son didn't know it: he had no answers for the men who came into the flat and asked his father's where-abouts. Nico's postal uniform hung on a hook by the door, but the boy shrugged and shook his head, and the soldiers moved on.

Each night, Cor knelt and prayed for her own brother Gerry, and gave thanks for the relative safety of the rest of her family's men: Gerrit, Nico, Jacques, Tom, and Nicolaas. Stories had reached Leidschendam of a town called Putten, whose men had not been so lucky. Some weeks back the place had been terrorized by the Wehrmacht after an attempt to hijack a German truck had gone awry for the resistance, and a soldier had been killed. Officials had ordered the town burned, and though the command was only haphazardly carried out, nearly six hundred men – the entire male population – were rounded up and sent to Germany, with their wives, mothers, and children watching them go. White sheets sagged from the windows of the remaining houses, evidence of the people's bid for mercy.

In Leidschendam and beyond, men scurried from place to place disguised in ladies' clothing, looking, Cor thought, like the chatty old woman from the Broekweg who had posed for Henny so long ago, stroking her greasy curls. She rarely saw *de prater* these days, and won-dered how she fared. It was God's blessing, perhaps, that her own parents had been spared enduring times like these. With the men and boys in hiding, and the women guarding their places, the very old and the very young were forced into service. Children took on the task of foraging in miserable weather, walking hours for a bit of wheat, and sometimes coming home with nothing. And Vader den Hartog was among the elderly picking sticks in the Vreugd en Rust park, his gnarled fingers feeling for the spongy ones that wouldn't burn and discarding them.

Despite Allied successes freeing places like Nijmegen, Maastricht, and Middelburg, progress was not fast enough for the Dutch living north of the Maas River. Although Seyss-Inquart's ban on shipping had ended, all-out plunder of the country's railway tracks, train cars, machinery, and equipment meant little could move anyway. The Netherlands' intricate canal systems became the best method to transport food, and men from Leidschendam steered barges of food to town when someone located a food source. In doing so, the men chanced being pulled from the streets in one of the sporadic *razzias* that still occurred, but when temperatures plummeted and the *sluis* froze up, even the barge trips came to an end. So began the coldest winter in years.

A Central Kitchen opened in Leidschendam, and a caravan parked at the end of the Broekweg, dispensing bowls of either *hutspot* or watery pea soup in exchange for two potato coupons at certain hours of designated days. Raised with soldiers strutting the streets, having no memories of other times, Koos blithely stood in the lineup, his too-small jacket stretched tight as he lifted the pot Cor had given him to collect the family's ration. He placed the filled container into Niek's empty pram and wheeled it carefully down the Broekweg, one eye on the pot. He loved the challenge of not spilling a single drop. Lately he dreamed about soup, and chocolate, even fish swallowed whole from the *tuin* stream. The smell of the soup's steam told him that this batch would be almost as good as the potato and turnip dish his father had cooked a few weeks ago when his mother was unwell in bed. Today it was his responsibility to bring home the meal: eldest son, puffing with pride. But as he turned into the Tedingerstraat, he saw his mother waiting on the front step and felt a rush of indignation – did she think he would spill the soup, or dawdle while it grew cold?

Koos was oblivious to his parents' real concerns. In mid-November, rations were cut yet again, so that each week an adult – if he could get it – was entitled to one and three-quarters small loaves of bread, less than half a litre of skim milk, and two kilograms of potatoes. No meat, no fat, no eggs. In The Hague, where it was harder still to get food, the malnourished were easy prey for pneumonia and tuberculosis. Diphtheria lurked in the canals, and families hid their dead in order to keep their ration coupons, thus spreading more disease. As Cor lifted the pan of soup from the pram, she suddenly recalled her own words to Bep, around the time that Henny had gone: *Take comfort in the fact that the eternal life has a larger charm than this one.*

In London, Prime Minister Gerbrandy could not accept such fatalism, reassuring though the sentiment might have been for those who saw starvation looking back at them in the mirror. Over the course of the fall, he'd fought doggedly to bring attention to the situation in the Netherlands, and though the press liked to describe him as Wilhelmina's little gnome, papers worldwide printed the chilling messages he offered with all seriousness. Now that part of his country had been liberated, he paid a visit considered unwise for Wilhelmina, and what he saw prompted a letter to Eisenhower. "After my journey, during which I have seen how slowly progress is being made, what difficulties have still to be overcome, what dangers still threaten us, my conviction that everything will come right in the end is gone." He stressed that special measures needed to be taken to avoid a disaster of frightening proportions. "Relief for the occupied Netherlands at the time of the liberation must have priority above everything, even the slogan: *First of all defeat the Germans.* The Netherlands Government cannot accept the liberation of corpses."

Though Juliana was still with her, Wilhelmina wrote of a miserable Christmas in England, gathered around a tiny tree with one candle. She delivered a radio speech intended to be uplifting – calling Christmas the "feast of promise" – but afterwards, she sat slumped in a chair by the window, a blanket drawn around her, and confessed to her closest aide a feeling of helplessness, knowing that, at home, people were dying in the streets. It would have incensed her to learn of the meaty dinner put on by Arthur Seyss-Inquart for his staff, and of the huge tree hewn for festive purposes. To his guests, he read Hitler's Christmas message, containing good wishes for the Germans who resided in the Netherlands. In the liberated part of the country, along the front, soldiers of the First Canadian Army settled in at a farmhouse to eat a Christmas dinner that had come out of cans and was served up in their mess tins – turkey, creamed potatoes, Christmas pudding, accompanied by fresh fruit and a glass of beer. Back in Canada, Prime Minister Mackenzie King recorded in his diary that all day he'd thought of these men and their comrades on the front. As night closed, he opened the door at 24 Sussex Drive and admired the tranquil evening. "I wonder," he wrote, "if the day will ever come when that loveliest of hymns, *Silent Night*, will come into the minds of people throughout the world to express the German heart. I believe it is the expression of the heart of many Germans . . . [and] of most people throughout the world. That is the appalling tragedy of all that we witness today."

The spirit Wilhelmina described in her Christmas address – a light in the world, a love of one's fellow man – seemed anything but everlasting. In Nieuw Beijerland, Leidschendam's ex-mayor Simonis had reached an all-time low, and had taken to foraging with a firearm in hand. He divided the food he procured between himself and his son, and also his family who remained in Leidschendam, still living in the mayor's residence, though a new mayor had been appointed. The local resistance despised Simonis and beat both him and his son, who had joined the Dutch SS. To heighten the humiliation, their bruised, naked bodies were left in the street, and the need to avenge kept cycling.

Just outside of Leidschendam, an SS man had made contact with the local resistance, and asked for help deserting the Grüne Polizei. The resistance obliged him, and he was sheltered with a family in the area, but after a while got restless and sensed an opportunity. He wanted better accommodations, he said, more food, and "visits" from girls, and if he didn't get those things, he threatened to turn on his helpers: after all, he could easily claim he'd been captured and held against his will by the resistance. His contacts made reassuring noises, and one evening in December they came to get him, implying they'd sneak him off to a preferable spot. Instead he was shot and dumped into a shallow grave. The following morning a farmer discovered the corpse, haphazardly buried. The unidentified body travelled by manure wagon to the police station, and then on to Saint Antonius Hospital in Voorburg, where an autopsy was performed – but by this time, the resistance had made contact with the doctor charged with the task, and put in a gruesome request. The doctor complied: he carefully covered the bullet wound, removed the dead man's SS tattoo, and then performed a circumcision. With those telling details taken care of, he reported that the corpse was of Jewish origin, and had likely died of a knock on the head. Authorities quickly lost interest in the case.

The autopsy was not the first subversive act to take place at Saint Antonius Hospital. Forty *onderduikers* lived there, and the wards were raided often because the Germans suspected something was afoot. Each time, the *onderduikers* scuttled into the many nooks of the building, or donned hospital gowns to look like patients in their sickbeds.

Early in the new year, Prince Bernhard toured flooded Walcheren, film camera's viewfinder pressed to his eye and his little dog Martin at his side. Scheldt seawater lapped at mailboxes and fish swam through living rooms, but with his easy smile, his smoothed-back brown hair, and his gregarious manner, Bernhard seemed untainted by the destruction he recorded wherever he went. He stood beaming for group shots amid serious officers or craggy resistance fighters still adjusting to liberation, and wrote to Juliana, who had returned to their children in Canada, "Take lots of photographs or have them taken of all of you together – the people here are desperate for them." Many of the royal portraits that came out of this time were artistic compositions taken by the world-renowned photographer of celebrities, Yousuf Karsh, but only a disgruntled few found it offensive when beautiful images of exiled princesses were dropped from planes into a dirty, broken country. Among the masses, the royal family – German Bernhard included – was more popular than ever.

Far away as she was, Juliana pushed for liberation. On her way back to Ottawa from England, at her mother's request, she detoured to Washington to visit President Roosevelt, who had been elected recently for an unprecedented fourth term. She intended to personally under-score the plight of the Dutch people, and to plead for immediate, ongoing aid if an invasion of the Netherlands was low on the list of Allied priorities. But she was concerned when she saw Roosevelt looking depleted and tired. In Canada, as she settled back into a life of mothering, volunteer work, and lunching with the elite, she confided to Prime Minister Mackenzie King that the president seemed unwell, and looked like a different man.

As usual, Ottawa was white with snow this January. In the Netherlands, too, where snow was normally less abundant, a severe winter raged, and the Allied soldiers hunkered down, staking their positions. The Canadians had been tasked with holding the line that stretched more than 360 kilometres from Dunkirk to Nijmegen, and they waited, while the daring Montgomery and his American counter-parts devised the next plan of attack. Some regiments received white fatigues that helped them blend into the frigid landscape and ward off the cold. Most were not so lucky, and shivered in summer battledress. Foot patrols were a challenge because of the drifting snow, and tanks and Jeeps slid off the icy roads. At places along the front the enemy was so close that the men could see German faces. Occasionally someone lobbed a grenade to land near a latrine as a German soldier entered, or exchanged taunts with the other side about who belonged in the chicken coop that separated the German and Canadian trenches. At Christmas, the Canadians had watched as the Germans climbed unprotected to the top of a dike and sang carols.

The waiting was tedious, but for the Dutch behind the enemy line north of the Maas River, desperation grew. Official rations dropped to less than a quarter of what a normal adult needed to maintain his body weight, and many were living on bread and potatoes. Victims of hunger oedema bore the telltale signs of swollen faces, limbs, and bellies. Cor scanned the legal newspapers – no more than a single sheet now – for tips like using stinging nettle as a vegetable, or grating dahlia bulbs into soup. Each issue told people to guard their ration coupons: *Hide them carefully. Don't leave them lying around in your house when you go out. Watch out for thieves.* Advertisements offered shoes, suits, dresses, and fur coats in exchange for food, and there were desperate requests for insulin – "my life depends on it" – and thinly veiled accusations such as, "Looking for Meneer J. Veen of Rijswijk, regarding a sack of potatoes which my brother L.C. de Geer gave to him for me but which has not to this day been delivered." Little booklets appeared, explaining how to prepare tulip, daffodil, and crocus bulbs – though Cor knew experts had labelled them unfit for human consumption back in 1942. The tulip, peeled, cut, its bitter core removed, could be boiled like potato, the recipes said, or browned with onion and curry-substitute. But the bulbs would either sprout or wither by the end of February, so had to be thinly sliced and dried on the stove before then. There were frequent warnings against consuming bulbs and seeds that could be poisonous, especially for the challenged digestive system, and Cor was cautioned when she brought a bag of spinach seed to the local baker and asked him to make it into bread. "Mevrouw den Hartog, you can die from eating these," he told her. She nodded to show she'd heard him, but answered firmly, "If you'll pardon me, Meneer, one can also die from eating nothing." The baker relented, and mixed the seeds with some of his own precious potato flour to fulfill her request.

Whatever the food, it was hard on the body. Gerrit's parents joined them at mealtimes, to make the most of the wood used by cooking, and to spare the elderly couple the difficulties of procuring and preparing food themselves. Moeder den Hartog was often unwell these days, one of a growing number of old people languishing at a faster rate than younger adults. Frequently, Bep came to stay. Cor put before each of them a teacup saucer that held several large white beans garnished with chopped onion, and Koos hummed through each bite – a habit she'd once admonished, but that now lifted her spirits for the briefest moment.

Queen Wilhelmina heard from the *Engelandvaarders* about families like Cor's, and those much worse off in the cities, where the death toll climbed. In The Hague, corpses were left above ground for days on end, because there was no wood for coffins, and no way to transport the bodies – the horses that pulled the hearses were dead themselves by now, or too weak to move, or deep in hiding. Together with Prime Minister Gerbrandy, Wilhelmina implored every powerful person she knew – kings, politicians, and military officials – to take action on behalf of the Netherlands, but each plan to move supplies into the occupied zones got caught in the snarl of bureaucracy. Back in October, when it had become apparent the country was headed for famine, the Dutch government-in-exile had appealed to Sweden for aid, but only now, at the end of January, did the ships arrive in the far northeast, loaded with food and medical supplies. There was flour and margarine, cod liver oil, tins of sardines for the school-aged children, and huge boxes of matches. Yet none of it moved, and the weeks stretched on, with the Germans preventing distribution.

Throughout the winter, ever since the weekly NSB newspapers had printed gloating reports of food rotting in the north thanks to the striking railway workers who wouldn't ship it to where it was most needed, women and children had been trekking far distances, hoping for a bit of cheese or flour or meat to sustain hungry families. By

February, Cor's shelves and cupboards were all but empty, and she knew she would have to join the foragers. Impatiently, she pushed away the image that kept invading: Gerrit in the backyard last fall, giving away the potatoes. They'd done the right thing. At least the drip-drop of the thaw had begun, and it was not as bitterly cold as it had been.

Truus came from Overschie to join Cor for the journey north, arriving by bicycle, wet and cold. She told of taking shelter several times as planes flew low, drawing gusts of icy wind over her, and Cor, towelling her sister's hair, nodded. "The planes come all the time now," she said, "but it doesn't stop the rockets lifting off." They shared a cup of weak rose tea and made a plan to leave the following day for Drenthe in the northeast, a trek of two hundred kilometres or more. It would be a dangerous journey – likely taking weeks to complete – with the possibility that they'd go from farm to farm finding nothing, but they had to try. They spent the evening sorting the things they'd take with them to barter: a small sweater Cor had knitted for the baby who'd died – she hadn't been able to give it up until now; fancy table linens Truus brought from Overschie that had belonged to their mother; Sunday clothes the children had outgrown, and an embroidered mantel cloth that not even Paulien Quartel could fashion into something useful. At the last moment, Cor threw in her favourite dress, seldom worn these days, because its pattern of anemones seemed inappropriately cheerful. "Are you sure?" said Truus, fingering the fabric. Cor nodded. Their sister Maria, at home with Truus's girls, had contributed items as well, and Cor and Truus would be sharing their bounty with her and her husband Nicolaas. Their chatter was light, but both were aware of the enormity of the task they were undertaking, and when it was time to say good night, Truus pulled Cor close and hugged her.

In the morning, a watery sun made an appearance as Cor got dressed in the silent household. It was still early, but Gerrit was up and had already gone downstairs. He'd been overly quiet last night, and Cor knew he hated the idea of her going, hated that it would be even more dangerous for him with the roundups and deportations, hated that she was right to insist he stay here in Leidschendam, where his exemption certificate carried more weight and he could begin to prepare the garden for spring. She glanced out the window and saw him in the backyard, bent over her rattly old bicycle, checking the chain and the brakes.

The children were still sleeping, and Cor stepped softly as she paused by their beds, kissing each small forehead. They understood that Cor would be gone for a while, but they were too young for details. Only Koos stirred, his eyes opening briefly, and Cor whispered, "Be good." She went quietly down the stairs, tugging her coat over layers of shirts and sweaters, wrapping a scarf around her head. Her stomach knotted with the thought of leaving, but she knew it was the only recourse if her family was to survive. At least she didn't have to go alone.

Outside, Truus and Gerrit stood holding the two bicycles. Jannie, a neighbour's teenager who like Mar's daughters often helped Cor with the cooking and cleaning, would join them on the trip, and came in the back gate with her mother. Gerrit tied the suitcase into the basket of Cor's bike, and Jannie's mother hugged her and told her to be careful. Cor looked over her shoulder as they rode away. She saw Gerrit standing outside the gate, one hand raised.

The riding was difficult because of the bare rims that skidded easily on wet roads, and sometimes it was easier to push their bicycles along. Cor thought of her last long-distance ride, when she'd gone to find Gerrit in Strijen. In nearly five years, so much had changed. Then, the countryside had staggered from German attacks, and now the rubble-filled roads were a result of Allied bombs. These days her bicycle had no tires, her shoes had holes in the soles, and she was stick-thin. People all around her had died, and two of her children had never known peace. Standing in a long line at one of the frequent checkpoints, shivering from the cold, Cor held her identity booklet ready, the cover closed on the smiling photograph inside.

One of the stops along the way was in Tienhoven, Utrecht, at the farm where Truus and Jacques had sent their oldest daughter, Nel, some weeks ago. Cor watched while Truus hugged Nel and buried her face in her hair. She thought of her own children, happy enough with Gerrit watching over them, and the grandparents just a street away. Moeder and Vader den Hartog would be at the house often in her absence, she knew, looking out for Gerrit and the children, and after years of simmering rivalry with Gerrit's mother, Cor surprised herself by feeling comforted by that thought. It no longer bothered her to share her family with Gerrit's parents. She thought suddenly of her own sixth child, a boy mourned wordlessly, wrapped in blankets and taken away before she could hold him. He had a name – Teunis – but beyond that she knew nothing about him.

At Tienhoven, Nel's host offered Cor, Truus, and Jannie a place to sleep in the attic, where rows of strangers' clothes exchanged for food hung from the rafters. As they bedded down on straw mattresses, Cor looked up at the empty skirts and blouses, the men's suits that at first glance made an eerie queue, as though right in this room with them a silent line of people waited. But then fatigue took over, and she slept soundly beside Truus until dawn, when they were quickly on their way. Leaving was hard, though, especially after Truus pulled back Nel's filthy collar and saw a neck red with flea bites. "Look," she said to Cor, eyes flashing with anger. They rode away and for a long time no one spoke, until Cor offered the weak reassurance that although Nel wasn't being well cared for, at least she was eating, and God would watch over her.

But for much of the morning, Truus stayed quiet. The metal rims of their bicycle wheels clattered over the rounded brick of the road, and the suitcase bumped in the basket. The noise kept conversation to a minimum. Before long they were pushing the bikes through an area of white sand dunes and tall trees, and Cor was reminded that the royal palace of Soestdijk was nearby. To get Truus's mind off Nel and her own off her throbbing legs and sore feet, Cor began to sing a psalm, and soon Truus joined in. Their faces beamed as they sang for God, but neither sister seemed to realize how off-key their voices sounded: perfectly matched in their tunelessness. Jannie began to laugh, and Cor and Truus stopped, puzzled. "I'm sorry," Jannie said, when she was able to do so, "it's just that – *och*, never mind." And then she helped them along with their terrible singing.

At the top of a hill they climbed onto their bicycles and coasted down, the tiny thrill as welcome as the pale sun that broke through the clouds, and they stopped at the bottom to share a biscuit, blowing into cupped hands to warm them. Then they turned north towards Spakenburg, a fishing village where many of the inhabitants still wore traditional dress, the women with white lace caps and a perfect roll of hair in front. Visiting was like stepping back in time, Truus said later, and added a wish that that were possible.

They stayed a short night near here with some friends of friends, and started before dawn for the old trade city of Zwolle, travelling along the edge of the Veluwe, an area of forested hills and ridges that would have been beautiful in a different season. Cor wasn't moved by scenery – she never marvelled at the different shades leaves could take before they fell, or the soft, rustling sound the new ones made in the spring. She didn't notice which side of a tree trunk the moss grew on, or if it was vibrantly green or dark, pumpkin orange. And even though Truus commented that the Veluwe was breathtaking when the leaves were on the trees, to Cor it was just a forest that went on and on, the farm country they sought somewhere beyond it. Neither Cor nor Truus knew that last fall, their cousin Cornelia had camped out in a shed in the woods they passed, still in the butcher's company then, her aching feet healing. Now it was Cor, Truus, and Jannie covering great distances in wind and rain, limping from blisters and cramped calves. Cor took to praying as she walked or rode, and tried to keep her mind off the things they hoped to barter for – cheese, rye, bacon. The thought of food made her lose concentration, and once she'd nearly steered into Truus. An injury so far from home would be a disaster.

In spite of Cor's vigilance, disaster struck. The three women were talking about the success they'd had at the last farm, where they'd exchanged Rige's velvet-trimmed Sunday coat for a slab of cheese.

With the rattle of the bike rims on the road and the sound of a train passing, the planes were almost on top of them before they heard the familiar drone. As the ground was peppered with machine-gun fire, the women ran for cover. Cor saw Jannie fall, and the bicycle land on top of her. The planes veered off, their underbellies grey as the sky, and Cor and Truus pulled the bike off Jannie. The basket that held the suitcase was broken, but worse than that, so was Jannie's ankle, and they were too far from home – more than halfway to Germany, in fact – to go back. Somehow Cor and Truus, dragging the suitcase and wheeling three bicycles, managed to get Jannie to a nearby farm, where she was graciously taken in to convalesce with a Christian family. Cor and Truus stayed the night with her, and satisfied themselves that they were leaving her in good hands. "You'll be safe here," Cor told her, as the farmer's wife wrapped Jannie's ankle. The farmer smiled and nodded at Cor and Truus. "Don't worry," he said. "In the end, we are safe anywhere."

Cor and Truus travelled on alone, going all the way to the heathlands near Camp Westerbork, knowing next to nothing about that place, where the population had dwindled to less than a thousand people. By this time, more than one hundred thousand Jews had been funnelled through Westerbork to Poland on the Tuesday trains, the last of which had left in September. Gemmeker had long ago cancelled the cabarets and deported the performers he'd favoured in earlier days. Heading for death, they and regular citizens like Henny's father had crossed the same terrain Cor and Truus approached as a means of survival.

The region seemed a different country than the one Cor knew. At the farms where they bartered for food and shelter they had trouble understanding the various dialects they heard – sometimes people shouted, and they found themselves shouting back, as if increasing the volume would help the listener decipher the words. Cor thought of Moeder den Hartog, whose river dialect she'd first found strange. But Cor had never had trouble understanding her, as she did these people.

And words were not the only mysteries: at one farm where they'd sought shelter for the night, the farmer grabbed Truus, pressed her to the wall of the room where they were to sleep, and kissed her. He drew back, then leaned close again, and in a husky voice warned her not to tell his wife. Cor looked on, frozen, as Truus flushed with fear and rage. Neither of them said a word as the farmer left the room, but the moment he was gone, Cor blurted, "How dare he! We shouldn't stay here –" But Truus interrupted. "It's dark," she said. "I'm tired. There's nowhere else to go." Together they crawled into the *bedstee* the farm couple had given them, and Truus scrambled over Cor to be near the wall. "You take the outside, Cor," she whispered. "If he comes back it's your turn!" And in spite of themselves, in the pitch dark, they laughed until their stomachs hurt. At least it was a bed, Cor thought, as she finally drifted off to sleep. The night before, at another farm, they'd stayed in the hayloft of the barn, and once they'd climbed up, the farmer had taken the ladder away. "I'm sorry," he'd called to them, "but I'm tired of people stealing from me." Exhausted, their breath white in the chill, they hadn't stayed awake for long, but before they slept they checked their stash of food and knelt together to pray.

They went as far as Stuifzand before they turned homeward, rushing to cross the bridge at Zwolle, since they'd been told the Germans had threatened to blow it up. Even intact the crossing was risky. The guards were known to search bags and suitcases and take what they liked. Well before the lineup came in sight, Cor and Truus stopped and hid what they could, strapping bacon into a corset, tucking cheese into coat sleeves and the precious tobacco Truus had found for Jacques into her bra. They couldn't afford to lose any of their lot, since it would go quickly shared among so many mouths. They passed through the bottleneck without incident, and considered themselves lucky. They stopped to check on Jannie, whose ankle wasn't healed, but she was well and had managed to get word to her family. Cor noticed that the farmer's son, just Jannie's age, hovered protectively. The sisters' journey home was faster than the first trip, and the success of the mission had Cor and Truus singing once again as they rode.

Cor was still away when Reverend Rietveld stood on the street across from the parsonage, hat shading his face, collar raised. The door of his lovely stone home stood open to the cold air, booted in by the SD, an intelligence branch of the German police. Uniformed men moved in and out, carting his furniture to a waiting truck. For some time Rietveld had suspected a raid was coming, so he and his family had become *onderduikers*, learning first-hand what it was like to live in hiding. He watched, one in a small cluster of shuffling onlookers. When one of the policemen emerged from the parsonage with a German uniform in hand, Rietveld slipped out of the crowd and hurried away. The clothing wasn't his, but it did belong to a member of the resistance group he helped. With its discovery by the Germans, the stakes of his cat-and-mouse game had suddenly risen.

News of Rietveld filtered through to Gerrit, who held the reverend in high esteem. Each night before bed he knelt on the floor and prayed first for Cor and Truus and then for men like Rietveld, for Henny and the rest of the disappeared, but also for the enemy. In recent days Gerrit had heard about Leidschendam's ex-mayor Simonis in Nieuw Beijerland, and how he'd taken his revenge for the beating he and his son had received. The police had detained men eighteen and older in the local church, two of whom were shot trying to get away. Others were transported to work on an island in Zeeland province. The resistance group was furious, and in short order, select members waited for Simonis on a deserted road, killed him, and threw him in the water. But it didn't end there. The Nazi reign of terror was in full swing, and as payback for the crime, ten prisoners were hauled out of their cells in Rotterdam, transported to the road on which Simonis had been killed, and executed. Gerrit wished Cor were home – he needed to know she was safe, and he selfishly wanted her company, though some time ago, he had stopped telling her everything he heard. There was simply too much, and so nothing, to say.

He found it almost unbearable when he was home and the air raid sirens went off, and all of them – often Vader and Moeder too – squeezed into the small washroom under the stairs, trying, for one another's sake, not to show their terror. Vader's bloodshot eyes darted, avoiding Gerrit's. Gerrit thought of Cor, alone with Truus, taking on a duty that should have been his. He wondered, huddled in the tiny room, if there were sirens whining where Cor was, and if she felt as he did when he was away from home and the warning came, mixed with the heavy drone of the bombers. In those moments, he felt helpless and beaten, wondering where his family was and if they had followed the precautions. So many didn't any more. The raids came so often, they couldn't be bothered.

During such hideous times, the bland colour of February leached into everything. Faces turned sallow, streets and canals were filthy, clothes were dingy and patched. Nevertheless, spring was coming, accompanied by murmurs of a large-scale Allied offensive. But when the waiting ended for the Canadian soldiers camped out along the Maas River, they didn't push north into the occupied Netherlands. Despite the pleas of Juliana, Wilhelmina, and the Dutch government in London, the Allied Command decided that the invasion of the occupied country was not a strategic priority, and the Canadians were ordered west towards the Siegfried Line. Here, they formed the northernmost link in a chain of Allied armies poised to attack along this line, a snake of wire entanglements, forts, pillboxes, and concrete "dragon's teeth" that followed the German border from Switzerland to the Netherlands south of Nijmegen. The plan was to attack in large numbers and with lightning speed, but mud and floodwaters sometimes a metre deep hampered progress of the armies up and down the line. While the Americans stalled in the south because of the flooding, the Canadians, bolstered by their experience in the Scheldt, made impressive gains and earned themselves the nickname

"Water Rats." By February 21, the Canadians had breached the touted Siegfried Line, and pressed on towards the Rhine.

Farther west, 2,690 tonnes of Allied bombs had fallen on the German city of Dresden, a place of little strategic importance but so overcrowded with refugees that the number of dead was impossible to estimate. The Germans were losing ground everywhere, yet the attack wouldn't be hotly debated in the international press until the sober light of post-war, when some called it a necessary move and others a slaughter of civilians that proved the Allies had sunk to the Nazis' level. Most reports from the time made note of the bombing almost gleefully, as a comeuppance to an enemy who wouldn't quit. When a German reporter called it an unparalleled catastrophe, he was dismissed by *Time* magazine as exaggerating.

As the assault on Germany progressed, the Spitfire crews continued to target rockets and other sites in The Hague. The civil registry office beside the Peace Palace had been hit, as had the telephone exchange building. Some residents scurried to shelters, and others slept or stood in doorways, waiting with seeming apathy for the planes to do their damage. And all the while, as Gerrit worried about Cor, she got closer and closer to home. Ironically, the food and medicine shipment from Sweden arrived before her, travelling in roughly the same direction. The supplies that had been held up in the northeast were finally being distributed, and just days before Cor made it back to Leidschendam with her goods, Gerrit collected the family's allotment of bread in a pillowcase: half a loaf for each person over four years of age, and a ration of margarine. The flour had been shipped to a local baker, who'd transformed it into puffy white loaves that were unfamiliar to the children. Gerrit tore an end off and gave each of them a taste. "It's soft like cake," said Rige. Gerrit's eyes pricked with tears. He wanted to warn them not to make too much of the food, or want it too badly, for while he hoped there would be more, he didn't dare believe it.

The next morning, after Gerrit carefully sliced the bread and set a thin piece on each plate, he left the room to gather his brood for breakfast. Niek circled the table with his chin lifted, to better see and smell each slice. He pushed the soft white bread into his mouth piece by piece, until all of it was gone.

On arriving home, Cor leaned against Gerrit and breathed in his comforting scent. She looked in on the children, tucked into bed, as they'd been when she'd left. She herself wanted nothing more than to sleep for days on end, but there was little time for rest, and her days quickly resumed their old busy pattern. Each night, when she did lie down and close her eyes, her mind swarmed with a repetitive cycle of worries, and her muscles ached as though she was still walking. The food that she had procured would go quickly; they'd already used up most of the margarine that had come from Sweden – but how delicious it had been. One night, as she portioned out the meal, she'd placed a small *klont* of margarine onto each plate. Koos, smiling, carefully separated the creamy yellow dollop from the hot vegetable, saving it as if for dessert, and the meticulous action, combined with his private happiness, had caused Cor to stand and leave the table, pretending to be busy in the kitchen until she'd composed herself. The children looked thinner, to her, despite the food that had come. And the house felt colder, despite the approach of spring. She had read in the underground paper that the lack of food harmed the soul as much as the body, because a starving person stops caring about anything other than his immediate needs. She prayed for greater strength, but the bombs kept falling.

On March 3, the RAF made a disastrous blunder. Aerial photos had revealed a cache of V2s in the Haagse Bos, the little forest surrounding Wilhelmina's Huis ten Bosch palace, and the RAF determined to wipe out the rockets in a single attack that employed fifty-six Mitchell bombers. But when the planes arrived, their explosives fell on the heavily populated Bezuidenhout quarter next to the forest. Unlike the smattering of small but lethal attacks the residents here had become used to, this was a heavy bombardment, and the fires it started engulfed the neighbourhood, which held more people than usual because such huge numbers had been relocated to make way for the Atlantic Wall. Flames licked from the belfry of the Catholic church, yet the roar of the blaze and the cries of the wounded and frightened didn't carry as far as the Tedingerstraat, three kilometres away. Seven-year-old Koos, rolling marbles in the gutter, smelled smoke on the cold breeze that lifted the hair from his forehead. He glanced up to see black clouds billowing over the rooftops to the west. Along the street, curtains moved in windows and doors opened as people peered out at the sky. Overnight, fires continued burning and the glow obliterated the stars.

Wilhelmina was outraged, and let Churchill know. The prime minister insisted on an investigation, and eventually released a letter apologizing for what he called "an erroneous execution of the task." Leidschendam swelled with 1,400 refugees, and when the flames were extinguished and the five hundred dead had been counted, the RAF dropped leaflets admitting their error.

Though the disaster looked bad on the Allies, Arthur Seyss-Inquart could see the end coming for his own side. A visit with Hitler in February had briefly rejuvenated him, and when he stopped in to see Gertrud in Mattsee, he told her, "That man is energy personified." Gertrud had agreed; in her opinion, the führer had an awesome magnetism and "such wonderful eyes." She felt lucky he liked her husband as much as he did, and remembered the early days in Berlin, when the führer would spot them at receptions and come straight for them through the crowd, clasping their hands in his. Those days were over, of course. Hitler rarely went out in public now, and Gertrud had few chances to attend soirees on Arthur's arm, or even to sit quietly with him through difficult days, such as the ones that closely followed the Bezuidenhout bombing, when Police Leader Rauter was badly wounded in an attack by the resistance.

Late one night, a group of armed men lay in wait for a German vehicle said to be carrying a shipment of meat. But the wrong car –

Rauter's – was ambushed. His driver and orderly died in the shootout, but Rauter, though seriously wounded, hung on. Seyss-Inquart groaned upon hearing that Rauter lay near death. He was no fan of Rauter's overtly aggressive tactics, and yet he knew the uproar this would cause on both sides. Executions must necessarily take place, but as he told Gertrud, "these Hollanders" baffled him. They'd continue their attacks in spite of the reprisals. In fact, the more prisoners were blown away, the more zealous the resistance grew. His challenge now was to punish but not overly provoke the resistance, and to satisfy Berlin that the matter had been appropriately handled. SS Chief Himmler ordered five hundred shot to avenge the attack, but contact with Berlin was sketchy these days, and with Rauter's deputy, Seyss-Inquart risked changing the number to less than half, using prisoners already condemned to death in order to fill the quota. He prided himself on the reduction. But he also believed that, however unpleasant the task, the resistance movement had to be suppressed at all costs. It presented an increasingly serious danger to the occupational forces.

And so the spring was off to a grim start. In her diary, Rie Batelaan wrote, "There are moments when the distress around us moves me so deeply that I feel choked. . . . At times I ask myself: Why do I write this down anyway? It can't take away the distress. And if the generation after me should read this they will not get a complete picture of the difficulties we experience at this time, because there is so much that happens to us that I could write for days on end to tell it all. . . . The miseries repeat themselves."

Sunday
MARCH 1945

THE FIRST WEEKS OF SPRING were gruelling for the Allied armies. The Germans resisted at the Rhine River, where craggy hills and thick forest lined the banks, and the river itself was treacherous, its currents swift. Montgomery and the American generals, George Patton and Omar Bradley, argued over strategy and who should lead which divisions. Almost childlike in their competitiveness, neither the British nor the Americans wanted the other to capture Berlin first, but nor did they want the Russians, making rapid progress from the east, to beat them to the prize. For the infantrymen fighting through the tangle of coniferous trees, the immediate concern was living long enough to see Berlin, never mind who got there first. The frightened inhabitants of the German towns and cities in the armies' path buried their valuables in their gardens, just as the Dutch had done as the Germans advanced.

Retreating Germans left an obstacle course of blown bridges and breached dams, but by mid-March, the Allies were in control of the east banks of the Rhine. The Canadians, fighting in the northernmost sector, turned north, back to the Netherlands, minus several infantry divisions and a parachute battalion that crossed the river and pressed farther west with the Americans and British into Germany.

By this time, Wilhelmina – who had been urged to put off such a dangerous excursion – could wait no longer to visit her liberated provinces. She flew from England accompanied by twelve Spitfires, and touched down in Belgium, where a motorcade transported her to the border town of Eede. Once there, she directed her driver to stop the car before the white chalk-line separating Belgium and the Netherlands. She stepped out, a stout figure in a fox stole and woollen jacket, and walked slowly across the border. In a photograph taken that day, Wilhelmina's smile beneath her black hat is wide, betraying a poignant moment for the queen and the dignitaries behind her and the orange-clad crowd. The celebrations continued as she wound her way slowly through this small stretch of home, liberated only a few short months ago by the Canadian Water Rats. She made frequent stops in her limousine, sharing her army rations with her hosts, shaking hands with resistance fighters wearing BS armbands, taking the marguerite flower from her coat and laying it on the spot where four Dutchmen had been executed. She listened to the stories: this woman lost her husband to a firing squad; this man's son was taken in a *razzia*; another lost all his children when the occupiers blew up a town hall filled with people seeking shelter from an air raid. Boys and girls climbed onto rooftops to get a look at the queen, and the smallest children, who saw her as a stranger, stared up at her from below.

For Wilhelmina, it was a moving, difficult week, permeated by the stench of drowned cattle in flooded polders, by the sight of shelled villages and people who'd lost everything waving and smiling at her from all sides. At a church in Breda, just south of Dordrecht where Gerrit had fought, she settled into a pew and lowered her head in prayer while across the Maas River, the bombs continued to fall. It was Sunday, March 18.

The men piloting the Spitfires that took off that morning from their bases in England reported some light haze and cloud cover, but by the time the afternoon flights departed from Belgium, the skies were clear and the visibility good, perfect weather for bombing. The planes glinted in the sunlight, and as they approached their targets – railways that carted the rockets, suspected V2 launch sites, factories making fuel – the commander ordered the planes into formation. One by one they began their dives, plummeting from about 2,500 metres, and the ground seemed to race towards them at a dizzying speed. Flak came too, little fireballs shot from the anti-aircraft guns below. At about 900 metres, just before they pulled out of their dives, the pilots released their bombs and climbed again. Before returning to base, they circled, making note of the success or failure of their mission for later record-ing in the squadron's Operations Record Book: *bombed NW to SE . . . one bomb seen to burst on track . . . bursts seen to N of line 75 yards away . . . crossed out at Katwijk.*

Today, as on every Sunday, Rige attended the afternoon church service with Cor. Her brothers, having gone to the morning service, stayed home with Gerrit. Lately the house on the Tedingerstraat was full, with Tante Bep visiting from The Hague, and Oma and Opa den Hartog living temporarily on the main floor, as Oma had fallen ill after a diffi-cult winter. Until yesterday, one of Tante Mar's daughters had been with them as well, filling the role of mother's helper, and Rige was sorry to see her go. She liked having her girl cousins around, and sometimes pretended they were her sisters. At two-thirty on this sunny afternoon, Rige and Cor began the walk to the Damlaan, slipping into their pew on the balcony shortly before three o'clock. Rige barely noticed that Rie and Henk Batelaan hadn't arrived yet, because she knew her friend Ineke wouldn't be with them; she was away in Zoetermeer, where there was more food. Jaap Quartel took his place at the organ as the congregation settled, but there was no music yet, only the shuffling of feet and creak of the wooden benches. Minutes before the service began, Rige heard the moan of air raid sirens in the near distance, and the sound of bombs falling: first the high-pitched whine and then the *boom* of impact. As always, Rige counted: *one, two, three, four, five, six.* But these were not uncommon sounds – they heard bombs every day. Last week, one had fallen on the tram-rails beside the Parkweg, the route to Emmaschool. The railway beams had flown up and landed on the housetops, and the sidewalk tiles and manhole covers were upturned and strewn about. Now, as then, the raid was noticed, but the day's events continued.

The service began, and the room flooded with Jaap's music. Reverend Feenstra stepped behind the pulpit, in place of Reverend Rietveld, who was still in hiding but sent messages to the congregation through the church bulletin. Rige read one now as the paper lay in her mother's lap: *Not one bicycle tire has been donated for those who have worn theirs out in the service of Mutual Assistance. The congregation is not going to disappoint us in this, is it? R.* The bulletin, called the "*Kerkkrant,*" had been her mother's favourite piece of reading in earlier days, but lately it had shrivelled, like other papers, to a single flimsy sheet, printed front and back.

The sermon began, but soon the sexton appeared at the end of their pew. He leaned in with a grave expression, tapped Cor's shoulder, and whispered in her ear. Rige watched the back of her mother's head as she listened to the sexton – the swirl of her pinned-up hair, her dark blue Sunday hat. The sexton stepped away quietly, and Cor took Rige's arm, urging her out of the pew and into the one behind, where Jaap Quartel's mother and sister sat. Cor murmured to Jaap's sister Paulien, but said nothing to Rige. Her shoes made barely a sound on the floor as she left the church without her daughter. Rige blinked. She faced forward, and watched the reverend's mouth open and close.

Minutes before three and almost late for the service, Rie and Henk Batelaan were rushing to church when they felt the ground shudder from the impact of the bombs. They knew the hits had come from the direction of their own home, and they turned back, Rie holding onto her hat as they ran. They found their house spared, their family safe with the *onderduikers*, a burgeoning group that now included three generations. Today the Reverend Rietveld was with them too, but as Rie and Henk arrived home he pulled on his coat and hat. From the balcony at the back of the Batelaan home he had seen where the bombs landed, and now he sped on his bicycle to the Tedingerstraat, though he was meant to be keeping a low profile. By the time Rie got to the church, hoping to hear the last half of the sermon, Reverend Rietveld was there too, breathing hard, waiting at the door while the sexton alerted Cor. Rie watched Cor come through the door and climb onto the back of the reverend's bicycle. The next day she'd write in her diary, "I just can't forget the face of that mother as she left the church fearing the worst."

Next door to the den Hartogs, Piet Blom was in the kitchen, thinking about the pot of soup made that morning. He took the lid off, and the aroma made his mouth water. He, his mother, and his sister Corrie had savoured one bowl at lunch so that the rest could be saved for supper, but already his belly rumbled. His father had been away for several days now, looking for food, and Piet hoped for a good haul, and that it would come soon. The squeal of children's laughter drew his attention, and he looked out the window at the clear afternoon. In the neighbour's yard he could see little Gert on a swing, pumping his legs to make himself go higher. Koos was there too, and the Meulenbroek boys from 59. Yesterday the den Hartogs' cousin had gone back to Rijswijk, to Piet's disappointment – she was a pretty girl with long shiny braids. The sudden wail of an air raid siren interrupted his thoughts and sent the Meulenbroeks racing home. He called to his sister Corrie, standing just outside the door to the backyard, but his voice was lost under the siren and the screaming planes. The impact of the first bomb moved the stove at his side, and in the split second before the glass in the kitchen window blew in on him, he saw Gert fly from his swing.

At Tedingerstraat 57, on the other side of the Meulenbroeks, sixty-three-year-old Gerritje Poldervaart turned towards the window when she heard the planes. Seconds after the bomb hit, she was wounded in the temple and died of an arterial hemorrhage. An official report still exists, and details the investigation of her death – giving time, date, and the eyewitness account of her daughter – but there is no document to explain what happened at the den Hartog house, just two doors down.

The family version has Niek, almost three, napping at the time of the explosion. The blast woke him in a crib littered with glass. He climbed out of it and walked over the shards downstairs to the devastated rooms below. But he himself has no recollection of this, and pictures it differently. The scene in his mind is brief but specific, and because it is so fleeting, and at odds with the accepted version, he doesn't like to call it a memory. But it persists. He sees himself sitting downstairs with Rokus, playing a board game. A shadowy figure – a woman whose name and face he can't recall – stands in a doorway nearby. Rokus holds a game piece and accidentally drops it on the floor, and when he stoops to retrieve it, a jagged slice of glass soars through the space where he was, and here, as Rokus pops back up before him, Niek's version fades. Rokus cannot deny or corroborate Niek's account. He remembers nothing from the day, and the family version says only that he was reading the children's Bible at the time of the blast – and it's true that as a boy he loved looking at the pictures of Moses and the tables of stone, the angel visiting Mary, and David overwhelming Goliath.

In the backyard, four-year-old Gert on his swing saw his father in the doorway, yelling, "Run! Come now!" He looked up and saw the flash of a plane in the clear blue sky. Then there was dust, and nothing. He didn't see the woman who rushed towards him, the same shadowy figure who, moments before, appeared in Niek's periphery, but she was surely Tante Bep. A bomb shard had pierced her abdomen, but her nurse's training helped her focus on the wounded boys. With a twist of hot metal inside her, she leaned over the two limp bodies on the ground, pressing her fingers against the slowing pulses.

Koos was steps from the door when he heard the whistle of the bomb dropping, and the *whoosh* as it neared the ground. He turned his head, looked over his shoulder, and saw the ground erupt in a spray. Dust and debris ballooned beyond the wire-mesh fence of the yard, the force of it blowing him backwards. He felt no pain, but something caused him to look down before he fell. The skin of his leg gaped open, and he saw blood, flesh, and his shinbone. One foot was planted on the patio tile, the other on the bright green grass.

Somehow he found himself on a cart, bumping over the brick roads. Who pushed him Koos didn't know – it seemed he was flying in a dream. But the pain now was excruciating, and the air raid siren played over and over in his mind. He could picture Gert's pale face and the whites of his eyes, though he wasn't sure he'd seen him. Still, he had heard somewhere that when your eyes roll back in your head, it means you're dying.

Across the way, at 86, the house where the German soldiers had been billeted, Mevrouw van Kampen had sprung into action when she heard the bombs falling – five, perhaps six of them in the immediate neighbourhood. She looked through her shattered window and then ran over the broken glass to pull her old beige stroller out of the upstairs closet. Her daughter was an adolescent now, and there was no reason to keep a stroller, but she was glad she had. She filled it with towels, and hauled it back downstairs and across the street, and through the narrow space between the blocks of houses to where the boys lay, tended by Bep, who held a hand over her own wound. She and Bep tried to get both boys into the stroller, but they didn't fit, and there was blood everywhere, so Mevrouw van Kampen had to choose. She took Gert, who had lost consciousness. She laid him in the carriage and pressed towels over his wounds, and then she ran, not stopping to think where the boys' father was, or what had happened to the Red Cross men who lived at 72. Later she told her daughter Jeanne that she'd only done what was necessary. "The people who counted," she said, "panicked."

Down the street at number 15, the milkman Piet Rehling had been in the backyard with his son Jan – a boy about Koos's age – when the planes came over. Just as the boy's face turned skyward, his father grabbed him and yelled, "Hurry!" and pushed him through the kitchen door. The blast threw them both into the hallway beyond the kitchen, and they lay listening to the sound of glass falling out of window frames. But the milkman was up again soon. He could hear screaming and hollers for help. He placed an old door over the bed of his milkcart and wheeled it to 61, veering around bricks and smashed tiles. And it was he who pushed Koos to Saint Antonius on this unwieldy invention, though when Koos learned this, more than sixty years had passed.

As Rige walked from church with the Quartels, no one spoke. They hurried along the Damlaan, and Rige saw her mother's hat lying in the street – an impossibility that meant something she couldn't find words for. When they turned into the Tedingerstraat, they stopped at number 9 where the Quartels lived, and Rige was told to come inside. She looked farther down to number 61, but couldn't see through the crowd of people. Jaap urged her through the front door. Once in the Quartels' house, she noticed that there were too many places set at the table, but she didn't dwell on the reason; her thoughts were of her own family. She sat silently, hands pressed between her knees, having no knowledge of Louis or his sister Flora, the *onderduikers* who lived here and who hid somewhere in the small house for the duration of her stay.

How the rest of the day passed escapes her now, but at some point, Rokus arrived. She wondered about Niek, Koos, Gert, and their father, and about Tante Bep, her grandparents, and the house itself, but when her parents finally arrived late that night and spoke to the Quartels, she was still told nothing. She watched them – the two people in the world most dear to her – wearing the expressions of strangers. Her father's face was covered in tiny red cuts, which must have stung from the salt of his tears. The skin around her mother's eyes looked pink and swollen, and she couldn't stop sobbing. Her face twisted with grief as she asked,

"Why didn't God make this happen to me instead of my children?" Rige
looked away. She had never heard her mother question God's will.

Piet Blom must have lifted his hands in defence, for his palms and his
arms were wounded. The pain throbbed in the cut nerves and tendons,
but he was not among the first load taken to Saint Antonius Hospital in
an array of makeshift ambulances. As his gravely injured sister was
wheeled away in a cart pushed by a bicycle, Piet was placed on the divan
in his living room and watched the Red Cross workers in their blue coveralls move through the house. His mother had gone with Corrie, his
father had been away for days looking for food, and because of Piet's
pain and shock he had difficulty telling the workers how to find what
they needed. *Do you have bandages?* they asked him. *Yes*, he answered.
Where are the bandages? they asked. *In the cupboard*, he managed.
Which cupboard? And on it went. It seemed a long time before he went
to hospital. Outside, with crowds still hovering, neighbours placed him
in a horse-drawn wagon, and just as it began to move along the
Tedingerstraat, Gerrit den Hartog climbed aboard with him – he'd been
to the hospital already, but had come home to check on the rest of his
family, and now headed back to be with his sons. Piet grimaced as the
wagon moved over the uneven road. He remembered the boys playing in
the yard as the bomb hit, and Gert flying through the air like a tossed
doll. He thought of the look on his own mother's face when she found
him and Corrie, and moved from one to the other, trying to decide which
child to help first. "How are your sons, neighbour?" Piet asked. But
Gerrit – face bloody, eyes glazed – didn't answer. As he stared ahead, a
look of confusion came over him, and he turned and jumped off the
wagon. Piet, propped up with pillows, watched Gerrit, who stood
unmoving in the middle of the street, looking towards his house.

The hospital in Voorburg, with its cache of *onderduikers*, was twenty
minutes away, a chaotic place that smelled of blood, decay, ether, and

burned skin. With the recent bombing of the Bezuidenhout district and a glut of patients suffering from diphtheria and oedema, the already challenged staff members were overworked and had scant supplies, including light, heat, and even fresh blood. The bomb shards embedded in Piet's hands and arms were difficult to remove, but afterwards he was given a piece to keep. The souvenir sat in his pocket as he rode home that night, prone on a stretcher pulled by a bicycle. The sky that had been so blue earlier in the day had turned black, studded with stars, and Piet felt oddly peaceful beneath it, even when a German soldier stopped the bike's driver and asked, "What have you got there?" He peered down at Piet, who lay with his arms bandaged, and motioned them on. As he continued his journey, Piet remembered the soup made earlier that day – plain but delicious – and hoped for a warm bowl upon arriving home. But the soup, he soon discovered, had been ruined by glass and debris. He lay down on his bed, trying to ignore the chill night air that wafted through the gashes where the windows used to be.

Somewhere in the hospital, both Gert and Koos moved in and out of consciousness. Each boy sensed a breathing body lying beside him, a rush of warm blood that must have been a person-to-person transfusion, though the donors remain unknown.

The next morning, Rige woke up in her grandparents' house on the Broekweg, as though magically transported. She was in the backroom in her own bed with her red and white blanket, and the beds of the others were there too. Opa was in the kitchen, and Oma – lately so unwell – must still have been in bed, as the door to her room was pulled closed. Either that day or the next, Rige was taken to the hospital, and she looked through a window at a figure she was told was Gert. His tiny body was cocooned in white bandages; he lay so still she could not see him breathing.

The days passed in a fog. With the intuition of someone beyond her years, Rige remained quietly in the background, filled with unspoken questions yet not daring to beg the attention answers would require. Only from the snippets of overheard adult conversation did she piece together the enormity of the tragedy that had befallen her brothers, and then, with an eight-year-old's logic, guilt and fear nudged her. Perhaps if she'd been at home that day, things might have turned out differently.

People visited and offered words meant to comfort, but if they helped her parents, Rige couldn't tell. When Reverend Rietveld came by with a church elder – not the annual family visit but an extra for these special circumstances – he reminded Cor and Gerrit that whatever happened to them – to anyone – was in God's hands. And somehow, sooner than expected, Cor had composed herself. There was a steeliness but no tears in her eyes when she told the Batelaans that Gert would lose his right arm at the shoulder and Koos his left leg below the knee. "We know," she said in a firm voice, "that in all things God works for the good of those who love Him."

For weeks, Tedingerstraat 61 stood empty. The three eldest Batelaan boys had nailed boards over the holes where the windows used to be, so that the inner rooms, when Cor finally went there with Rige to retrieve a sewing kit and some clothes, were dim. Light slanting between the planks fell on clots of dried mud, splintered wood, and furniture shifted by the blast. Glass crunched underfoot. Until now, there had been no time to think of the house. Gert and Koos needed all the energy the family could muster, though Cor had already felt tired for two years. She spent most of her waking moments at the hospital, relying on Gerrit and his parents to look after everything else. Lines that would become permanent etched her face, though she was only thirty-six years old. Her devotion was fierce, and when the pain in Koos's leg became extreme, she told him to bite her hand, to bite as hard as possible, as if she could take on his suffering. He only did it once, and after that said "No" when she asked him, and looked away from her. She studied his face – the freckles that sprinkled his nose and the stubborn cowlick – and sat at his side saying nothing.

When she was gone, Koos lifted the covers and looked at his bandaged half-leg, soaked in blood. All his life he'd been told that God was listening, that God loved him and would protect him. That if only he believed – truly believed – then God could work miracles. So night after night, while he breathed in the metallic smell of blood, he closed his eyes and prayed to have his leg back. But as the days and then the weeks passed and nothing happened, he came to a new understanding. God didn't care about him, or perhaps wasn't there at all. From that moment on, he never prayed again.

His quiet decision would have hurt Gerrit, who felt guilty enough for what had happened to his sons. With spring, only the hard work of the *tuin* – digging beds, spading manure, turning compost piles, hauling the glass of the hotbeds out of storage – helped keep his mind off Koos and Gert, the sight of bloody bedding, and the choking smell of ether. His own grunts of exertion muffled the groans of the sick and dying he could hear in his head, though worse, perhaps, was the complete silence of his sons, small in their hospital beds. He pushed those images away, but saw the boys anyway in all the corners of the *tuin*, once their playground. Over the noise of his spade he heard their voices and running feet, their shouts of protest as someone broke a rule of the game. Rinsing the muck from his spade in the narrow stream, Gerrit thought of the day Gert had returned home dripping with muddy water. He'd fallen into the stream and his chaperone Koos had hauled him out and sent him sloshing home alone. Gerrit recalled with a smile the baffled indignation on Koos's face when he'd been scolded rather than lauded as a hero for rescuing his brother. But good memories made Gerrit want to cry, and took him back to the blue afternoon of March 18.

He was glad his sister Mar's daughter had gone back to Rijswijk the day before, and that he'd not had to bear the responsibility for her injuries as well. Too clearly he recalled how he had made it as far as the door when he heard the sirens – he'd hollered both their names, shocked that his voice had come up past his fear. Koos had seemed close enough to grab, but in the end Gerrit had failed to do so. The rest was a blur – his old mother wailing, his father's voice in his ear. And then there'd been Cor at the hospital, running towards him, holding him, looking into his face for an explanation. That awful silence. Her whole expression a question he couldn't answer. "I'm sorry," he'd said. Every day he remembered that moment.

In the early evening, before he returned to his parents' house, Gerrit detoured to Tedingerstraat 61 and let himself in the front door. Fine grit – dust from the wreck of the bombs – had settled on every surface. Still, he removed the *klompen* he wore in the *tuin* and sound-lessly climbed the stairs in sock feet, feeling his way through the dimness and pausing below the flight to the attic. He lit a match and looked around. Glass covered the floor, and the rooms were empty of their beds. A torn curtain hung, stirring in the breeze that sneaked between the boards tacked over the window frames. Soon the workers would come and begin repairs that would make the house habitable again, though glass and other necessary materials were hard to come by. There was a heavy demand for the workmen's services, and because of the *razzias*, few men available. The legal newspapers stressed who was at fault: that due to the Anglo-American "terror attacks," there'd been heavy losses in the region between March 18 and 24. Gerrit knew the wording showed bias, but he couldn't deny that he had felt terror as the bombs dropped.

He climbed the last set of stairs, lifted the loose board in the attic floor and reached into the dark hole to reassure himself that the radio was still there. Because there was no electricity, he couldn't listen, but news travelled without it. If one resistance paper got shut down, another was started soon after. The new *Vlietstreek* – a paper that raised money for Reverend Slomp's LO through subscription prices – even had a temporary, secret office in the town hall, directly above the new mayor, until a safer location could be found on the Damlaan. A few clandestine radio sets were still operating – not at Gerrit's house, but elsewhere, rigged up through an ingenious splicing of telephone wires – and he'd already heard from Jaap that on the day the bombs fell, Queen Wilhelmina had been home, but had since gone again. The entire German defence in the west was crumbling, Jaap had told him. Gerrit knew it was good news, and meant to cheer him, but nothing could do that these days. He sat for a long time in the dark attic.

EIGHT

Cigarettes, Chocolate, and Flowers
1945

LATE ONE NIGHT IN APRIL, Gerrit lay awake in his parents' home, listening to vehicles pass on the Vlietweg. For a few nights in a row he'd heard the sound. Rumour said it was the Germans retreating, and Gerrit thought that possible, as they were still the only people allowed outside at night without permits. For several days the skies had been blessedly still. No V2s rumbling, no Allied planes droning, no bombs missing their targets. In his imaginings he moved the quiet back a few weeks, or changed the course of the Spitfires, and thought, *if only*. But wishing stoked bitterness, and he rolled over in the thin bed. He appreciated peaceful skies, and the progress being made in the east, strange though it seemed that freedom would come from the direction of

Germany. Still, it was about time. There was heavy fighting, he knew, near Arnhem where Cor's relatives lived. That was the cost of liberation, and daily he and Cor prayed for the family there. Another truck passed, and he wondered if it was possible that Leidschendammers had paid their price, that the Germans would simply drive away, leaving Henk Batelaan to raise the flag over the gasworks, and people to walk the streets when they chose.

Cor's relatives had not yet returned to their homes in Oosterbeek. Her cousin Cornelia and the butcher's family had found shelter in the attic of a shipyard building near Alkmaar, while Tante Ester and her family had stayed closer to home and were still living in their abandoned farmhouse, sleeping on straw put down on the floor. The two families were finally reunited there, running to the empty coal-cellar of a nearby school when the Spitfires and Typhoon fighters pummelled German positions nearby to ease the way for the advancing troops. These villages along the north bank of the Rhine were also the scenes of fighting between the Dutch SS division, Landstorm Nederland, and its Allied counterpart, the Princess Irene Brigade. There were stories of brother fighting brother, and of desertions and insubordination from the SS division when it became apparent that their German masters could not win.

In those early weeks of April, the list of places liberated by Canadian soldiers grew long. Fighting was sporadic; the advancing troops never knew if the Germans would dig in and engage, or turn and run, leaving any number of surprises. Sometimes there were blown bridges, ruined dikes, exploded buildings, or barns of livestock set on fire. Sometimes they found civilians with fresh bullet wounds, usually resistance workers murdered by a vindictive loser. But always, the people they freed were grateful, none more so than at Camp Westerbork, which Gemmeker and the guards had abandoned by the time Canadian armoured carriers rolled into the camp on April 12. Hundreds of inmates streamed from the barracks, crying "*Welkom, bedankt!*" and grabbing the hands of the men in army green.

The same day, while sitting for a portrait at the spa he owned in Warm Springs, Georgia, President Roosevelt collapsed in his chair, and later in the afternoon, he died of a cerebral hemorrhage. Messages of sympathy poured in from the upper-crust, more closely bonded because of the war. Prime Minister Mackenzie King had the flag on Parliament Hill in Ottawa dropped to half-mast, while from England, Wilhelmina sent Mrs. Roosevelt the message that the Dutch "will ever cherish his name." Churchill, setting aside the sandpaper quality of his relationship with the American president, wrote of feeling a "deep and irreparable loss." But in Berlin, Goebbels and an increasingly reclusive Hitler were giddy with delight, and wondered, ever so briefly, if the war might not be over after all.

Seyss-Inquart was more pragmatic. His earlier visit with Hitler had buoyed him, but since then he'd been unable to ignore the only obvious conclusion. When the führer ordered the full implementation of his "scorched earth decree" – stipulating that infrastructure in Germany and its occupied territories be destroyed rather than handed over as the Germans withdrew – Seyss-Inquart conferred with armaments minister Albert Speer in Germany, who confided he'd be going against the order, and told Seyss-Inquart that armaments production was dwindling. Germany's efforts, he said, couldn't last much more than two or three months. Seyss-Inquart decided he, too, would quietly disobey the führer. Such wholesale destruction seemed pointless now, with the war practically lost. After all the *razzias*, the confiscations and deportations, and the embargo that had led to famine, the Reich commissioner sat down to tea with members of the resistance, and began negotiations. He promised destruction would stop if the Allies didn't advance any farther until the war was declared over. Furthermore, he'd allow food drops for the starving population. But for weeks, both sides hemmed and hawed over each other's promises and whether they could be trusted, and all the while, people died. The final death count from that last miserable winter would surpass twenty thousand.

The Reich commissioner only had so much power these days, and the army continued to follow Berlin's demands in spite of his promises to the other side. They pierced dikes and flooded polders to prevent the Allies from landing or advancing. In a strange, mirror image of the 1940 invasion, the occupiers had been backed into an area roughly comprising the Fortress Holland of five years ago, but unlike the Dutch soldiers before them, the surrounded troops were not defending their own. The havoc wreaked as they continued to destroy locks, dams, and dikes prompted Field Marshal Montgomery to halt the Allied advances at the Grebbe Line, but already, as Rie Batelaan wrote in her diary, "The North Sea is streaming in. . . . We can hardly imagine that at the very last moment they would still do *this* to us." With the flooding of the Wieringermeerpolder, Amsterdam's last food supplies were cut off, and an already desperate situation turned dire.

In Italy, Benito Mussolini was captured and executed by resistance fighters who left his body hanging upside down for all to see. In Germany, two Soviet armies raced to be declared the conqueror of Berlin, in their exuberance sometimes shooting one another instead of the enemy. Squirrelled away in a multi-chambered bunker below the garden of the Reich Chancellery, Hitler plotted yet further schemes to turn the war around. But by the end of April, the Soviets were already hammering Berlin into submission in the streets above Hitler's head, the Americans were closing in to meet other contingents of the Red Army at the Elbe River in the south, and the British had captured the port of Bremen in the north. In the Netherlands, Seyss-Inquart had altogether abandoned Villa Spelderholt near Apeldoorn because of the Allies' steady approach, and found himself back in The Hague, at Clingendael. The Germans were trapped with their backs to the North Sea, but still held the most heavily populated area, one that encompassed Leidschendam.

On April 30, at a school in the village of Achterveld, a crucial meeting took place between the Allies and the Germans. When Seyss-Inquart arrived at the appointed time, escorted by Canadian soldiers and flying white flags from his motorcade, Prince Bernhard was already there. These days, he was staying in the residence Seyss-Inquart had quit, and today he cruised to the meeting place in a newly acquired vehicle: the spare Mercedes Seyss-Inquart had left behind. The prince parked it in front of the door of the school, so that Seyss-Inquart had to walk around it to enter the building. Inside, conference rooms had been set up in the classrooms and for hours the gathering of men negotiated a food truce.

Word spread about the pending relief for the three starving provinces of South and North Holland and Utrecht, and while the food was badly needed, the talk was discouraging, as people assumed it meant no quick rescue was at hand. Nevertheless, they poured into the streets when the heavy bombers sounded. This time, the planes carried food.

The bombers circled repeatedly, so there seemed to be hundreds of them, and from their hospital beds at Saint Antonius, Koos and Gert watched the packages fall from the sky. The sight terrified Gert, but Koos knew the packages contained food, and he thought of the doughy white bread that tasted almost like cake, thick smears of margarine, and curls of shaved chocolate. To him, the crates of food swaying down looked like so many babies' cribs, coming in for a landing. Back on the Tedingerstraat, young men clambered to the rooftop to watch the planes drop food, and since Piet Blom couldn't climb because of his bandaged arms, his friends tied a rope around him and pulled him up.

The food, of course, was welcome – egg and milk powder, biscuits, flour – but notices in papers and tacked to signposts gave precautions for shrunken stomachs: eat slowly, drink small amounts of water, and then wait before eating more. Much of the food was concentrated and needed to be diluted before being consumed, but not everyone understood this, and as the morsels swelled inside them, some were killed by the very thing sent to save. Cor followed the instructions to the letter, doling out small portions to her family and watching them sip their water. She was taking no chances now.

No surrender came of the meeting at Achterveld, though it may as well have: while the talks took place, Hitler committed suicide in Berlin, and Goebbels soon followed, taking his wife and children with him – five girls and a boy, who were injected with morphine to calm them before they swallowed cyanide capsules.

The following day, in a statement released in German only, Seyss-Inquart urged the German people in the Netherlands not to forget the man who had made their lives worthwhile, and to grace his portrait with flowers. Hitler's spirit, he said, would live on. And then, Seyss-Inquart himself disappeared from the Netherlands, speeding by boat to the northernmost part of Germany, where members of the Reich's new government had gathered. In his will, Hitler had appointed Seyss-Inquart foreign minister, likely recalling the moderate quality that had made him such a good choice for the Netherlands posting.

⚔

Wilhelmina returned home carrying the same small suitcase she'd left with five springs before, but escorted this time by one of the handful of Spitfire squadrons that had flown the anti-V2 missions over Leidschendam. Juliana, who'd been summoned to England when the win was certain, accompanied her. It was May 2, the grass was jewel-green, and flowers bloomed amid the rubble – though not as brilliantly as before, since bulbs had been dug up and consumed, and flowering trees had been cut down. Mother and daughter moved into temporary quarters at Anneville, a country home in the province of Noord Brabant that had housed German officers just weeks earlier. Wilhelmina seemed to have forgotten her aversion to accommodations inhabited by the Germans, perhaps because there was almost no building left standing that had not felt the German presence. Het Loo was north and east from there, and wouldn't be ready for her for some time. Bernhard, upon his recent arrival there, had discovered it in deplorable condition. Originally used by German officers, it had more recently served as a military hospital, and reeked of waste and gangrene. The cleanup began, and Bernhard situated his headquarters there while living at Spelderholt. Bit by bit, furniture was returned to Het Loo from houses nearby, and Bernhard was told that Willem Röell had helped it "disappear," a service he'd performed for all the royal residences. Bernhard's watches and cufflinks and fashionable clothes – all of it was waiting for him when he returned, though Röell himself was long dead and buried.

Wilhelmina made herself comfortable at Anneville, insisting on registering for rations the way any ordinary citizen must do, and filling in the card with her name, Wilhelmina, and her profession, "queen." With Juliana's girls still in Canada and Bernhard close to the action, the women waited for good news, which came two days later, when the BBC announced that enemy forces in Denmark, northern Germany, and the Netherlands would surrender unconditionally. For Wilhelmina, "an indescribable burden" was lifted, just as one fell upon Arthur Seyss-Inquart.

On his arrival in Germany after Hitler's demise, Seyss-Inquart met with the precarious new government of the Reich, which rescinded the führer's demolition decree. With that done, he tried to return to the Netherlands, not just to participate in the peace negotiations, but – on principle – to be present in what he'd later call "the hour of disaster," just as he'd been present in "the hour of triumph" in 1940. When a storm kept him from travelling back by boat, he chanced the journey over land, in spite of the Allies' presence. His place was there, he told armaments minister Speer in a mournful voice, adding that he knew he'd be arrested as soon as he arrived. In fact, it happened sooner, when troops caught up with him on the outskirts of Hamburg. He attempted to explain that he was on his way to meet with the other side, but was apprehended anyway, and taken to the Allies' headquarters at Hamburg's elegant Atlantic Hotel, a popular place for elite Nazis that now seemed grander still with the city around it so devastated. Along with the rubble, thousands of church bells sat on the docks in Hamburg, ready to be melted down. Between the car and the lobby, Seyss-Inquart was photographed as he walked towards the palatial building. He kept his jaw clenched, and his hands in the pockets of his long leather coat, neatly belted. Beneath his peaked hat with its gold eagle, his face was an unreadable mask.

In the Netherlands, the surrender negotiations happened without him at a small, dilapidated hotel in Wageningen, near Tante Ester's village of Oosterbeek. Its name was De Wereld, or "The World," but the *W* was missing from the sign, there were cracks in the walls, and windows had been blown out in the fighting. At this unlikely, soon-to-be illustrious meeting point, Bernhard's camp turned up with both of the Reich commissioner's cars, and the prince brought his dog Martin along too. Photographers snapped tiny Martin standing on the back of Seyss-Inquart's leather seat. The convertible roof was open to the spring day, and Martin yapped at Bernhard standing next to the car.

Inside the hotel, the Germans, headed by General Johannes Blaskowitz, sat facing the Allies at a long table. Members of the press surrounded them, flashes popping on their cameras, as the terms were laid out for surrender.

With the first news of the capitulation, bonfires flared in Leidschendam's streets, and the celebration continued all night, in the aftermath of Cor and Gerrit's tenth anniversary. Outside, strangers and friends danced and hugged, congratulating each other on their newfound freedom, eager for the arrival of the men they called *onze Canadezen*, "our Canadians." Some of the revellers had not been outdoors in years and were paler than the rest. Others were too weak to join in, or had lost too much to make the shift into happiness; they stayed inside their houses, and turned off their radios, which played the *"Wilhelmus"* repeatedly, but there was no shutting out the hollers and the singing that would stretch on for days.

Rige's best friend Ineke weaved through the throng, bursting with excitement. She could finally tell Rige about the Jewish family living with her own – six in all! – and especially the two girls she liked to think of as sisters: Jeanette, two years old now, and little Dolly, the baby delivered in April. She wanted to parade around with them and bring Rige along, and to explain the real reason Rige hadn't been able to play at the Batelaans' for so long. All of that would change now. She hurried to the Tedingerstraat and rapped on the door. "Quick, quick, come!" she said to Rige. "I want you to meet my sisters!" The fantastic secret she'd kept for nearly three years streamed out of her as she took Rige's hand and tugged. But Cor, standing behind her daughter at the door, interrupted the girls' chatter. "You have brothers to visit," she reminded Rige. "This day is for them as well, and they mustn't be forgotten." Ineke, she continued, could come along to the hospital if she'd like, and later, Rige could meet the sisters. Ineke tried not to show her disappointment. She'd been to the hospital before to visit Koos and Gert, but Rige had never met Dolly and Jeanette.

The atmosphere was less jubilant in the hospital than it was on the streets, but Corrie Blom was wheeled out on a gurney to hear the music, and the wide lawn of Saint Antonius Hospital was dotted with convalescents and the forty *onderduikers* who had taken shelter in the wards over the last years. Gerrit lifted Gert to his shoulders, not knowing that the moment would be one of Gert's few wartime memories – this and the "nice nurse" who inserted his needles with care, and the "mean nurse" who jabbed them in.

Koos, after almost two months, liked life at the hospital, with so many pretty nurses smiling at him, and the constant buzz of activity, even in the middle of the night when he lay awake, feeling impossible twinges in the leg that wasn't there. He didn't like the prescribed exercises – painful stretching of his stump to keep his ligaments from tightening and curling back – or the sick, hollow feeling he got when he woke from a good dream in which he had two legs, and saw the contour of only one beneath the blanket and a flat space beside it. Visiting hours were his least favourite time, because of the inevitable arrival of his sad, serious mother, but at least she brought him wool and a corking tool that Gerrit had made by hammering nails into a wooden spool, and she showed him how to weave long, lacy chains by looping the yarn over the nails and pulling it out the hole in the bottom. Even better than this, she brought stamps that over the months formed an impressive, colourful collection, and made him want to travel the world.

Right away, the Allies trekked food to the cities in long convoys, and with the BS began rooting out the Germans and the Dutch collaborators. Traces of them turned up everywhere. In the tower at Emmaschool, the soldiers were gone, but had left behind helmets, a gun, and a chair placed by the small window. Mussert, too, stayed ahead of the troops as they arced north and west, but at the end of it all he found himself back in The Hague, cornered, a detested man whose party had disintegrated in the last months of the war. On May 7, members of the BS caught up with him in the Queen's Office, the place he'd lovingly remodelled a couple of years back after the Germans had turned it into a casino. Then, he'd envisioned a different future, himself at the helm of the Netherlands. He was taken to Scheveningen Prison – the Oranjehotel where Cor's cousin Dirk had been tortured. Here, with other Dutchmen, the Nazis' notorious Police Leader Rauter, and Gemmeker from Camp Westerbork, he awaited trial.

Not all surrenders were free of violence. On the day of Mussert's arrest, a massive crowd gathered in Amsterdam to greet Canadian troops, whose arrival had been rumoured by the newspaper *Het Parool*. A street organ piped happy music, and the people filling the Dam Square in front of the Koninklijk Palace wore orange sashes and waved their flags. Above them, drunken sailors of the Kriegsmarine, the

German navy, awaited arrest by the BS on the balcony of a club over-looking the square. Their capture was a mere formality now, but shortly after men with BS armbands arrested German officers below, some of the sailors opened fire from the balcony. Panic replaced the revelry as people ran for cover in the wide, open square, forming huddled lines behind the street organ and the skinny lampposts, or crouching in doorways. When the shooting stopped, the square was empty but for trampled hats and sashes, abandoned bicycles, and twenty-two lifeless bodies. More than one hundred were wounded in the short span of time that the shots rang out.

Two days after the carnage, with the violence still fresh in their minds, people packed the streets again, anxious for confirmation that the war was really over, and refusing to be fearful. The first Canadians did arrive, their vehicles rolling over the recent bloodstains. In an effort to keep the tanks and Jeeps moving, the soldiers threw cigarettes and chocolate into the mob, as they did in The Hague and Rotterdam. The ecstatic crowd swarmed the vehicles, tossing tulips and lilac blooms, hugging the soldiers and shouting, *"Thank you, Canada – onze Canadezen!"* until their voices turned hoarse.

Leidschendam was among the last towns to be liberated, but when word finally came that the Canadians were on their way from Rotterdam, the community gathered to give them a hero's welcome, clamouring to ride on Jeeps, waving hats and throwing kisses, just as in the cities already freed. A Jeep stopped in front of the doors of the Gereformeerde church on the Damlaan, and someone snapped a picture as the soldiers passed chewing gum to the people clustering around. One young boy held up a plate on which he had written a message in quasi-English: *Ol Kniedi-juns Welkum!* Across the street, the parsonage was occupied again. Reverend Rietveld and his family had moved home.

Three of the Canadian trucks continued on through Leidschendam to neighbouring Wassenaar, and several people were still along for the ride when the liberators happened upon a contingent of German soldiers at the Valkenburg airfield. An officer stepped forward, holding a white flag aloft. Their guns, bayonettes, and helmets were lined up neatly on the ground, and they themselves stood at attention, rigidly silent.

Arrests continued during these bizarre days, but angry groups found baser ways of punishing the collaborators living among them, ignoring posted proclamations that urged the newly liberated citizens to oppose any temptation to take revenge. Girlfriends of the occupiers – like the girl Gerrit had seen leaning against the factory wall in the moonlight – were publicly humiliated: heads shaved, they were dressed in German soldiers' clothing, and shoved through the streets weeping, forced to hold out an arm in the *Sieg Heil* salute. The vengeance satiated some, but others turned away in shame. At the end of the Broekweg, near Moeder and Vader's house, Gerrit noticed a patch of grass that had been burned for some reason, the remaining vegetation a black, woolly stubble; every time he passed the spot, he associated it with the hair of the young women, and his stomach turned. He waited for questions from Rige or the boys, for there was so much happening in the streets now that he couldn't control what they saw. But nothing was asked of either Cor or him. His little girl was painfully quiet, his boys, to his amazement, oblivious.

Once again it was spring, and Gerrit's busiest season, but he didn't work at the *tuin*, though there was plenty to do. Instead he fulfilled his role as a BS section commander, wearing an armband stamped with ORANJE and overseeing a group of Leidschendam men. Together they arrested members of the NSB and tried to prevent violent responses from angry townspeople who'd been hungry for what they called *bijlt-jesdag*, or hatchet day, when they could do horrible things to their oppressors. Gerrit thought it had to be God who'd kept him free of such black hatred, which surely destroyed the soul. He felt more shame than venom as the offenders were rounded up and horse-drawn carts were loaded with a mountain of stolen Jewish property. Looking at the tee-tering stack of tables and chairs, he wondered what had become of the people who rightfully owned them. At the mayor's residence, where Simonis's family had remained after he'd gone to Nieuw Beijerland, BS workers uncovered a wealth of stolen goods. One of Simonis's sons was photographed awaiting arrest, standing outside the house with a small, wrapped parcel and looking just like a labourer complying with the German conscription months earlier. There was no glee in Gerrit's job, the way there was when he popped a potato beetle or obliterated a weed invading the garden. But he tipped his hat to a man who stood in an upstairs window, hanging a large sign on his house that boasted JEWISH HIDING PLACE IN THE WAR YEARS.

In Overschie, Jacques donned the dark blue overalls assigned to him, and got to work dismantling tangles of barbed wire and clearing the beaches of mines. To this day, his picture hangs in a corner of the local museum, and a biography acknowledges him as a long-standing member of the resistance whose own *volkstuin* at the edge of the Schie was used as a depot for the exchange of information. Just next door, a shipyard building was used for weapons training. Gerrit's connection to the resistance is less obvious: there is just a typed list of commanders that surfaced in the Leidschendam archives, and a photograph that might or might not be of him. The picture shows a group of BS men wearing ORANJE armbands, rounding NSB men into a low-sided cart. One man rests his hands on the wall of the wagon and leans towards it. The way he stands, arms outstretched, one thumb down, is startlingly familiar. The man's face is turned away from the camera, but his hair is shaved high on the sides and nape of his neck and left longer on top, and his ears stick out, like Gerrit's. Under the archives' fluorescent lights, his children – now in their sixties and seventies – lean close to the image, squinting, as if waiting for the man to glance around and reveal his true identity.

The Dutch traitors and German prisoners traded places with those they had incarcerated at the Oranjehotel in Scheveningen, and within weeks of the war's end, gangs were marched into the dunes with shovels over their shoulders and told to dig, their labour supervised by government officials, uniformed military men, and a white-bearded coroner. This place, Waalsdorpervlakte, is a secluded area of sand hills and scrub brush that hid the bodies of hundreds of dead men and women, mostly resistance fighters, who'd been executed there by German firing squads. Shrunken corpses in tattered clothes were pulled from sandy graves, since none of the victims had been given the dignity of a coffin. Some of the bodies were easily found because of the diligence of a man who'd witnessed many of the executions from a distance, and had marked the graves as soon as the Germans were gone. Now a photographer recorded the grisly task as one by one the dead were laid in caskets and set in a line on the sparse grass of the plain. At the end of each day, before the sun set, the workers hoisted the wooden boxes onto their shoulders and carried them out of the dunes.

Soon after liberation, a parade was held for the official re-installation of Leidschendam's Mayor Banning – the man who'd tried so hard to stay in office in order to sabotage Nazi efforts, but had eventually been ousted and replaced by Simonis. In a horse-drawn carriage, he was brought to the town hall with his wife at his side and a top hat on his head, and as he rode likely relished the news that his old nemesis De Regt had been arrested and would serve a lengthy prison term. Children decorated their bicycles and joined in the parade. Bursts of celebration over the course of the summer took place alongside the suffering: Corrie Blom, who'd dropped to seventy-seven pounds in the crowded, dirty hospital, watched covered gurneys pass her door every day; Bep recuperated in Cor and Gerrit's bedroom, having come close to dying from her wounds.

At the edge of the *tuin*, Gerrit watched Rige pick wildflowers and put them in her toy watering can for Bep, but later, when he returned home, he saw the wilted arrangement outside the bedroom door, and felt sorry for Rige that Bep hadn't answered her knock. He felt bad for Bep too, for he'd learned that the company of children was an unparalleled balm, and Bep's wounds, he knew, were emotional as well as physical. That was the way of the times, and would be, he suspected, for years to come.

Every day he noticed that some had fared the years of occupation and its vile finale better than others. His brother Nico reported that a teacher at Emmaschool had suffered a nervous breakdown, but at church, there were a handful of men around whom a prestigious aura hung. They walked tall, with their shoulders back, and people – Gerrit included – fell silent as they passed. These men commanded a reverence once reserved for the church minister. One had been held in the Oranjehotel, like poor Dirk de Korte; another had headed the local resistance. Everyone knew, now, what Gerrit had known for some time: that Henk Batelaan had been chief of transportation and materials. The *zonderlingen*, the neighbourhood eccentrics, had fared less well. *De prater* had survived the *hongerwinter*, as that miserable last leg of the war was now called, but lately she talked to herself as much as anyone else, trailing a cloud of body odour behind her. The dim-witted *schillenboer* seemed slower than before, but he still gave kids rides on the heap of potato peels that filled his wagon. He'd always been a gangly man – now he had the look of a cadaver.

Everyone talked about getting back to normal, though no one seemed quite sure of how to do so, and Gerrit was always aware of the fact that most of his children couldn't remember life before the war. Rige had been three years old when "normal" came to its abrupt end. Somewhere in that there was a blessing. Had the children been older, it would have been hard to keep things from them. It might even have been tempting to send them out thieving, as so many parents had done. But how could you teach a child, afterwards, that what had been right was now wrong? He agreed with Cor, that the best way through this time was a direct route with little reflection – they should proceed as an ordinary family, just as they'd done before the war.

When Truus and Jacques and their girls visited from Overschie late in May for Second Pentecost Day, Gerrit suggested they go on a family outing, as they used to do. He took Niek on his shoulders and the group followed the still unused train tracks that linked the *tuin* with Scheveningen and the stretch of coast marred by Hitler's Atlantic Wall. Over the course of the walk, he felt strangely elated, sorry only that Koos and Gert remained in hospital and couldn't be with them. He watched Cor walking arm in arm with Truus, and Rige running ahead with her cousins. He even laughed when Jacques called to Rige, "*Graatje*, don't disappear between the ties!" though he knew the nickname "little fishbone" – newly minted because Rige was so skinny now – mortified the child. But his mood changed when they arrived at the coast and stood looking through curls of barbed wire to the sand and the great expanse of water beyond. The beach was still mined, and there were long wooden poles sticking out of the sand.

"Rommel's asparagus," Jacques said, nodding, and Gerrit felt a prick of irritation. His brother-in-law's tone implied he'd coined the phrase himself.

Rige, for her part, pictured the feathery greens of asparagus, and the white asparagus deprived of sunlight under a mound of earth. This was her first trip to the beach; it was not what she'd imagined, and she couldn't get close to the water. The area had been evacuated when the beachfront had turned into a war zone, and the houses left were dilapidated, with blown-out windows that looked through to wallpaper hanging in pieces, and drifts of sand on the floor. Eavestroughs dangled and roof tiles lay broken on the ground. She heard Tante Truus whisper, "Horrible," and saw her mother lower her eyes. But the day was windy and warm, and tasted of salt water. There was a picnic lunch, and all of them sat on the unkempt grass of an abandoned house, eating sandwiches and watching the sun sparkle on the water. And Rige thought to herself, *No matter what, this is a happy day*.

By now they had moved back into number 61, but often there was no one at home. Cor still spent most of her time at the hospital, while

Gerrit worked at the *tuin* and Niek and Rokus played in his range of vision. To ward off loneliness, Rige formed a habit of going to her grandparents' house instead of home after visiting Ineke. Oma seemed better these days, but so old, and her eyesight was failing. She made tea with real tea leaves, pausing to smell them before she dropped them into the pot, and telling Rige how much she'd missed a good brew during the occupation. They sat close to each other on the divan, listening to choral music on the radio and sipping the hot drink. Neither of them needed to say a word. After the visit, Rige continued on to the Tedingerstraat, where she stood alone in the quiet kitchen and devoured bread slathered with margarine. Fresh plaster and paint covered the damaged walls, the rubble and dirt had been swept up, and new glass had been set into the window frames. Outside, ruined bricks had been replaced with new ones, giving the attached walls of this small section of houses a funny patchwork look. Decades later, the mismatched bricks remain a testament to the day the bombs fell.

Similar work went on in Wilhelmina's palaces, though the buildings were grander than the little rowhouse on the Tedingerstraat. Cracked walls were repaired, broken windows replaced, bullet holes plastered, and the stink of war scrubbed away. By mid-June, as the den Hartogs settled back into their house, Wilhelmina had moved as well, leaving Anneville, with its rhododendrons and frog pond, for a house in Apeldoorn. Nearby Het Loo would not be ready for another year, and though other places were habitable – Noordeinde, Soestdijk, Huis ten Bosch – the queen worried that moving into a palace while her people still suffered might jeopardize the informality she'd worked to develop during her time in England. Ensconced in smaller houses, Wilhelmina could continue the tradition of intimate receptions she'd begun in exile, inviting people from all walks of life to tea. In Anneville, people had come uninvited, shuffling in long, solemn lines up the drive, filing past the house and out the gate while she stood in the window, each paying silent homage to the other.

During the first summer of the liberation, the queen travelled the countryside in what she called "the strangest collection" of borrowed cars, because the Germans had taken her vehicles. Her old chauffeur drove her; he'd shown up for work directly after her return, as if she'd only been gone for a weekend, and since then had taken her on journeys wherever road conditions allowed. Her first stops were in the towns and cities that had seen the most adversity, and from the window of the car, she watched the cleanup going on around her and wondered how long it would take for her country to scrub the occupation from its streets and sidewalks. So much had happened in her absence. She visited what she called the "widows' village" of Putten, and was stunned by the hollow faces of people in Amsterdam, Rotterdam, and The Hague; they looked malnourished, as she'd expected, but also tense, she wrote, and wary, even now that the war was over.

The day she drove through Rijswijk, the Hague suburb where Gerrit's sister Mar lived, the crowds along KoninginWilhelminalaan were ten and twenty deep. Children pushed to the front to see more than the backs and elbows of the adults who stood with them. One of the girls here was Rige, who'd walked from Leidschendam with Ineke's family for a chance to glimpse the woman known as the mother of the resistance as well as queen. Rige was wearing an orange ribbon in her hair, but if she thought it would make her stand out from the rest, she was wrong. Everyone there wore orange; all of them must have looked the same to the queen as she went from town to town in a hand-me-down automobile. Rige waited. Finally the car came. The crowd strained like one huge person heaving towards the queen, and flowers and banners fluttered in front of Rige's face. Through the window she saw fingertips, feathers on a hat, a fluff of grey hair. And then the car was gone.

Juliana returned to Ottawa in July to close her life there and bring her daughters home. The recently re-elected Prime Minister Mackenzie

King attended her farewell dinner and noted as he arrived that the sky was black with a rainstorm in the east, and bright and sunny in the west. He imagined a rainbow stretching over them as they said their goodbyes, and decided it was a fine embellishment for the occasion. He took his seat at Juliana's left, and listened as Governor General Athlone toasted the princess, and Juliana, in turn, offered her thanks to Canada. But as Mackenzie King stood to praise Juliana's "simplicity of life and friendliness," he felt disappointed by the ordinary dishes and the humdrum food laid out before them – forgetting her modesty and extolling it all at once.

The princess brought her children as far as England, and when the palace at Soestdijk was deemed livable, the girls flew the rest of the way home. Irene sat quietly in her seat, eating candy and shoving the wrappers out through the plane's vented windows. Beatrix was less composed, and every few minutes asked, "Are we there yet?" When the answer was finally yes, and land was visible below, she turned to her younger sister and snapped that she should now stop throwing out her garbage lest it land on the Netherlands.

At a small airfield near Apeldoorn, Bernhard welcomed his family amid a gaggle of eager photographers. Margriet had never been to her country before, and Irene, who'd left in a gas-proof crib, didn't remember it at all. For Beatrix, the eldest, there might have been some hazy memories. The seven-year-old future queen already had plans for tackling the reconstruction: she wanted to become a farmer, she'd told her nanny, and deliver milk to the kids who'd done without it during the occupation.

Wilhelmina, too, seemed determined to take a practical approach. She hoped to have a simpler court and lifestyle now that she was home, but it quickly became apparent that she and the common man had different ideas. Deprived of royal pomp and pageantry for so long, most people wanted nothing more than to watch the glitter of a royal procession, and wave at rows of shiny cars flying the banner of the House of Orange instead of the hated swastika. On *Prinsjesdag* in September, the traditional procession to the Binnenhof was "adapted to the times," with the queen riding in a car rather than the horse-drawn golden coach – the Germans had taken her horses as well. Her escort comprised uniformed army, navy, and air force personnel, and lines of BS men in dark-blue overalls. Wilhelmina called it "the most beautiful opening of the States-General ever." But even she admitted that almost no one agreed.

Slowly and steadily, the country got back on its feet. Canadian soldiers helped rebuild houses, town halls, dikes, and bridges, and the bond between liberator and liberated tightened. To the Dutch, the uniforms seemed impressive rather than severe, as the German ones had, and many young women were smitten by the soldiers. The Gereformeerde community disapproved of the new sexual liberty that followed, but in much of the larger population, the women who fell in love with soldiers were teased happily, while the Germans' girlfriends hid their stubbled hair beneath hats and kerchiefs. Dutch children laid flowers on Allied graves dug in the Netherlands' soil, and their parents vied for the chance to honour the living men, for there was a certain prestige in having soldiers for dinner guests, and the men who came to the table offered a different perspective of the war – a picture of the Dutch themselves from the outside, embellished by stories from farther afield. In a way, the stories explained things: *This is what we went through to get to you.* The need to thank the soldiers on an individual basis grew into a broader need to acknowledge the country they'd come from, and a trend started: people began sending flowering bulbs overseas, and eventually so many packages clogged Canada's postal system that the army was called in to help open them. The official gift arrived more smoothly, from Princess Juliana on behalf of the people of the Netherlands – one hundred thousand tulip bulbs for Ottawa, a gesture that would continue over the decades, each spring filling parks with dazzling colour.

The war had had its dreadful finale in the east, too, with Japan's surrender. From various corners of the world, Dutch people drifted home.

Cor's cousin Teun arrived home from the Pacific, only to learn that his brother, Dirk, had been killed by the Germans. At least Teun could offer a happy story: the coincidental meeting he'd had with Marinus in the Indies.

Oom Marinus, who'd first gone to the Dutch East Indies at nineteen, was now a fifty-year-old man. After Singapore, he'd spent almost two years imprisoned in Osaka, Japan, which fell down around him, and then had been moved to bombed-out Nagaoka for the war's final summer. In September, he'd been found in Yokohama, suffering from malaria, anemia, and beriberi, caused by a diet of little more than white rice. He'd been given sick leave and allowed to return to the Netherlands, according to his military records, but for unknown reasons he didn't go. He didn't even make it back to his wife Fien and their daughter Corrie; by spring, he died in Makassar, Indonesia, as a result of his ailments. Only after he'd been buried did the Red Cross notify Fien. Apologetically, the military escorted Fien and Corrie to his grave, where Corrie kissed the white cross, one of identical thousands dotting the cemetery's graceful terraces.

Cor's charismatic brother, Gerry the mariner, had fared better, and arrived in Antwerp's busy port after a hiatus of more than five years. His wife and daughter made the trip to meet him, riding in a U.S. army Jeep driven by a black American soldier whose skin colour was still a novelty in the Netherlands. But Gerry's homecoming was not what his family had hoped. He'd met someone – a pretty English nurse named Nora Battle – and he wanted a divorce. Gerry and his suitcase ended up at Tedingerstraat 61 when none of the family in Overschie would have him.

"Why did you wait so long to write?" Cor asked, remembering how worried they'd been during the battles in the Atlantic, and how their mother had seemed to wither as the months with no word of either Gerry or Marinus went on. But Gerry explained that he and other Dutchmen had been warned against writing letters to family members living in Holland – it would only put them in danger, they were told.

The ruptures the war caused at a personal level were endless. If there'd been weak spots in the relationships of people separated by circumstance, they were irreparable now. Having heard Gerry's story, Cor was less surprised when Henny returned from Switzerland and announced he was in love with another woman. But it was a heartbreaking shock for Bep, who looked at Cor with bloodshot eyes and said, "Please don't tell me to pray." Cor could still picture Henny leaning over the fence and making faces at Koos and Rige. His magnetic personality had been like a bright spark on the Tedingerstraat, and he'd had a way with women that had given him the power to turn even *de prater* speechless. Men like that were exciting, Cor supposed, but they were dangerous too: someone else always wanted them. And Henny was ten years younger than Bep, still in his thirties. In his time away, as she'd awaited his return, Bep had begun the decline that follows middle age. Henny's years in Switzerland must have changed him – she supposed the war had changed all of them, and the people who'd failed to keep God as their centre were all the more vulnerable to external influences. Cor felt sorry for her friend, and offended by Henny's choices, but didn't know how to help other than to offer the higher path Bep didn't want. She knew this setback would complicate Bep's physical recovery, too, and now and then, the urge rushed up to reach out and hug Bep close, and let her cry and cry, but each time, Cor kept her hands folded in her lap, fingers entwined, until the feeling subsided.

Koos and Gert came home from the hospital within weeks of each other, and although Cor's stomach fluttered with excitement, she was apprehensive. She didn't have Bep's medical know-how if something went wrong, and even in the hospital her efforts at comforting had seemed inadequate. Nevertheless, she agreed with Gerrit that they must not make a fuss over the boys, so their homecomings were treated like any other day. Despite Cor and Gerrit's intentions, the neighbours peered from behind curtains, and openly curious children stood in the street and watched as first Koos, then Gert, arrived wan and thin, Koos with his half-leg dangling.

With the boys home and Gerry still living with them, the house was bustling. Rige gave up her bed and her red and white blanket for this uncle she didn't remember, and while her brothers were thrilled by his seafaring tales and quickly decided he was a hero, she was not so sure, watching him snore on her pillow each day until nearly noon. She was less wary of Oom Nico, her father's brother, who never made himself the centre of attention, and pitched in by putting a coat of emerald-green paint on Koos's homemade wooden wheelchair. The wagon had come from a great-uncle, and was finished with fat wheels from the baby carriage Niek had outgrown. Gert didn't need to ride, but sometimes squeezed in beside Koos, as at the opening ceremony of the playground built behind the Tedingerstraat, close to the spots where the bombs had exploded. Tante Bep stood behind them, leaning on the cart for support. No one recalled then how Tante Bep had rushed to the boys, or how Mevrouw van Kampen had tried to place them both in her stroller, side by side, and today they looked like their old selves, though their injuries were apparent. Rige watched as a photograph was taken of the gathered crowd, a group that included *de prater* and the van Kampens' daughter Jeanne. Gert peered out from behind Koos's shoulder, and Tante Bep smiled behind them, where a mother might stand. But Cor was outside the shot, like Rige, admiring her threesome. Rige saw her head drop to the side in that way she had when watching something that made her happy. Flowers graced the lectern where someone important would make a speech, acknowledging the milkman, who'd wheeled Koos to the hospital, the grocer, the cigar-seller, and so on – all the people of the neighbourhood who'd contributed time, experience, or building materials for the Speeltuin Kindervreugd, or Happy Children's Playground. The slide, roundabout, seesaws, and swings revitalized the atmosphere behind the houses.

Soon after the picture was taken, Gert left Leidschendam, his small hand in Oom Gerry's as they travelled by boat to England. There, the medical system was less burdened than the Netherlands', and with his girlfriend Nora's connections, Gert would get a better prosthesis and better care. Koos, too restless to sit overly long in his wheelchair, itched for an escapade that was not his. The muscles in his good leg grew stronger, and he balanced well, but he was not always as fast as he needed to be. One day, when the barrel organ returned to Leidschendam, Rige heard the music and rushed to the window to watch as the lovely old contraption was wheeled up the street. She saw Koos outside, hopping across the Tedingerstraat with his pant leg flapping, too fixated on the organ to notice the cattleman's truck returning home to the bottom of the street, and heading right for him. Rige screamed and closed her eyes just as Koos was hit. He disappeared under the truck, and she dropped to her knees to pray. Cor ran past her out to the street, but Rige kept her eyes squeezed shut, mumbling, *"Dear God, I'm sorry, please save my brother,"* convinced that she owned some blame for the accident, just as she did for the bomb that had dropped when she stepped out to go to church.

Koos, miraculously only bruised and scratched, lay on the divan for a few days, fussed over by his mother and oma, who blamed the cattleman for his reckless driving and his general disregard for the neighbourhood. Rige often pretended to busy herself in the back-room throughout Koos's short convalescence, but kept an eye on her brother through the glass door. Even his freckles seemed paler. But whether by prayer or good fortune, Koos quickly recovered. He read of his own mishap in *Trouw*, the underground paper begun in the war and now printed legally. YOUNG BOY RUN OVER IN THE TEDINGERSTRAAT, it reported, to Koos's delight. Worse than the mild concussion he suffered was the fact that his brother had gone to England with their gregarious uncle, and he had not. The news that the Dutch government was giving him a brand-new bicycle lifted his spirits somewhat, but the bike took ages to arrive, and his prosthesis would take even longer. Until he had two legs, a bike wouldn't do him much good. For now, he went to his physiotherapy appointments in Voorburg on the seat of his mother's bicycle, Rige his driver.

Rige didn't mind the job, until the day a group of kids laughed as they passed and yelled at Koos from the side of the road, "*Hinkepoot!*" – "Cripple!" Face burning, she waited for Koos to retort with something clever, as was his way, but he said nothing. She couldn't see his expression as she pushed harder on the pedals, and didn't want to. She let the wind in her ears smother the children's taunts. At the physiotherapist's, she sat on a chair by the door while Koos was taken to a room down the hall. She folded her hands in her lap and tried not to listen to her brother's cries echoing through the building.

Soon, the doctors informed Cor and Gerrit that Koos needed a second operation. He'd been so long without a prosthesis that his ligaments had contracted. Back into Saint Antonius he went, liking the hospital less this time than the first. So much had happened under this roof – the burn and starvation cases, the *onderduikers*, and the murdered SS man who'd undergone a circumcision. But Koos knew only of his own pain when his leg was reopened in two long slices – the scars from these would cause more problems when the prosthesis was finally fitted. Weeks later, he came home with an aluminum splint moulded in the shape of his stump. Each night, Cor and Gerrit began the agonizing routine of fastening the splint over his leg, sliding the flannel cover on, then binding it tightly with cloth as he writhed in pain.

Gert, meanwhile, had fallen in love with a girl named Patty. Though he rose only to her armpit, he stood grinning beside her in a photograph of his happy days near Liverpool in England. There, he'd learned to shout English cheers at soccer matches; he'd been interviewed for the

Hartlepool newspaper, outdoing Koos's own appearance in the pages of *Trouw*, and he'd been whisked to and from exotic London for fittings for his arm. Six months had passed by the time he returned from England with his Oom Gerry and the scandalous Nora, lipsticked and perfumed, her fingernails filed and painted. They came laden with decadent treats like oranges, peanut butter, and oily mussels in a tin. Nora bought bundles of cut flowers from the florist and placed them in rooms that had only known Rige's wildflower posies, picked from the meadows. She spoke no Dutch, and her strange words and ways fascinated the children. Gerrit, too, seemed somewhat charmed, and turned pink when he tried a "good morning" in English.

Cor feared divine retribution for letting the unmarried couple sleep in her attic, but she justified the decision on the basis that Gerry had already committed a sin by leaving his first wife, and by marrying Nora he would only commit another. Besides, he and Nora had taken good care of Gert, and though she didn't condone her brother's actions, she couldn't go as far as her siblings had in Overschie, and ban them from her house altogether. Her choice had ramifications. Rige's friend Ineke was not allowed to play at the den Hartog house while the couple remained, and a church elder paid Cor and Gerrit an unscheduled visit, insisting, like the family in Overschie, that Gerry and Nora marry, and that until they did so, Cor and Gerrit were harbouring sinners, no matter how temporary the stay. The visit weighed on Cor, as it was unlike the annual, confessional visits she had now become accustomed to. However uncomfortably those had unfolded, they'd always left her feeling cleansed, and closer to God. This was a different kind of discomfort, being at odds with the Church she revered. Yet she was resolute that Gerry should stay, and determined to stand by him, though the decision kept her awake at night analyzing the moral dilemma. Even when he and Nora moved out, taking an apartment above a bar in Rotterdam, Cor didn't believe the real problem had been resolved.

She discussed it with Bep, who said the Church didn't seem to know much about love and compassion, and Cor felt her indignation rise at the comment, but she let it go. Once, their difference over religion had seemed manageable, and one of many characteristics that had defined their relationship, but lately it loomed between them like a thick fog, through which it was harder and harder to see and be seen. One thing was sure, though: Bep still had not recovered from the loss of Henny – her house was messy and the blinds often remained closed to the sunny day. Cor was certain the only hope for Bep lay with God, that it was her job to help Bep see that. If she could do so, God might forgive the allowances she'd made for Gerry and Nora. And if she could not, she would sooner or later need to revisit the purpose of her friendship with Bep, as seen through the eyes of God, for it was He who played the central role in all of her relationships.

Koos paid little attention to the unwieldy troubles of adults, and the comings and goings of dour church elders. More worrisome than Oom Gerry, luscious Nora, and the increasingly absent Tante Bep was the fact that his so-called brother Gert had become a different boy. He had a strange haircut and a complicated new arm, and he spoke no Dutch in the first days of his return. He moved around the house like a whirlwind, with energy to spare. Koos shouted at Gert in Dutch and Gert barked back in English, each of them fighting the good fight but having no idea what the other was saying. Next door, Piet Blom watched them in their backyard as he stood in his kitchen, and was reminded of that other day he'd observed them from a similar vantage point before the planes had come. He smirked as Koos shoved Gert and limped past him to his bicycle, which had finally arrived along with Corrie's, courtesy of the government. Unlike the usual black bicycles with coaster brakes, which weren't yet available for purchase, these bikes were special, complete with hand brakes and metallic brown paint. They were tall, too, and Corrie and Piet's father had attached spiked metal blocks to Koos's pedals so his feet could reach. At first Rokus had had to hold the bike and run beside him, but the humiliation of that had been so great that Koos quickly left him in his dust. Now he did so to another little brother, spinning away from Gert as fast as he could, and revelling in the speed he could no longer achieve by running.

The Future

1946–1951

GERRIT'S WOODEN SHOES SANK SLIGHTLY in the moist earth of
the *tuin* as he walked between rows of new sprouts glistening with dew.
In the not-too-distant future, *klompen* like these would cover the walls
of souvenir shops, painted with stereotypical windmills and tulips. But
Gerrit's shoes were plain wood, darkened with mud, as practical as the
hat on his head and worn by every gardener around him. During the frequent Allied attacks at the end of the war, when Koos and Gert had
been injured, wooden shoes had become unexpected armour, especially
so close to the targeted railway tracks. Piet Rehling, the milkman who'd
pushed Koos to hospital, had been working a small family plot near
Gerrit's, and had had to dive for cover when the tracks alongside his

plot were bombed. Not until later, as he began to walk home, did he realize his foot was hurting. He'd wiggled out of his *klomp*, which was full of blood: a bomb shard had pierced his wooden shoe.

These days – May, one year into liberation – the plots along the railway tracks were mostly quiet. Working in the early morning near the reed-rimmed pond on his property, Gerrit listened to the croak of the frogs and the squawk of the black-and-white waterhens, which sound perpetually irritated. He and the birds and frogs had been up for hours, enjoying the peacefulness of the morning, and though he knew there were others who started their days as early, within the rectangular borders of the *tuin* he sometimes felt he was the only soul stirring. He whistled as he hung his hoe on a nail in the shed, just above the space that used to hide the pewter and the good silver. Those things had been moved back to their rightful places in Cor's kitchen, and order on the small and large scale was being restored. Train service had resumed in December, and with the return of stolen railroad cars from Germany, schedules were improving. The community was startled, though, when the *dronkaard* lay down on the tracks one morning as a train approached. The train sliced off both of his legs, but he survived. Nowadays, having failed in his mission, he whiled away the hours at the café at the end of the Broekweg, where he could fill himself with gin and prove a capacity greater than that of the boozing German soldiers who'd loitered there during the occupation.

These sorts of small tragedies continued, like aftershocks, while the country at large healed. The Heineken Brewery in Amsterdam would soon reopen, and the Phillips plant, once Europe's largest supplier of radio equipment, was operating again. Gerrit's radio had been brought down from the attic, and held pride of place once more on the main floor. The Netherlands had resumed its export of tulips, and Gerrit, who'd begun to take night-school classes in horticulture, read with interest about several newly developed blooms: the President Truman, satin-pink; the Field Marshal Montgomery, with red and white blotches; and the Joseph Stalin, fiery red with fringed edges. Walking between his neatly planted rows of vegetables, he wondered if the other *tuinders* would think him crazy if he sacrificed a few rows for some experimental flowers of his own. Last night he'd dreamed that the *tuin* was full of flowers, and as he'd gently worked the earth around them, surrounded by their heady smell, he'd heard a droning overhead, coming closer and closer. In his dream he'd been terrified to look up and see planes – his head like a dead weight, impossible to lift – but then something had brushed his hair and a single, fat bee passed across his line of vision, moving from bloom to bloom and taking the sound with it. Gerrit laughed, now, to think of his terror, and how in his dream his hands had gone damp with sweat.

In the dunes of Scheveningen, a few kilometres away from Gerrit and his musings, the morning's tranquility turned eerie, as if the unfound dead at Waalsdorpervlakte were watching the procession that snaked along the footpath. At this infamous Nazi execution site, still combed for bodies of resistance fighters, convicted traitor and NSB leader Anton Mussert came to a stop, his hands cuffed behind him. Though the death penalty had been abolished in the Netherlands in the last century, it was temporarily reinstated for men like Mussert. That day, May 7, 1946, marked one year since his arrest by BS members in The Hague. The court had rejected his appeal, and Queen Wilhelmina had just refused his last request for clemency. The Dutch marksmen's rifles cracked, completing the task, the sound muffled by the hills of sand.

If Wilhelmina had given any thought to the execution of Anton Mussert, there was no evidence the next day when Winston Churchill arrived in Amsterdam, a portly figure in a top hat. Riding in a flat-bottomed canal boat that had just recently been reclaimed from Germany, he poked his head up through the roof and beamed, flashing two fingers in his signature *V* for victory symbol. Crowds lined the canals to watch him float by. He visited the royal family at Soestdijk, and photographers captured them together on the lawn, little Margriet's hand tucked into his, as if he was a friendly old uncle. Cor and Gerrit, listening intently to the radio accounts of his visit, knew he was much more. When the rotund Englishman made a stop in The Hague, Cor went to hear him speak, and returned with her eyes shining.

Three weeks later, the *Canadezen* went home, many of them with Dutch brides and lifelong connections. The bodies of more than seven thousand soldiers and airmen remained, along with plaques and memorials that had sprung up around the country. In time, the burial places would be graced with neat rows of white stones marked with a maple leaf. In the largest war graves cemetery, at Groesbeek, words were etched in stone: PRO AMICIS MORTUI AMICIS VIVIMUS – We live in the hearts of friends for whom we died.

No such tribute would be paid to Mussert, whose body lay in an anonymous grave in The Hague. The Dutch courts would also try Police Leader Hanns Albin Rauter, executed in 1949, and Westerbork's "gentleman" Gemmeker, sentenced to ten years for his crimes. They wanted Arthur Seyss-Inquart in the prisoner's dock as well, but because of his crucial role in helping Germany take Austria, his fate rested with judges in Nuremberg, where the band of men accused of war crimes captured the world's attention. In August, William Lyon Mackenzie King attended the trial at Nuremberg as part of his European tour. In the upstairs gallery overlooking the courtroom, he took a centre seat in the front row, and looked down on the prisoners as the judges filed into the room. Following the morning's proceedings, Mackenzie King was given a tour of the prison. The door to Arthur Seyss-Inquart's cell was unlocked, and he stepped inside to get a sense of what the rooms were like from the prisoners' perspective. He eyed the narrow bed, a small table that held books, papers, and pictures of family – surely Gertrud and the couple's children.

At Nuremberg, Seyss-Inquart and the other party members had undergone intelligence testing by a psychologist, and the former Reich commissioner achieved the highest point score. In spite of his genius

status, he coolly testified that he felt "proud" of his record in the
Netherlands, and that under another man, the country might have suffered much more than it had. He claimed he wasn't responsible for
many of the crimes he was accused of, since they'd been largely orders
from above and carried out by the army and the police, who'd reported
to Himmler. And while the court agreed that he had sometimes
opposed extreme actions and managed to undermine Hitler's scorched
earth policy, "the fact remains that Seyss-Inquart was a knowing and
voluntary participant in war crimes and crimes against humanity." The
evidence was staggering: the prosecution reported that under his rule,
by the end of 1943, the Germans had already seized "600,000 hogs,
275,000 cows, and 30,000 tons of preserved meats." Over the years,
they had hauled away six hundred thousand radios and a million bicycles, not to mention thousands of human beings: Jehovah's Witnesses
and gypsies; men for forced labour. Excluding Poland, the percentage
of Jews murdered was far greater than in any other European country,
an uncomfortable truth that would haunt the country for decades to
come. Of the 107,000 Jews deported from the Netherlands to camps
like Auschwitz, which the Reich commissioner had deemed a suitable
holding place, only 5,000 returned. Of course the individual details
were not recounted here – that Henny's father died in one of those
camps, an old man whose only mistake had been forgetting his pyjamas.
Dead, too, were the siblings of Louis and Flora and their many nieces
and nephews, and the Rijssen shoemaker and his wife – Max's parents
– who'd turned down the Batelaans' early offer of a place to live, and
would never meet the granddaughters born in hiding. Not one of the
native Leidschendam Jews sent to camps had survived, but all thirty
onderduikers, who'd come to the town from elsewhere, made it through
to the end of the war.

On October 1, Seyss-Inquart was summoned into the courtroom at
the Palace of Justice to hear the verdict: death by hanging for him and
eleven others, including Hermann Goering and Martin Bormann,
although the latter had been tried in absentia, and was suspected to be

dead. After learning his sentence, Seyss-Inquart shrugged resignedly and told the prison psychologist he hadn't expected otherwise. He was fine with it, he said, but his voice sounded uneven. He asked if he'd still be entitled to tobacco, and then apologized for the question, which he admitted must have seemed petty under the circumstances.

The deed happened just over two weeks later, on a night pulled from a gothic novel: cold, with a wind howling around the prison walls, and complete with a suicide sideshow. Goering escaped the noose by swallowing potassium cyanide just hours before his scheduled execution. For the remaining men, scaffolds were erected in the brilliantly lit gymnasium of the Nuremberg jail. A crowd of thirty gathered, including journalists chosen by lottery, a priest, and a chaplain, and shortly after one o'clock in the morning, the first prisoner, Joachim von Ribbentrop, climbed the gallows stairs. With his manacles removed, he voiced a wish for an understanding between east and west, then a black hood was pulled over his face and the trap door opened beneath him. Nine more followed; as one prisoner dangled on his rope behind a dark canvas curtain, the next was brought in, and when both ropes were taut, the first corpse was removed to make way for another. Seyss-Inquart was the last to die that night. He limped his way slowly up the scaffold's steps, helped by two white-helmeted guards. With the noose slack round his neck, he spoke in a low voice: "I hope that this execution is the last act of the tragedy of the Second World War and that the lesson taken . . . [is] that peace and understanding should exist between people." After the executions, Seyss-Inquart and the others were placed in coffins, loaded into two trucks, and taken in an armed convoy to a crematorium in East Munich. Later, the ashes were scattered in secret in the nearby river Isar.

What *was* revealed was the last photograph of Seyss-Inquart, showing the knot of the noose still tight to his neck, his crisp double-breasted suit neatly buttoned, his arm dangling over the edge of the black box where he lay. The picture seemed of a different man than the one in the portraits in Gertrud Seyss-Inquart's living room six years later, when

Dutch historian Louis de Jong arrived to interview her. One photograph sat on the piano, and showed the SS officer looking stern in full uniform. The other peered out from the bookcase, depicting a gentler Seyss-Inquart in civilian clothes. "I'm collecting everything about him," said his wife to de Jong during the interview. And at the end of the visit: "I have tried to tell you some things about my husband who I love – who I loved – so that your work may be truthful."

In February 1947, soon after Koos's ninth birthday, Princess Juliana delivered her fourth daughter, Marijke, at Soestdijk Palace. Gerrit remembered the celebrations for her sister Beatrix: church bells pealing, people toasting the birth outdoors with nips of *jenever*. Beatrix had been the first royal baby of her generation in a line not known for being prolific, and would someday be queen if her parents didn't produce a son. There had been a headiness to those celebrations, but also a giddy undercurrent of fear that wasn't there this time. Now, people paused for the fifty-one–gun salute honouring Marijke, and then got on with the business of rebuilding their lives. The day was officially declared a national holiday, but because the weather was bitterly cold and there was a coal shortage, the schools were already closed.

Koos was not interested in baby princesses, but he was pleased to miss school, since the pond near the *tuin* had iced over. He couldn't skate with his prosthesis, but he zoomed over the frozen surface on a *prik slee*, a sled that he propelled using two sticks with nails fitted into the ends. His artificial leg laced around his thigh like a boot, pulled over a "sock" knitted by his oma. In spite of this padding, the casing frequently chafed the scars on the back of his thigh, and phantom pains still twinged in the missing lower half. But he was rarely helped or coddled, and rose to physical challenges with his adrenalin pumping. When the weather warmed, he raced to be first through the reed fencing that surrounded the playground behind the backyard, passing the places where the bombs had fallen, and never for a moment think-ing that because he wore an artificial leg he might not win. He gave little consideration to the bombs either, and may not even have realized that more than one had dropped so close to him. One had landed in mud, and when it exploded, its pieces were smothered, sending out nothing but a spray of earthy splotches that covered the backs of the houses. The other had done the damage. It slammed into the brick street and down into the sand beneath, hurling metal fragments and debris everywhere. But in Koos's house, none of that was discussed in the children's presence, making it easier for everyone to act as though it hadn't happened.

Only when the children were in bed did talk turn to the war and its aftermath, and even then it was the bigger stories that were told and retold, as if to mask the existence of the ones that had occurred closer to home. During visits to Overschie, or when the relatives came to Leidschendam, the men leaned forward with their forearms on their knees, and the women crossed their ankles and frowned. When one discussed a lingering resentment of the German people, another chided him and said the Nazis were to blame – that when two countries were neighbours they had to be practical and find a way to get along. They discussed the war's toll, lost relatives and friends, but focused more pragmatically on the slow economy, the lack of jobs and opportunity, and their worries about the future.

People wanted so badly to forget this time and get on with a new era that a woman living across from Gerrit's parents on the Broekweg was repeatedly ignored when she told authorities there was an unexploded bomb under her house. It had fallen the same day as the bombs in the Tedingerstraat – there'd been six altogether – but had plunged intact into the garden, where the ground closed over it. With the war still underway, such potential problems were regularly ignored; and after-wards, the workload was enormous. The woman's warnings went unheeded until the 1980s, when the municipality was upgrading the sewers. "You can't dig here," she said when they got to her place, and finally someone listened. The little row of houses had to be demolished, and forty years after the fact, the delicate procedure of removing a 250-pound bomb began.

While the idea of abdicating was out of the question during the war years, Queen Wilhelmina began to consider this possibility over the summer of 1947. The new era was not what she'd thought it would be, with a more central political role for herself and the former resistance, and she was both frustrated and tired. After forty-nine years on the job, she felt entitled to a rest. She appointed Juliana temporary regent and moved to Het Loo in October, soon after Marijke's christening. The Germans had used it, but she still loved this residence because it reminded her of her childhood and how she'd toured the grounds in a wicker carriage with her mother. The palace was nestled at the edge of the Veluwe parklands, the same forested area Cor and Truus had traversed on their trek to find food, and where their cousin Cornelia had lived in a shed during the *hongerwinter*. Wilhelmina considered it one of the most beautiful parts of the country.

Her perspective, of course, differed from Rige's. By coincidence, Rige spent the autumn months not far from the queen, in a grand old mansion that had been transformed into a sanatorium. Like the Austrian girl who'd come to stay with Cor's family after the First World War, Rige had been shipped off for a change of air and peaceful surroundings. She was what the Dutch then called a *bleekneusje* – literally a "little pale nose" – rail-thin and unhealthy. The mansion was a fattening camp of sorts, where she'd get regular exercise and good food, but as she approached the imposing building with its tall windows and double doors, she was already homesick for her cramped house and her noisy brothers. The hall where she slept had eighteen beds on each side of the room, and a double row of six in the centre, but it was terribly quiet. The girls – she knew none of them – were told to sleep on their right sides, that it was better for their hearts and their circulation, but Rige lay awake, thinking about the blood pumping through her and waiting for the tall girl with the shaved head to sleepwalk towards the door. She heard the bed creak, and turned to see her paddle out. The door was open, and the light streaming in defined the girl's silhouette: her bald head, her long nightgown. Just as she moved through the doorway, a nurse arrived and silently steered her back to bed. Rige closed her eyes and waited for morning, and in the morning she waited for afternoon. She felt a sinking unhappiness in this place that was meant to make her strong, and when the allotted six weeks passed, she was weighed and told she hadn't gained enough, that she needed to stay six more. She remembered Oom Jacques teasing her on their last trip to Overschie, when Tante Truus was assigning beds to the guests. "It's convenient you're so skinny, *Graatje*. You can sleep in the eavestrough." Everyone laughed, because everyone always laughed at the things Oom Jacques said, but Rige had felt herself shrinking.

In the afternoons, she wrote letters home, sometimes risking an honest line she never would have said to her parents out loud – *I miss you*, she wrote. But the letters were censored, and expected to convey pleasantries – *the food is good, I'm having a nice time* – and she was told to redo what she'd written. She wondered how the brothers fared without her, and who would polish their shoes on Saturday so they'd be shining for church. They all had new shoes now, and Rige knew the importance of taking care of things, that nothing should be taken for granted. It seemed she'd been away an awfully long time, and sometimes, just for a moment, she forgot what her mother looked like now, and an earlier image came instead: her mother turning, the fabric of her dress swinging, and her hair uncoiling in a fit of laughter. Rige remembered the dress vividly – it was covered in anemones, beautiful even hanging loosely in her mother's closet – but she had not seen it in years.

Having been away twelve weeks, Rige came home by herself on the train. No one met her at the station, so she walked the familiar brick streets with her small suitcase, increasing her pace as she thought about seeing her family. She stepped in the door just before dinnertime. The pot on the stove was boiling over, and Rokus and Koos were quarrelling.

Her mother looked out from the kitchen. "Good – Rige – hurry up and get your coat off," she said. "The table needs setting."

Rige went to work diligently, trying to make up for the chores she had missed, and pushing the dismaying homecoming far to the back of her mind.

The tranquility of Het Loo was precisely what Wilhelmina needed to make a final decision on abdication, and apart from her personal reasons, she cited her country's law on retirement age, recognizing that "many old people were no longer what they had been." She made the announcement on radio the following May, waiting until late afternoon so that most working people would be home to hear her. Juliana would become their queen in September, she declared, after her own Golden Jubilee festivities came to an end. She told her listeners that it seemed just yesterday that she'd stood in Amsterdam with her father in 1889 commemorating his fortieth year on the throne, yet "I must accept reality," she said, and explained that age had worn her down.

Cor was worn down too, though she was not yet forty. Soon after the queen's announcement, the den Hartogs walked to Scheveningen again, with cousins, aunts, and uncles, and Cor watched the Blauwe tram pass and wished they were on it, no matter the cost. The occasion for this trip was the beginning of the herring season, a festival that would come to be called *vlaggetjesdag* – Flags Day – in honour of the hundreds of fishing boats clogging the harbour, their flags fluttering in the stiff wind. Jacques and Nicolaas slurped back the traditional *nieuwe haring*, not cooked but preserved in brine, and when all of them went out on the water in a fishing boat, even Cor found herself relaxing as the wind combed her hair. By the end of the day, their noses were pink from the sun and the wind, and the kids were tired. But there was more to come. In the dark, people had gathered along the boardwalk, and the family sat among them on the steps leading down to the beach. Cor took her shoes off and rubbed her feet. An air of expectation settled over the crowd, and then fireworks lit the night sky. With the first bang Cor saw how Rige jumped, and Gert clung to Gerrit, but then relaxed when he realized no one was running or afraid. Cor recognized his fear because she felt it too – the lights and the noise took her right back to the many nights she'd stood on the balcony with Gerrit, watching the glow of war; or the times they'd laid in bed, hearing the planes approach and whispering to each other, trying to decide whether to wake the children and rush them down to the shelter below the stairs. Cor looked around. Who else was thinking these thoughts and doing their best to hide them? The crowd whistled and clapped, and on the beach, a huge reproduction of the Dutch crown and lion emblem was set ablaze.

When it was over, she was glad of the late hour, which justified taking the tram home. A tram ride alone would have thrilled the children, because normally they walked everywhere to save money. Niek climbed over her for a window seat, but was asleep moments after the tram started rolling, his head resting in her lap. She rubbed his cheek and recalled a day, weeks back, when he'd gotten up to no good. Near the Tedingerstraat, he'd latched on to the tram's exterior, intending to go for a harmless little scoot – no more than a few hundred metres as the tram turned itself around for the return journey. Niek had likely watched the tram do this so many times that he believed it never deviated from its routine, but that day the driver had finished his run and shot past the loop, and Niek found himself hurtling along the tracks, clinging to the tram as the neighbourhood blurred by. The tram had been moving too fast for him to risk jumping, but his friend Wim van der Panne – a slow, pudgy boy moved to action – hollered on the platform, and as if by his call alone, the tram came to a stop. An angry streetcar official escorted Niek home and told Cor the whole story. She could still picture Niek, white as a sheet, his hair in a stiff fan as if raised by terror or wind. It seemed funny now, but then she'd been aghast at Niek's mischief and embarrassed by the appearance of the tram worker on her doorstep. She had tied Niek to a chair – harsh punishment, but the first thing that had come to mind to make him stay put. And as he'd sat there crying, she'd nearly cried too, and wondered in exasperation what she would do with all of them – the boys especially. Koos and Rokus, sharing a bed in the attic, often climbed out the narrow window onto the roof tiles and sat revelling in their small transgression, watching the world with a bird's-eye view until Cor came up and found their bed empty. Even Rige had been involved just a few weeks back, when all five children had pressed the white moons of their bare bottoms to the upstairs windowpane, eliciting howls of laughter from the kids in the street below. Gerrit had spanked each of them, catching them as they dove under the blankets to get away, but the punishment had been nothing compared to going to bed at night hungry as they'd done in that last year of the war, knowing there'd be little food or warmth with morning.

Throughout the summer, the country prepared feverishly for celebrations to mark Wilhelmina's sixty-eighth birthday and her fiftieth year as queen of the Dutch people. At the Leidschendam town hall, new stained-glass windows were installed to commemorate the queen's reign, and a booklet was printed listing those who'd helped pay for them, including Rige's Bible group, Gerrit's *tuinders'* co-operative, and the association that had erected the playground behind the den Hartog house. Koos and Rokus missed much of the activity. In June, Rokus went to a Scouts camp in Drenthe, where he got to wear his green uniform, and earned badges for his sleeve. Cor and Gerrit hadn't approved of the Padvinders before the war: the organization had English military roots and allowed heathens to join. But this was a different world, and scouting was enjoying a new popularity in part *because* of its "Englishness," and the fact the Nazis had outlawed it. So with other boys his age, Rokus hiked through fields of heather, learned to stand at attention, and at night slept in a room much like the one Rige had stayed in, with twin beds lined up in neat rows. Koos too joined Padvinders, and would have been with Rokus in Drenthe, but was spending the summer instead in the small village of Kleinditwil, Switzerland. The train trip was costly for Cor and Gerrit, but they managed, since the doctor had prescribed mountain air for Koos's asthma. Cor felt a small stab of jealousy as she read Koos's postcards referring to "Mama and Papa" Geissbühler, and describing his room with its view of pastures and hills and snow-capped mountains in the distance. Mama was kind and cooked delicious meals, Koos wrote, and Papa, who owned a hardware store, let Koos try out all the tools. Some days, Koos and Mama walked a hillside path to a farm where they earned a bit of money plucking fat June beetles from the plants and collecting them in pails. Cor pasted on a smile and wrote back: *Niek picked this card for you,* mooi heh? . . . *Tante Maria's new baby Hansje is a real treasure. . . . The boys have been to Overschie, fishing and more fishing!* She wrote to the Geissbühlers too, dutifully thanking them for caring for "*mijn zoon,*" and suppressing a shiver when their replies came in German.

Soon after Rokus returned from Drenthe, the sky over Leidschendam turned copper green. All afternoon the air had been heavy and thick, and Rokus watched the storm roll slowly in. He pictured his oma closing the windows of her house on the Broekweg and fretting over God's wrath. His father was still at the *tuin* by early evening when the fat raindrops began to fall, and Rokus, peering out the window, hoped he'd taken shelter in the shed. Yesterday, his father had brought home one of the melons that had been ripening in the warm August sun for the last while, and they'd sliced it open on the kitchen table and shared the juicy hunks with listless Wim van der Panne and the milkman's son Jan. Rokus wondered if he'd bring another today, but then the sky opened and egg-sized hail pelted the ground. Rokus stared through the window as the falling balls of ice flattened flower beds and dented the metal roof of the toolshed in the Bloms' backyard, and snapped branches from the shrubs near the *kinderpark*. He thought of the window he'd smashed with a ball at the Scouts camp. He'd been hauled down to the leader's office and had stood with his hat crumpled in his hands, awaiting punishment. But instead, he'd been made to say *I'm sorry* – a simple penance he hadn't expected – and that had been the end of the incident, unlike the time another ball had smashed Mevrouw van Kampen's window, just after the war. No one had owned up to the deed, so no one had been made to apologize then either, but Koos, still travelling in his green cart, had wheeled from door to door down the Tedingerstraat and the Broekweg, collecting enough money to repair the window.

When the storm ended, Gerrit came home from the *tuin* and flopped into his armchair, closing his eyes. Most of the seven hundred windows he used as covers for his hotbeds, stacked for storage by the shed, had been shattered, and much of his crop destroyed.

His voice, as he told Cor the news, was leaden. She took off her apron and walked to the *tuin*, her shoes crunching over the hail that lay melting on the sidewalk. At the gate, she stood staring at the mess of glass, the mangled vines, and the flesh of the hacked melons, thinking what Gerrit hadn't said – that nothing was insured. The sense of defeat winded her, and she sagged against the gate, the wood wet beneath her palms. There was no future here, not now. But at the same time, starting over somewhere else would be equally difficult with such a setback. Cor bowed her head, thinking.

When she returned home, she stood in front of Gerrit's chair and said that tomorrow all of them would get to work in the *tuin*; they'd have a sale on melon, direct to the consumer, sold by the piece. There was nothing to do but inch forward in baby steps, which was just what had been happening all around them every day since the end of the war.

Gerrit's disaster didn't stop the nation's celebrations. They bid Wilhelmina farewell with parties and parades awash with orange lights, streamers, and flowers. Barrel organs churned out music and banners fluttered from rooftops, and in Amsterdam, where the queen would say her final farewells, the population swelled to twice its number, so that people slept in the parks and on boats and in hotel bathtubs. From the balcony overlooking the Dam Square she accepted a choral serenade by nineteen thousand children and adults, and, caught up in the fun of it, waved her arms as if conducting them. Later, at the Olympic Stadium, Wilhelmina took in the festivities standing in a box festooned with gladioli and greens. Wearing a coat covered in stars and a hat with a flopping feather, she laughed and clapped her appreciation.

Four days later, in a solemn, late-morning ceremony that took place in the Moses Room of the Koninklijk Palace, Wilhelmina signed the abdication paper and was queen no more. The palace belfry pealed out a tune, dying away as the clock chimed noon, and on the twelfth stroke, Wilhelmina grasped Juliana's hand and stepped through the balcony doors, followed by Bernhard. "One could have heard a pin drop in the Dam at that moment," Wilhelmina later wrote. The crowd in the square below – the scene of tragedy when people had hidden behind lampposts to avoid the spray of bullets – waited expectantly. They seemed unsure of the protocol of losing, but gaining, a queen. Wilhelmina felt no such uncertainty, and announced her abdication in a clear, forceful voice, thanking the Dutch people for their confidence, affection, and sympathy over the years. "Long live the queen!" she shouted, flinging her arm in the air as if brandishing a sword, then turning and hugging her daughter while the crowd echoed the cry.

Wilhelmina's reign ended in a sea of orange, the mounds of marigolds and zinnias a floral tribute to her golden jubilee and the House of Orange she had represented for fifty years. But Juliana, with Bernhard beside her, began hers by sending a subtle message of change via the pink begonias that adorned the church for her formal inauguration. Reserved and compassionate, and having her own ideas about colonialism, she would be a different queen than her bold, unyielding mother. At the inauguration, she surprised Wilhelmina by bestowing on her the Military Order of Willem, the country's oldest honour, awarded for exceptional courage. Touched by the gesture, Wilhelmina accepted it as "a tribute to all my brave fellow-fighters during the war."

It seemed there were more and more of these heroes all the time. With the danger over, people liked to stress that they had been on the right side, often underplaying collaboration with the Germans and exaggerating acts of resistance. But an ugly reality has emerged with the passing years, and hundreds of thousands have been counted as active collaborators. No other Western European country had proportionally as many volunteers for the Waffen SS as did the Netherlands. Wilhelmina's own decisions continue to be questioned as the country examines its past. Some ask how different the occupation would have been if she had remained among them throughout it. Of course each resister and each collaborator has his own story, with its myriad reasons, as do those who straddled the middle.

Gerrit may or may not have been courageous during the occupation years, but either way, he would not have included himself in Wilhelmina's tribute. There were no medals or high honours to say he did anything out of the ordinary, and he never spoke to his children about his brave deeds or his cowardice. The armband he must have worn in those weeks after liberation has long since disappeared.

Now and again, Gerrit stole a few hours from the *tuin* and took the boys fishing for *snoek*. In the sunshine, legs dangling over the canal wall, the den Hartog men sat in a tidy line, jigging their garden stakes with the floats tied on. Koos fished the way he did everything, with enthusiasm for the task and a determination to make the first catch, or at least the biggest. Gert's head swivelled towards his bigger brother frequently, and he mimicked Koos's swaggering banter, deftly handling the rod with one hand and his knees. Rokus seemed less concerned about fishing, but liked the competition, while Niek often used his rod to snare bits of weed or flotsam from the water, and then inspected them close up. Finally, Gerrit thought in these moments, his children were enjoying a childhood.

Cor took them often to Overschie, and if Gerrit wasn't too busy he joined them. There, Jacques also fished with the boys, but right off the back stoop, which was as much a treat for them as Jacques's boisterous personality. Rige loved going to Overschie too, but Gerrit suspected she found her larger-than-life uncle overwhelming, since he filled the room with more than his size. Maria's husband Nicolaas, less ostentatious, had to work harder for the children's attention, but child and adult alike were surprised when the little man flipped himself over one day and stood on his head – all the blood rushed down to his face, and change tumbled out of his pockets.

If it was sunny, the adults would loll on the neighbours' barge that floated in the Schie, a pastime they jokingly called "going to sea." Occasionally someone got a dunking, and it occurred to Gerrit that a passerby might think that the lot of them were carefree. And now and then he supposed they were. After the children had been sent to bed, someone would pass the *advocaat*, recalling Neeltje as they sipped the sweet, strong liqueur, and how she'd made her batches on the back stoop – tastier than anyone's, they agreed, and Jacques suggested Schie water had been her secret ingredient. Maria's husband Nicolaas liked something a little stronger, a neat shot of *jenever* that he downed with one twist of his wrist. Once, he made the mistake of leaving his just-filled glass unattended while he stepped out of the room, and Jacques, grinning, holding one long finger to his lips to signal the others to go along with his prank, replaced the glass of liquor with one filled with water. Nicolaas returned, tossed back the shot, and spewed the water across the room to the delighted howls of the rest. Incidents like this kept the children creeping back to spy from the top of the stairs, and Gerrit noticed them crouching there, where cigarette smoke rose in a blue curl. The young were so resilient, he thought to himself, glad that adult concerns were mysterious to them now that there were no German soldiers in the streets.

These days there were syrupy treats, pet rabbits in a cage at home, and, that Saint Nicolaas Eve, a black puppy named Molly, and he wondered if they'd forgotten the nasty German shepherd that had guarded the *tuin* for a while during the occupation – nearly three years had passed since the war's end, a long time in the lives of children. Molly arrived in a cardboard box, and Rige and the boys shrieked happily as she scrambled out of it and raced through the house, tail wagging. Cor wasn't thrilled, Gerrit saw, especially when Molly peed on the carpet, but Cor's own sister had made the offering, so how could she say no? Molly outdid all the other presents: the elaborate dollhouse Rige had wished for years earlier, and for which she was likely now too old; the miniature village for the boys that spread through two rooms, complete with tiny roadsigns, green-painted bridges, and strips of black paper for roads. But the warplane books for Rokus and Koos were a hit, as Gerrit had expected. "What if they trigger bad memories?" Cor had asked him, but Gerrit doubted that – he understood his boys' fascination for planes, and for collecting, whether it be pictures of Spitfires, cigar bands, stamps, or the Padvinder badges Cor sewed on their sleeves. He knew that Koos's great mission was to acquire more badges than Rokus, who seemed to come by them easily though he was a year and a half younger and should have been – at least in Koos's opinion – a year and a half less adept. The emblem on their Padvinders hats said *Je Maintiendrai*, but neither of them pondered it. Dressed in their identical uniforms, they attended the meetings, vowing to outdo each other. Life was good to them in the post-war era, and that made Gerrit vicariously happy.

He and Cor, though, were ever aware of the underlying struggles, of financial difficulties both personal and national as the months and years wore on, and they each feared the future held no reprieve, since potential buyers for the *tuin* were few and far between. The American Marshall Plan was in effect now, giving millions of dollars in aid to countries devastated by the war, but the rebuilding was a massive endeavour, and both he and Cor agreed Europe's convalescence was and would continue to be painfully slow. They worked and survived, and made enough to ensure that Koos went to Switzerland in the summers for his asthma, that the children were decently clothed, that Moeder and Vader's rent was paid. But there was no feeling of progression; worse than that, they shared a sinking sense that their children, Koos and Gert especially, wouldn't flourish here, where there were so many needy people and not enough resources to go around. Gerrit thought of the garden, and how blight crept from plant to plant, spreading past the boundaries, even, to the meadows where only wild things grew. Often, he remembered the storm, which had revived their old wish to emigrate. At times during the occupation and immediately afterwards, leaving the Netherlands had seemed a silly fantasy, but now, little by little, it seemed sensible, and therefore possible. When a poster went up advertising Esperanto lessons given in the Tedingerstraat, Cor suggested they go, and once a week, the couple studied the "international language" once outlawed in Nazi Germany. Gerrit glanced at Cor during the classes, and loved to see how she paid such close attention, lips mouthing the words as if everything depended on this strange new language. Also in attendance were Mevrouw and Meneer Blom, as well as their daughter Corrie and the girl Jeanne van Kampen from across the way. Sometimes Gerrit looked around at the others, and it unsettled him to think that if he and his family left, the people of his past would not be part of his future.

As they lay in bed each night, Cor and Gerrit recited *kie, tie, ie, ĉie, nenie*, the Esperanto words for where, there, somewhere, everywhere, nowhere, and had halting conversations that usually declined into laughter – Esperanto meant "hope," but they were both hopeless when it came to learning it. Still, when the chuckling subsided, they talked about leaving: where they would go, how they would get there, what it would mean for their families. And each time, Cor offered the surety that God would provide, just as he always had, and would give them a sign as to when and how. So when an official notice came from the public works department, Cor said it was actually a message from above. A large portion of the *tuin* land was needed for a major highway, the notice said, and the municipality would purchase the property from him. Gerrit could easily sell the leftover parcels for family plots, and these amounts combined would be just enough to fund a move overseas. Gerrit knew, too, that the auction building would move to Delft within five years, increasing the cost of moving his produce beyond profitability. He knew the time was right. His scalp prickled with nervousness at the thought that their plan was now fully in motion, and that he was running along after it, trying to catch up. Cor, once the deed of sale was in hand, looked as happy as she had the day she'd held the deed of purchase. Gerrit remembered how much it had meant to her that they were landowners – how proud she'd been.

In that last season, his cucumbers were selected to be shipped to England for an exhibition, and Jacques jokingly called him the *Komkommer Koning*, but his reign of that domain was short – with winter, he'd have to find work in a lumberyard, or take anything that came until the myriad details of emigration had been sorted. As he walked the rows of the *tuin*, he thought of his favourite days there, when Cor as his new wife had brought him lunch and coffee, and then a little later when Rige was small and he'd held her to his chest, taking her up and down the length of the property as he sang the old lullaby "*Slaap, Kindje, Slaap*" in her ear. Somewhere there was a picture of them, father and daughter with the *tuin* behind them, snapped by his old friend Henny Cahn.

He'd own no small parcel of land in his new country. He'd start right at the bottom and work his way up, though he was middle-aged now and had a brood of children. The old choices of South Africa or Australia had been set aside for Canada, revered in the Netherlands since the days of liberation. Gerrit knew by now that it was a huge country, ripe with possibility, where many Dutch families had already settled and started Gereformeerde churches, and urged more families to come. The paperwork to get there arrived in thick packets from Ottawa, painstakingly translated by Rige, who'd learned her piecemeal English in school. "We will have representation to meet you in Halifax," she read. Gerrit and Cor looked over her shoulder at the mystifying words and letters, more foreign to them than Esperanto. "We will give you labels whereon is your name, destination station where you have to get out, and the number of the wagon wherein you shall travel. Wear these labels inside and attach them at once in the buttonhole of your coat. . . . We wish you a pleasant journey and every success in your new country."

All of a sudden, it was upon them. Their belongings had been crated and taken to Rotterdam, and Molly the dog had been given away, though the boys cried and didn't see why she couldn't come on the ship with them. Cor's brother-in-law Nicolaas arrived in his car to pick them up and take them to Overschie, where they'd spend their last night. On the Broekweg, Gerrit held Moeder, then Vader, and stood back as Cor and each of his children embraced them. He knew he would never see his parents again, and that the youngest of his children would barely remember them: an old man with a groove in his lip and a missing ear, and an old woman, arthritic and nearly blind. "Don't go too far into the bush in Canada," joked Vader to the boys. "Otherwise the rabbits will eat you." Moeder smiled and let the tears pour down. She gripped Vader's arm as they drove away, and Gerrit, watching in the mirror until the car turned the corner, wondered if she could even see them as she frantically waved goodbye.

On the morning of their departure, as they stood outside Cor's family's bookstore, Niek – almost nine now – ran off down the street to the corner store, clutching the bag of marbles his friend Wim had given him when they left the Tedingerstraat. He used his last thirty-seven cents to buy a Donald Duck figure for his Tante Truus, and ran back swinging the marbles and cradling the duck in his palm. Truus bent to take it and embraced her gangly nephew. Jacques towered above them, grinning, and asked Niek, "Why are you going to Canada? Why would you go so far away?"

Niek looked up with a serious expression. "Because there's no future here," he said, repeating words he'd heard at home.

Everyone laughed, but an uncomfortable moment hung between those who were leaving and those who were not. Behind them, the row of crooked houses on the Zestienhovensekade still stood after everything, looking as unchanged as the greenish canal waters that had carried Cor's belongings to Leidschendam. Cor could smell the Schie with every breath, which was strange because she couldn't recall having noticed it before – an organic, funky scent that brought on a well of nostalgia. A memory flashed, of herself as a girl, laughing while brother Gerry held her by the armpits and dunked her in the water again and again.

There would be no dips in the Schie this morning. It was a bright, sunny day in March, but chilly too. Cor was wearing a new chartreuse-green coat that had been sewn by Paulien Quartel in the popular swagger style. Cor had picked the fabric herself, and the pattern, but suddenly it felt wrong, and didn't seem to suit her. It was more a coat that Truus would wear, or Bep, and she wished for her old blue one that had worn through at the elbows. She wished she'd been able to say goodbye to Bep, properly and in person, but the rift between them now seemed unmendable. Visits over the last while had become more strained, and eventually Cor decided she was unable to continue a friendship with Bep if her friend wouldn't let God help her. Maybe she'd gone too far – certainly it seemed Bep thought so. She'd written a letter, but Bep had not responded. Ignoring the guilty feeling that pulled in her stomach whenever she thought of her old friend –

whenever she pictured her leaning over Koos and Gert as they lay in the yard – Cor resolved to leave things in God's good hands.

With relatives in tow, and Rige's girlfriends Ineke and Willy, they took the train to the pier, and the crocuses that had just begun to bloom showed themselves in a vibrant blur. At the crowded dock in Rotterdam, the *Volendam* stood waiting, still rigged as a troop carrier used to take soldiers back home. Cor's brother Gerry may have known the old ship's war stories – how it had attempted to escort English children to Canada but had been torpedoed by U-boats. But today, most thoughts were of times ahead. He gave Gert his gold watch – clunky on the boy's wrist – and someone took a picture of the seven travellers looking into the camera with their arms around one another, lifejackets visible in the rafters above them. Each had new warm clothes, carefully chosen for weather they hadn't experienced. The boys were wearing matching bomber jackets in the style of the day, and Rige's was similar, but fashioned for a girl. Gerrit wore a dark beret, and Cor a scarf tied turban-style. Husband and wife look almost sophisticated in this shot, and confident of their decision to start over, with their life's possessions crammed into a single wooden crate.

Below on the pier, friends and relatives stayed from morning until late afternoon. Jacques kidded Truus, "Do we need to watch them cross too?" and Truus smacked him. But all playfulness disappeared when the heavy ropes were cast off, and Truus began to cry. "I'll never see her again," she said, and Jacques put his arm around her, pulling her close. He looked up to the *Volendam* and saluted Gerrit, the *boerenjongen*, as the ship eased slowly away.

On board, Gerrit stood behind Koos, who waved like mad as Truus, Jacques, and the rest diminished into dots of colour. He knew that for Koos, the waving and shouting was less a goodbye than an outlet for the boy's excitement as they floated through the long waterway that opened into the North Sea, and he envied that uncomplicated enthusiasm. Koos would miss summers in Switzerland, but Canada was better, he'd told Gerrit, "because it's farther away" – whereas that, for Gerrit, was the worst thing of all.

Rige, on the other hand, understood the implications as well as Gerrit did, but had none of her parents' vision of a better future: they would likely never be back, and she would never see Ineke and Willy again, and this might be her last glimpse of her family and the flat, green country behind them. He felt sorry for pulling her away from everything she knew and loved, and sorrier still when she got queasy on the first day of a long crossing. But her brothers were aching for the adventure, and for the sight of the broad sea with no land visible for days. They gaped over the rail at the sea foaming against the ship's sides, and wove between the other passengers as they explored the decks. Koos, thirteen by now, was hardly held back by his artificial leg, and eleven-year-old Gert had proven more than resilient – the kind of boy who'd easily learned to shoot a bow using his foot, and found it gave him greater range. Once, while playing at the *tuin*, he'd pierced Wim van der Panne's lip with a homemade reed arrow, and Gerrit had seen how his son had marvelled at the accuracy of his shot when the bubble of blood appeared against Wim's pale flesh.

The passage was rough, and soon Rokus was so violently ill that the ship's doctor suspected something contagious, and confined him to the hospital at the boat's stern. Niek loved the vanilla wafers said to ward off seasickness – though they didn't always work for him, he spent his time hunting out empty bottles and cashing them in so he could buy great stacks of the thin, delicious cookies. Koos liked them too, and swiped them when Niek wasn't looking. As he munched away in the salty air, streams of yellow vomit fell from the decks above, interrupted here and there by a hat or a set of false teeth twirling down. "He has a pirate's leg," Gerrit said to Cor, "and a sailor's stomach." He leaned back in his deck chair and waited for her to laugh, but she stayed silent, and when he turned and looked at her, he saw that she, too, had gone waxy and pale beneath her dark turban. Over the entire trip, only he and Koos managed to dodge seasickness. One day – at breakfast, lunch, and dinner – Koos and Gerrit sat at the table assigned to them in a vast, otherwise empty dining hall. Almost everyone on board was seasick, and by dinnertime, when Koos and Gerrit strode into the quiet room to fill their bellies, they and the superfluous white-clad waiters shared a fit of laughter at the telling scene. The two of them clinked their glasses and pompously dabbed the corners of their mouths with the thick linen serviettes. Koos hummed through the rich, unfamiliar food – "Cream Martha" soup, steamed cod fillets, carrots in butter, and English cakes. Koos didn't know it, and Gerrit wouldn't tell him, but the "den Hartog table," clothed in white like the waiters and laid with gleaming, heavy utensils, was a point of pride for Cor and Gerrit. They found themselves seated in these wide, comfortable chairs only because they had paid their own passage: three thousand six hundred and thirty guilders and seventy-four cents by ship and train. Had the family's fare been subsidized by the Dutch government, they would have been eating down below at long tables, elbow to elbow with other passengers.

But the accommodations were not otherwise grand. Rige and Cor shared an overcrowded cabin, and the boys slept in the hold with Gerrit, lying in tiered bunks as strangers snorted and mumbled. He thought back to his time in the barracks at the farmhouse in Strijen, and he wondered if Cor, too, thought of that period of separation, for it had been one of the few times they'd slept without each other in the years of their marriage. "I missed your snore," she said to him one morning when they'd come midway across the ocean. "It reminds me that all is right with the world."

For Rige, almost fifteen, things couldn't have been more wrong. Every wave took her farther from home, farther from friends like Ineke and Willy, to a place she didn't want to go. Against her parents' rules, she'd sat in darkened cinemas a handful of times with her friends, admiring Rita Hayworth's lips and eyebrows and the backdrop of New York City – but glamorous as that had seemed, she still didn't want to move to North America. The only thing that made the trip bearable was a tall, blond Frisian boy she met and sneaked off with between bouts of seasickness, but the boy would go to Alberta when they reached Canada, and she'd never see him again. She was with him when they drew close to Newfoundland, distracted by her first try at romance; her brothers were equally distracted by a game of cowboys and Indians, the kind of fun they expected to have in their new country. None of them paid attention when the *Volendam* sounded its horn, or when the great ship in its path answered. The two drifted so close that a person could jump from one deck to the other. On either side, crowds of passengers gathered, holding their breath as the crews strove to keep the ships from colliding. Cor slipped her hand into the crook of Gerrit's arm as they watched, and kept it there as the ship passed and the *Volendam* headed for shore. The sun shone on the coastline, revealing blackish-green conifers, bare maples, grey rock. Patches of earth smudged the snow brown.

On a Saturday morning, they moored in damp, chilly Halifax, after nine days at sea. Still on board, Cor and Gerrit joined the horde holding immigration papers and sorting out crates and destinations, and confirming the next part of their journey. They'd requested a change from their assigned posting of Cochrane in northern Ontario, hoping for something closer to Toronto so they could more easily address Koos and Gert's growing needs for new prostheses. The plans took time to arrange, but the children kept busy watching the goings-on, and looking out at Canada. Koos gawked at the dockworkers in their peculiar red and black wool jackets, and Rige started when a crate – not theirs – plunged into the water as the cargo was unloaded. It was here, when Rige's head was turned, that Niek wandered off for a snoop around the harbour. Still holding his bag of marbles – Wim van der Panne's entire collection, now his – he headed down the ramp and onto land without anyone seeing him go. Once they discovered his absence, Cor and Gerrit panicked, and the family spread out to look for him. Cor thought of the size of the country, and the dark forest Vader had joked about, and worried they'd never find him. Rige feared he'd dropped into the water, like the crate, and bubbled under. But Niek didn't think he was lost. He wandered into a building and down a hall where two official-looking men sat at a desk. Strangely, one of them offered a cigarette, and Niek accepted, feeling eighteen rather than eight in spite of his marbles. He inhaled the potent smoke and his head swooned, but he puffed again as he stepped out-doors, and the sky spun above him. The clouds swirled like the patterns on his marbles, and he felt himself turning green as he drifted back on to the boat, searching for the washroom. Over an all-too familiar basin, he threw up again, though the boat trip was over.

Cor gripped his arms when she found him, and flashed back to the time she'd tied him to the chair. She held her face close to his and tried to think of something to say, but instead just hugged him, hard and fast. She gripped his hand that evening, squishing the bones, as they all walked to town to pass the time. The shops had closed for the day but offered a picture reflected in their windows: the seven people trudging past looked like immigrants here, despite the attention paid selecting new clothes. The boys' knickerbockers and long socks shouted out their foreignness. Even in March, the coats were insubstantial, and the hats didn't cover their ears, and the thin-soled boots slipped on snow and mud. "Where are the horses?" Gert asked Cor, and she remembered the pictures of prairies in his books at home. There was no sign of cowboys and Indians in Halifax, but after their last night on the docked *Volendam*, Gert still woke up hopeful, and told her he'd watch for them on the train to Ontario.

The train had none of the comforts of Dutch trains. Together they sat on slatted wooden benches for the journey through a drab landscape in which trees had not begun to bud. They slept in their seats, leaning up against one another, and waking to the long, melancholy sound of the train's whistle in the middle of the night. The journey took three days, brightened by a short stop that gave Gerrit time to step out of the train and come back with sweet, delicious bananas. Soon, they were underway again, passing nothing but trees and more trees. To Cor, it seemed unfathomable that this was all part of one country. She sat with Rige and looked out, tapping on the glass and pointing to the plain white clapboard houses. "Those," she told her daughter, "must be where the immigrants live."

It was night when they were deposited in Aylmer, Ontario, two hours past Toronto. Their wooden crate was stored at the railway station, and they stood at the roadside, waiting for their contact as the snow fell in slow, bright flakes. Gerrit's new sponsor was a dairy farmer – the job was one he'd never done, but he and Cor had agreed he should take what was offered to get them farther south than Cochrane, which looked on the map to be in the middle of nowhere. Now that they were here, Aylmer, too, looked like nowhere. Cor thought of the flower vendor bicycling by, and his cry of "flowers in all colours!" and how out of place it would seem here. They waited a long while in the quiet night until a Dutchman pulled up in his pickup truck, and said he'd take them to their lodgings on the farm. Gerrit rode in the back, crouched down with the boys and their luggage, and Cor and Rige climbed into the cab with their driver, a friendly man who belonged to the Gereformeerde church started there. Hesitantly, he told Cor that the farmer who would be Gerrit's boss had already gone through several helpers, and Cor understood his tone of warning.

It hardly prepared her, though, for the accommodations assigned them when they arrived: two rooms filthy from their recent use as chicken coops. There were two double beds for all seven of them, and the pots and pans were rusted through with holes. The fatigue that had been with her for nearly a decade swelled, but there was nowhere clean to lie down, and there were the children to think of. She divided the duties, as they'd done at the *tuin* after the hailstorm, and everyone got to work to make the place bearable.

Dinner that first night was a piece of meat, stalks of celery, mashed potatoes, and something called Jell-O, courtesy of their hosts, a skinny old man with missing teeth, his wife, and their thirty-ish son, a sluggish fellow with cruel eyes. They ate in silence. The elder man inhaled his food and finished before the rest, then scraped his chair back and retired to his rocker, belching. Cor looked away in distaste. They were expected to stay for a year, to fulfill the contract Gerrit had signed, and once more Cor found herself surveying her new home and thinking it wouldn't be possible. Nor did she see how they'd acquire another, but she reminded herself that God always provided. All that they needed would present itself in due time.

The kids started school in a one-room schoolhouse that served eight grades, but all five of them read Dick and Jane, puzzling their way through a foreign language and a culture much less formal than their own. Cor, too, had trouble adjusting, and couldn't run her household the way she always had. Money for food was subtracted from Gerrit's wages rather than given as cash, which meant the old farmer took Cor to the grocery store and told her, "Choose what you need," but when she placed the items on the counter in front of the cashier, the farmer picked through her selections, removing things randomly until he found the cost satisfactory. Cor stood at the farmer's elbow, seething and humiliated, but with her head held high. She'd been through worse during five years under the Nazis, so she knew she could withstand this boor.

Little by little, spring arrived and the slush disappeared. Gerrit worked long hours and earned a paltry amount, but they managed to give Niek, growing quickly, new jeans for his birthday. Cor noticed his swagger and the way he hooked his thumbs into the belt loops, while the bag of marbles from pale Wim lay forgotten in a corner, an old game from an old world he was no longer part of. But Rige's letters flew back to Ineke and Willy, pages long, each one dutifully answered. With equal frequency, notes came from Moeder and Vader den Hartog in Leidschendam, always short, starting with a few lines from Gerrit's mother: "I would like to knit a sock for Koos, but I can't even see well enough to write," she confessed, and passed the pen to her husband. The letters had the tone of finality – "We hope you may live in that new land for many years, and that your life goes well" – but also brought everyday news from home: auction prices, hellos from the Batelaans and the Quartels, and a message to Cor that, no, they still had not heard from Tante Bep. Moeder told of a wild rainstorm that caused her to step into her wooden shoes and put up her umbrella in the house, and Vader said the sight made "quite a movie." But the overall message of every letter was melancholy: they missed their family and wished they would come home. "Say, Cor and Gerrit, the *Volendam* has left again with 1,200 passengers, that is the third time already since you! But you are having some bad times. We hope you will soon find something better. If that doesn't happen then you'll just come back. You can move in with us so long as we are healthy, and by the Koop factory they are going to build thirty-two houses. This will provide work. Say, Cor and Gerrit, you shouldn't think it bad to come home. So many are coming back. Paulien Quartel told us that a family with ten children returned. Anyway. It is cold here, but things are growing well. The auction prices are uneven. Lettuce three cents. Wagonloads go to the cows."

Cor folded each letter and tucked it away like a keepsake. As bad as things were at the farm, she wouldn't consider moving home. Rige would have gone in a minute, she knew, but the boys were happy enough, especially Niek and Gert, who came home after school chanting new English words: "chalkboard," "strawberry," "sandwich." Some, like "chipmunk," they repeated endlessly, snorting with laughter. Gert had a head start with the English he'd learned in England, and though the vocabulary hadn't stayed with him, he picked it up easily now. He started calling himself Gerry, an easy enough change. Niek became Nick, thumbs tucked in the belt loops of his treasured blue jeans. But Koos went further upon discovering how ridiculous his Dutch name sounded to him in this new environment. The kids pronounced it *Koos*, like loose, with their lips puckered. So he leafed through the English Bible to find the right translation for Jacobus – likely the last time, he says now, that he used the Bible as a fount of knowledge. He was surprised to come upon James rather than Jacob, and soon shortened the moniker further to Jim. And it was this "Jim," eagerly shedding a skin, who merged the cumbersome *den* and *Hartog* to Denhartog, amazed by how different it looked on the page. He felt lighter and suddenly more confident once he'd made the change.

One day in May, as he walked home with his brothers and sister, he lagged behind enough to be out of earshot, and practised saying his name with a hard *r* and *g*. But as they approached the barn, he rushed to catch up – it had become their habit to stop and see their father before going home. They watched him scraping straw-caked manure off the barn floor or filling the cows' feed troughs, the big beasts lowing softly as he elbowed his way between them. Seeing their father acting like a farm-hand was strange after so many years of seeing him in the *tuin*, but it didn't occur to any of them that he, too, was reinventing himself. Koos liked being near the big cows with their long eyelashes and swishing tails. He even liked the smell of the cow dung that lay in flat discs called "patties," and he loved to torment Gert, who still had the picture of his so-called girlfriend Patty from England. "Watch out!" Koos shouted. "Don't step on Patty!" But Koos stayed quiet inside the barn, as did the others, since the farmer and his son were so unfriendly.

Today, the older man sat milking a cow, and the milk squirted rhyth-mically into the bucket. His stout son carried another pail of milk to a calf in a stall, who had to learn to drink from the bucket rather than from his mother. The man leaned into the stall and offered the milk, and the calf lapped noisily but shook its head when the droplets tickled, and the pail fell to the ground. The milk seeped into the carpet of straw on the barn floor, and before anyone had time to speak, the farmer's son grabbed a plank of wood and swung, bringing it down on the calf's head. One blow knocked the animal to the ground, where it lay dead and bleeding. Koos felt sick to his stomach. He saw his father drop his broom and look at the son and then the farmer – the older man stopped milking but then started again. Koos stood rigid. He saw that Rige and Niek were crying, and sensed that, behind him, Rokus and Gert hovered in the doorway. Suddenly his father stood and moved in front of the children. He said to the men in his awkward English, "I will not work tomorrow." His voice was clear and even, and Koos stared at his ears, red beneath his cap. "I will look for another job," he said, and his hands at his sides opened and closed nervously.

The younger man scoffed, but it was the farmer who answered, hardly glancing up from his chore. "In that case you can go look for one right now," he said flatly. "And don't come back."

Koos's father turned and looked at each of them. "Go and tell your mother to pack the suitcases," he said to Rige.

Rokus was sent to fetch a church friend who had a car. Within the hour, they were gone.

❧❧

The friend didn't have room for them for long. Cor and Rige stayed in the house, sharing a narrow bed, and Gerrit slept with his boys in the barn. But the late Canadian spring had finally begun, so the nights weren't overly cold. He remembered Cor's foraging trip with Truus, and how they had slept in a hayloft in February – that it should have been him and Jacques. Jacques had been livid when Truus recounted how the farmer kissed her. After the war, he had said, he'd find the man himself and wring his neck. But it had been too long a journey. Now the distance seemed short by comparison. He listened to his sons breathing, trying to gauge whether they were asleep or not. He could hear Koos sucking his thumb, and smiled. The habit had almost disappeared but sometimes came back in his sleep when the boy was nervous or scared, even now that he was "Jim," barrelling into adolescence. Gerrit sighed. The hooting owls and flapping bats were comforting sounds, and while he had just thrown away his only income, his family's lodgings, and the sponsorship that made his status in Canada legal, he felt good. The night smelled of hay and freshly turned earth, like the *tuin*.

The next morning, Gerrit's friend took him to McConnell's nursery to apply for a job, but Gerrit's hopes weren't high. He knew the busy season, early spring, was over, and that now was the time people were let go rather than hired on. As the car travelled along the gravel driveway towards the nursery, Gerrit saw the greenhouses spread out before him, and off to the left, a beautiful two-storey home where the owners lived.

He met with the foreman first, and was taken through the packaging room, where the plants were bundled for mail-order. The smell of cut greens and flowers hung in the air as the man in charge of the flower department introduced himself and showed Gerrit the time clock and how it punched each employee's card. Gerrit's English was still poor, but he understood that, against the odds, he had gotten the job.

Each day, he tended long rows of flowers in the humid green-houses. He made chrysanthemum cuttings with a sharp knife and dipped the stems in rooting powder, and he unpacked roses that arrived from the Netherlands, surrounded by mulch. His horticulture studies and his experience as a *tuinder* carried him, and he learned the work-ings of the nursery quickly. Before long he found himself offering tips that helped the fussy plants bloom, and throwing horseshoes with the head of the department at lunch hour. In the afternoons, the owner began stopping by the greenhouses to see his work, and calling him "Garrett," as if they were friends. The informality seemed strange to him, but he liked it.

With Gerrit's job secured, he and Cor quickly found a house, and the nursery's truck picked up the crate from the railway station and brought it home. Gerrit pried open the wooden slats. Inside was the oak table that had travelled by barge to Leidschendam when Cor and Gerrit were married. The crate also contained small items, carefully wrapped and boxed: the pewter pitcher and fluted cups Rokus had spotted in the shed; a packet of photographs and the Swiss postcard from "José"; the old queen and the new queen's portrait; the mill in which Rige and Cor had ground peas and beans; the small metal lockbox with its old, soldered coins and spent bullets; Gerrit's sharpshooting certificate, and the ID cards they had carried during the occupation. As he and Cor drew out the items and unwrapped them, it occurred to Gerrit that these things represented what already felt like a past life, and that now, a new one would begin.

Epilogue

OPA DIED OF CANCER in 1982, but by that time his dream of flying had been realized several times over. On his first flight back to the Netherlands – one he'd never imagined taking – he sat beside Oma, alternately staring out the window and recording his impressions in a notebook. "It is a beautiful sight," he wrote. "The river goes like a snake through the land." And also: "I feel superb."

Weeks before he died, when we went to Aylmer to say our goodbyes, Opa lay emaciated in his hospital bed, his hands big and callused though he'd retired from the nursery years earlier, head of the flower department by then. His bosses had given him an easy chair and a big party on that occasion, and Oma, in her proprietary way, had placed an ad in the local paper to express their gratitude: *I, his wife, appreciate this token of love for my husband very much*. Opa had retired and gone home to tend his fragrant rose bushes in the modest garden outside his house. There, after he died, his son Rokus crouched on his knees, pulling weeds, and as he worked he sensed his father beside him.

After his funeral, in a rare moment of candour, Oma sat on the porch with Rige's youngest daughter, crying. "I shouldn't have tried to control everything," she said. "I should have let him make more of our decisions. He deserved that." She looked down at her hands and turned the ring on her finger, perhaps recalling the time, a few years before, when he'd been asked by the church to become an elder. The honour had thrilled Oma, but he'd turned it down, saying he hadn't the gifts that that function required. Despite her disappointment, he'd stood his ground.

Oma missed riding with him in their brown car to and from church, for which she'd worn hats with spotted veils and he'd shined the good shoes that now sat empty in their closet. She missed lying beside him at night, with their noses pointing at the ceiling. She had become old. Her white hair dipped down on her forehead in a widow's peak, but Opa's, even in his last days, sprang back from his face, and accentuated the look of optimism that was almost always with him.

Five years after he was gone, Oma, too, became ill with cancer. But death had lost its terror. "Eternal life," she said, "is the greatness that gives this difficult one its splendour" – which was not something most of her children believed but it seemed to give her peace. In her last weeks, her sister Truus visited from Holland, and Rige, staying with her mother in Aylmer, woke each morning, hearing them whisper and giggle in the next room, just as they had as girls, and later as women shocked by the kissing farmer.

Oma seemed to soften at the end of her life. Her closeness to God became more personal, and less of a fixation. It was a great disappointment to her that all of her children's marriages had ended in divorce, that four of them had turned away from the Church, and the other,

Rokus, practised a new religion that seemed at odds with her own. To say she had tried for a different outcome would be an understatement. Only after her husband's death did she understand his warning that she would push their children away entirely if she kept forcing religion on them, and that the grandchildren would then be lost to her also. In her own way, she began mending fences. Weeks before she died, she received the fiancé of a granddaughter – a man she hadn't met before because they'd been "living in sin" – and she grasped both his hands and whispered, "Be a good husband." And when our sister, Heidi, visited, she sat on the edge of the hospital bed that had been placed in Oma's living room, feeling sad and awkward, but Oma smiled with her eyes sparkling. "It will be all right," she said. "I'll be with Opa soon." What stayed unspoken was her conviction that she was also going to God.

Her last wish was connected to her lifelong evangelism, and a realization, perhaps, that it had hurt people more than it had helped them, whatever her intentions: "If you want to do something for me," she told Rige, "find Bep, and tell her I'm sorry." For Rige, Bep was a distant memory. She didn't ask for details, but kept Oma comfortable until she died. Then she washed her and dressed her, gently combing the white strands of her hair into the bun she'd stopped wearing during the last weeks of her illness, and sliding her glasses on: her mother's face seemed too soft and vulnerable without them. When the funeral home brought her casket to the house, Rige slept in the living room beside it. She drew the doors to the room closed, but we, who had arrived for the funeral, heard her talking and singing to Oma late that night, and again in the morning. We thought it was strange then, but now it seems right, and beautiful.

Afterwards, in Oma's papers, Rige came across a picture of Henny, and a letter from Bep that had been sent in care of the Bloms in Leidschendam and forwarded to Canada. "I received your letter," she wrote, "but could not make myself answer. I found it too difficult. I'm sure you know that, Cor. I want to emphasize that I know how much you and your family loved me, but I never heard talk of 'love' in the church. *You* gave me love. I will always think of you and remember that." Rige wanted to deliver her mother's apology, whatever it meant, but she couldn't find "Tante" Bep at any of the addresses listed in Oma's book, and when a query she placed in a Dutch magazine went unanswered, she stopped looking.

Oma had been dead for nearly twenty years when we came to Rige and told her we wanted to write about our grandparents. She told us everything she knew, and tirelessly hunted for the answers she didn't have. The search also resumed for Bep, or some trace of her. It turned out she had died before Oma had, but her daughter was still alive, and offered what she could remember. We found Henny's son by his second wife, and discovered Henny had died only a few years earlier, at age ninety-one, and that late in his full life he'd written the account of his escape in a journal, which he gave to the Jewish Historical Museum in Amsterdam. We pored over the pages, fascinated by his story, but looking also for some mention of his life in Leidschendam. Had he ever spoken of our grandparents? we asked the son. But the answer came back no. From Rige's old friend Ineke – their friendship spans almost seventy years – came the diary of Rie Batelaan, Ineke's mother, an intimate piece of writing that brought us moments we'd never dreamed of finding: *I just can't forget the face of that mother as she left the church fearing the worst.* And there was the packet of letters from Opa's parents that gave us a glimpse of the heartache of leaving family behind, the final letter coming less than two years after our family moved to Canada, when Moeder den Hartog died. "The first thing that I must do," Vader den Hartog wrote in a shaky, barely legible hand, "is to give you the last greetings from your mother. That she must have asked of me a hundred times. I have had to give her up, but I am thankful that I was able to look after her until the last moment." Two months later, he also died. These personal accounts have been like lanterns for us, lighting an otherwise dim route into the history of ordinary people.

In the summer of 2006, we found ourselves in the Netherlands at Corrie Blom's, eating cake and drinking coffee with her and her brother

Piet, our father Koos, and Aunt Rige. In Dutch and broken English, Corrie and Piet shared their memories of their old neighbours, the den Hartogs, telling us how Opa couldn't answer the question "Neighbour, how are your boys?" in the hours after the bombing. Our sister was with us too, and the three of us watched our father's body language – the way he leaned forward towards Piet and Corrie, and then back, pressing his spine into the sofa. We sensed that he both longed to remember this time himself, and felt reluctant to do so. Piet said, "How is it that you don't know these things – how is it you weren't told?" but nodded when given the answer, as though of course he should have known. Oma and Opa were not unique in their unwillingness to share their experience. It was typical of their culture and their generation, and a reaction to horrible times. On top of that, the den Hartogs were known in the street for being a *terughoudende* family – reserved and restrained. Oma especially was *fel Gereformeerd*, fierce in her religion. The visit with Corrie and Piet was an emotional day, especially for Dad, who reacted with the same speechlessness upon hearing how Opa couldn't speak, and how his face, pale with shock, had been covered in abrasions. Even after having his own children, Dad had never thought of the day from a father's point of view – hearing the planes coming, having only enough time to run to the door and yell.

Except in the obvious way, Dad has always claimed to be unscarred by that 1945 Sunday. Since the mid-1990s, he's lived aboard his sailboat, travelling the world and enjoying one adventure after another. Like his brother Gert, he's never considered himself handicapped. The two of them may even have been more determined to ski, cycle, swim, and sail their way through life because of what happened to them as boys. Both thank their parents for this, and laugh about the time a stranger told them, as adults, "It'll cost you an arm and a leg," before noticing those bits were already gone. But over a lifetime, the curiosity of strangers can grow tiresome. Once, a woman in a bar blurted to Gert, "What happened to your arm?" and he answered wryly, "I lost it," and turned away from her.

To us, the missing parts were ordinary, but we sensed the fascination of other children. We used to invite friends into our parents' room early Saturday mornings to peek at Dad's leg lying under the bed as he snored away beneath the covers. The leg was our link to a foreign, dramatic time full of goose-stepping soldiers and raining bombs and princesses hastening across the ocean. We laughed when Dad walked around with his foot on backwards, turning heads on the street, and sending the message – to us at least – that he was comfortable with his body. Years later, while sailing in French Polynesia, he wrote to say, "Today I broke my toe. It bent so far backwards it almost broke off, which wouldn't be so bad except that a few weeks ago, I broke my ankle. So, mindful of my religious upbringing and remembering that an offending eye ought to be plucked out, I took a very sharp scalpel and, gritting my teeth, amputated my leg just below the knee. Instant peg leg. Call me Ahab. Finally I will be able to jump out of the dinghy into the water, splash in puddles, or sit in the bowsprit with a sea running. And that after only 67 years!"

When we began this project, Dad told us he had "no problem" talking about any of it, but in the middle of recounting by e-mail his memories of the day – the sight of his shinbone, and Gert's eyes rolling back in his head – "I suddenly got tears in my eyes and had to keep from crying," he wrote. "Amazing."

After our visit with Piet and Corrie Blom, we ventured out without our Dutch-speaking guides and noticed a resistance monument marked on our bicycle map of Scheveningen. We decided to find it, but there were no route markers to guide us, no obvious entrance, no access for cars or parking rack for bicycles. We stumbled upon the path and a tiny sign after wondering if we'd lost our way, having passed vine-covered bunkers and tall barbed-wire fences. Gunfire rang in the distance and we could only guess that it came from a military range, yet it seemed we'd been transported back to the 1940s. We had no idea what to expect at the end of the hushed, sheltered path that led through the dunes. The trail opened into a small glade, bare but for a couple of benches and four narrow, bronze crosses on a grassy mound. A stone marker added to the mystery: HIER BRACHTEN VELE LANDGENOTEN HET OFFER VAN HUN LEVEN VOOR UW VRIJHEID. BETREED DEZE PLAATS MET GEPASTE EERBIED. Here many countrymen gave their lives for your freedom. Enter this place with appropriate respect. We realized later that we'd followed the same route as hundreds of resistance fighters, and also the traitor Anton Mussert. This was their place of execution, Waalsdorpervlakte, famous among the Dutch but new to us, who'd grown apart from our history.

Dad says that as a child, he always "knew" Opa belonged to the resistance, but that later he wondered if maybe all children of his era thought that about the parents they loved, wanting to believe they'd been courageous. When a document surfaced at the Leidschendam Archives confirming Opa had been a section commander for the BS, we had a small amount of proof, but few anecdotes to go along with it. We knew that because he'd been a gardener, he would have had a permit that allowed him to be out past curfew, and that such permits were gold for the resistance. And the list is long of the people close to him who were deeply involved in subversive measures: in Leidschendam there was Reverend Rietveld, the Batelaans, and Jaap Quartel, who with his family followed Gerrit to Canada. In Haarlem, another of Cor's de Korte cousins had been one of many people involved with the legendary Corrie ten Boom and her safe haven for Jews. And in Overschie there was Cor's brother-in-law Jacques, another cousin Dirk – the man tortured at Scheveningen – and Dick Zandbergen, who, with his wife Marie, remained a lifelong friend of Gerrit and Cor, and visited them in Canada.

If they were still alive, what would these people be able to tell us about Oma and Opa? Old letters only beg more questions. Reverend Rietveld wrote to Oma after Opa died, and said that he remembered Gerrit "with sympathy and respect." And in another, earlier letter, responding to Oma's first contact with him in decades, he wrote, "This morning I received your letter . . . and I hurried to write you back. Of course I have not forgotten you. The years in Leidschendam were intense; etched in stone in our memories." But in the letter itself there are no details of those memories. At times we craved evidence of grand, heroic gestures on the part of our grandparents during the war years, but in the end, their courage was less meaningful to us than their emotions, and their means of enduring first the occupation, and then the events in their own backyard.

Before the idea for this book came about, we were in London, Ontario, visiting our mother's side of the family, and on a whim, detoured to Aylmer. Meandering on back roads through hardwood forests that opened onto fields of fruit trees, we stopped at the shores of Lake Erie, where Dad and his brothers learned to swim. We found the nursery where Opa and, for a time, Rige had worked, and the white farmhouse where the family had picked strawberries and cucumbers to supplement Opa's earnings at the nursery. But these places belonged in *their* memories, not ours. Only when we drove into the town of Aylmer did we feel a rush of familiarity. It was surprising how easily we found our way, knowing almost instinctively when to make a left and when a right, though it had been nearly twenty years since our last visit, and that a brief one for Oma's funeral. There was the ramshackle building – a smoky taxi stand now – where Oma had opened a dry-goods store and travel bureau. There was the little grey brick house where they'd lived in later years, but the lace curtains were gone from the window and Opa's roses no longer grew in the flower beds. We found the church where we had sat on Sundays, bribed, or perhaps rewarded, for our stillness with Wilhelmina Peppermunts from Opa's pockets.

Our last stop that day was the cemetery. None of Oma and Opa's children had lived near Aylmer in decades – in fact, at this point, all of them lived out of the country. It took a long time to find the graves, since the shared marker lay flat on the ground, and when we came upon it we saw how the grooves of their names were muted with moss and lichen. We searched for small sticks to clean the stone, and worked side by side, gently scraping until the names again became clear.

NOTES

CHAPTER ONE

20   "life was a pond without a ripple": Wilhelmina, Princess of the
     Netherlands. *Lonely But Not Alone*. Trans. John Peereboom.
     London: Hutchinson & Co. Ltd., 1960

21   "the greatest debauchee": *New York Times*, September 26, 1897

23   "together with the misery": *Lonely But Not Alone*

23   "What a burden": *Lonely But Not Alone*

25   "carrying a message of peace": www.olympic.org

26   "Nazi Prince Bernhard": *Time*, January 18, 1937

38   "Our good intentions": *Lonely But Not Alone*

38   "asleep on the pillow": *Lonely But Not Alone*
41   "twilight of the neutrals": Goebbels, Joseph. *The Goebbels Diaries: 1939–1941*. Trans. Fred Taylor. London: Hamish Hamilton, 1982. November 11, 1939
41   "Worried Queen": *Time*, November 27, 1939
46   "an adventurous journey": *Lonely But Not Alone*
47   "miniature war council": *Lonely But Not Alone*

CHAPTER TWO
61   "to spare further bloodshed": *Globe and Mail*, May 15, 1940
63   "Not a single house": *New York Times*, May 23, 1940

CHAPTER THREE
70   "My name is Juliana": *Globe and Mail*, June 18, 1940
72   "Nothing should prevent us": reprinted in *Over, door en om de Leytsche Dam*. Dams, F.H. Chr. M., and de Kort, J.D. Leidschendam: Gemeente Leidschendam, 1988
72   "When all is said and done": *The Goebbels Diaries: 1939–1941*, February 27, 1941
80   "My compatriots": www.nationaalarchief.nl
83   "reduce consumption": Nazi Conspiracy and Aggression documents, Volume 11, www.nizkor.org
84   "the greatest mass destruction": *New York Times*, July 17, 1940
85   "musical chairs": *Lonely But Not Alone*
86   "Tom's flat in Lincoln's Inn": Bernhard, Prince of the Netherlands. *Het fotoarchief van prins Bernhard*. Uitgeverij De Verbeelding. Amsterdam, 2005
88   "the only man": *Time*, June 3, 2002
88   "a doubtful kind of product": *Lonely But Not Alone*
99   "He is no real Nazi": *The Goebbels Diaries: 1939–1941*, February 26, 1941
100 "absolute peace": *The Goebbels Diaries: 1939–1941*, March 1, 1941

100   "the Jews, for us": Nazi Conspiracy and Aggression documents, www.nizkor.org

100   "And then things went on": Nazi Conspiracy and Aggression documents, www.nizkor.org

103   "a typical young Englishman": *Hamilton Spectator*, June 11, 1942

103   "any young Canadian airman": *Globe and Mail*, January 15, 1943

104   "I think they are going to": *New York Times*, June 12, 1941

104   "A prince": *The Goebbels Diaries: 1939–1941*, June 15, 1941

105   "The beginning of the end": *Lonely But Not Alone*

105   "Already our eyes see": *Hamilton Spectator*, August 30, 1941

105   "We stand here in dark times": *Hamilton Spectator*, August 30, 1941

109   "quiet knocking": http://home.luna.nl/~arjanmuil/radio/museum.html

111   "What excellent care": Batelaan, Rie. *The Diary of Rie Batelaan*. Leidschendam": 1941–1945. September 16, 1941

111   "I shall try to keep up": Cahn, Henny. "Autobiographical account of 1942 flight to Switzerland." Jewish Historical Museum. Amsterdam, 1990

111   "In spite of all the rumours": *Het Parool*, September 11, 1941

CHAPTER FOUR

116   "We are not beaten": *Lonely But Not Alone*

116   "This Wilhelmina is surely": Goebbels, Joseph. *The Goebbels Diaries: 1942–1943*. Trans. Louis P. Lochner. New York": Doubleday & Company, Inc., 1948. March 5, 1942

127   "pigheadedness . . . Seyss-Inquart is pursuing": *The Goebbels Diaries: 1942–1943*, February 15, 1942

128   "a woman of real character": *The Diaries of William Lyon Mackenzie King*, www.king.collectionscanada.ca, June 18, 1942

129   "archaic, medieval empire ideas": Roosevelt, Elliott. *As He Saw It*. New York: Duell, Sloan and Pearce, 1946

129 "strong personality": *Lonely But Not Alone*
129 "We want nothing": *Hamilton Spectator*, August 6, 1942
130 "I did not find the queen": *The Diaries of William Lyon Mackenzie King*, August 11, 1942
131 "Dutch churches": as recorded in *The Diary of Rie Batelaan*, July 26, 1942
132 "It sounds like a mockery": Nazi Conspiracy and Aggression documents, www.nizkor.org
135 "Not Jew-friendly . . . I cannot do this": all from de Jong, Louis. "Twee gesprekken met Gertrud Seyss-Inquart, Salzburg, 30 September 1952." *Oorlogsdocumentatie '40–'45": jaarboek van het Rijksinstituut voor Oorlogsdocumentatie*. Zutphen: Walburg Pers, 1989
136 "What is it that a human being . . . *Vous êtes libre là*": all from Cahn, Henny
142 "Invasion jitters": *Globe and Mail*, December 7, 1942
145 "The ghost of conscription": *The Diary of Rie Batelaan*, December 14, 1942
146 "Who does not remember": *Lonely But Not Alone*

CHAPTER FIVE
151 "our fallen comrades": *Over, door en om de Leytsche Dam*
151 "There is only one answer": reprinted in *Over, door en om de Leytsche Dam*
152 "If all the Dutch houses could speak": *The Diary of Rie Batelaan*, February 16, 1943
153 "The question has been put to me": *The Goebbels Diaries: 1942–1943*, May 9, 1943
156 "I don't mind the loss": *The Diaries of William Lyon Mackenzie King*, June 10, 1943
157 "Each Sunday is an oasis": *The Diary of Rie Batelaan*, January 17, 1943

159 "How much good": *The Diary of Rie Batelaan*, July 12, 1943

161 "I have the impression": *The Goebbels Diaries: 1942–1943*,
     September 8, 1943

162 "I felt as if I were in a golden cage": "Twee gesprekken met
     Gertrud Seyss-Inquart"

163 "By and by they are being seized": Seyss-Inquart's letter to
     Martin Bormann, https://www.jewishvirtuallibrary.org/
     jsource/Holocaust/Inquartreport.html

166 "little country place": *Lonely But Not Alone*

168 "on principle": Nazi Conspiracy and Aggression documents,
     www.nizkor.org

172 "People of Europe": *New York Times*, June 6, 1944

173 "We will give you precise directions": *The Diary of Rie Batelaan*,
     June 8, 1944

173 "entirely unhurt": Shirer, William. *The Rise and Fall of Adolf
     Hitler*. New York: Random House, 1961

175 "our boys": *Lonely But Not Alone*

175 "Huns in Full Retreat": *Globe and Mail*, August 24, 1944

176 "Keep to the instructions": *Globe and Mail*, September 3, 1944

178 "a difficult town": *Over, door en om de Leytsche Dam*

CHAPTER SIX

180 "To Her Royal Highness": *The Diaries of William Lyon
     Mackenzie King*, September 9, 1944

182 "devilish": *The Diary of Rie Batelaan*, September 12, 1944

190 "There could be no graver accusation": Nazi Conspiracy and
     Aggression documents, www.nizkor.org

197 "an illegal army": Nazi Conspiracy and Aggression documents,
     www.nizkor.org

201 "After my journey . . . liberation of corpses": letter reprinted in
     United States Army in World War II, Center of Military History,
     United States Army, Washington D.C., 1992

202 "feast of promise": *Lonely But Not Alone*

202 "I wonder if the day will ever come": *The Diaries of William Lyon Mackenzie King*, December 25, 1944

204 "Take lots of photographs": caption from photography exhibit *Het fotoarchief van prins Bernhard* at Verzetsmuseum, Amsterdam

217 "an erroneous execution": Churchill's communiqué reprinted at http://www.v2platform.nl/bombardement.html

217 "That man . . . such wonderful eyes": "Twee gesprekken met Gertrud Seyss-Inquart"

218 "There are moments": *The Diary of Rie Batelaan*, December 21, 1944

218 "At times I ask myself": *The Diary of Rie Batelaan*, January 18, 1945

CHAPTER SEVEN
223 "I just can't forget": *The Diary of Rie Batelaan*, March 19, 1945

CHAPTER EIGHT
236 "will ever cherish his name": *New York Times*, April 14, 1945

236 "deep and irreparable loss": Churchill, Winston S. *The Second World War: Triumph and Tragedy*. Boston: Houghton Mifflin, 1948–1953

237 "The North Sea is streaming in": *The Diary of Rie Batelaan*, April 22, 1945

237 "We can hardly imagine": *The Diary of Rie Batelaan*, April 18, 1945

240 "queen": Hazelhoff Roelfzema, Erik. *Soldier of Orange*. Toronto: Hodder and Stoughton, 1972

240 "an indescribable burden": *Lonely But Not Alone*

240 "the hour of disaster": Nazi Conspiracy and Aggression documents, www.nizkor.org

251 "the strangest collection": *Lonely But Not Alone*

251 "widows' village": *Lonely But Not Alone*

252 "simplicity of life": *The Diaries of William Lyon Mackenzie King,* July 10, 1945

252 "adapted to the times": *Lonely But Not Alone*

253 "the most beautiful": *Lonely But Not Alone*

CHAPTER NINE

265 "We live in the hearts": reprinted in Goddard, Lance. *Canada and the Liberation of the Netherlands.* Toronto": Dundurn Press, 2005

266 "The fact remains that Seyss-Inquart": Nuremberg trial transcripts, The Avalon Project, www.yale.edu/lawweb/avalon/imt/proc/judseyss.htm

266 "600,000 hogs": Nazi Conspiracy and Aggression documents, www.nizkor.org

267 "I hope that this execution": International News Service, October 16, 1946

268 "I'm collecting everything about him": "Twee gesprekken met Gertrud Seyss-Inquart"

272 "many old people were no longer": *Lonely But Not Alone*

277 "One could have heard a pin drop": *Lonely But Not Alone*

278 "a tribute": *Lonely But Not Alone*

PHOTO CAPTIONS

ACKNOWLEDGEMENTS

Many people shared memories, expertise, and invaluable translation skills, chief among them Rige den Hartog, whose courage and energy in large part made this book possible. We are also indebted to our father, Jim, and uncles Rokus, Gerry, and Nick for answering what must have seemed like an endless stream of questions, and for responding so candidly. To the long list that follows, *hartelijk bedankt*: Ineke Batelaan, Joost Batelaan, Piet Blom, Willy Boss-Mol, Wendy Broer at the Waalsdorp Memorial site, Denise Bukowski, Leo Cahn, Marilyn Charbonneau, Evert den Boer, Tonny den Boer, Helen den Dekker, Heidi den Hartog, Linda den Hartog Austin, Simon de Korte, Hajo Groenman at the War Over Holland site, Arigje Jol–de Vos, Gene Kasaboski, Ineke Kranendonk–van Veenendaal, Jennifer Lambert, Corrie Landman-Blom,

Allyson Latta, Liesbeth Meijer, Jeanne Opdam–van Kampen, Schil Overwater, Trudy Pronk, Johanna Quartel, Jan Rehling, Corrie Ruis–de Korte, Gerrie Schipper-Post, Cor Scholten, Oeral Thus, Henrika vande Burgt, Ken vande Burgt, Jan van de Graaf, André van der Zee, Adrie van Everdingen of "Het Land van Strijen," Carla van Gent–Warnau, Bep Warnau-Hefting, Trena White, Jeff Winch, Aad Zandbergen and the Leidschendam–Voorburg Archives, Nel Zwolsman–van Veenendaal. A special thank you, too, to Jeroen Dewulf, who holds the Queen Beatrix Chair at the University of California, Berkeley, and who checked the manuscript for historical accuracy.

The number of books, websites, archives, and museums consulted is great, but the following condensed list proved indispensable:

Batelaan, Rie. *Diary of Rie Batelaan.* Trans. Tanny and Joost Batelaan. Leidschendam, 1941–45. (Late in 2007 the diary was published in its entirety in the Netherlands as *Verborgen Dagboek 1941–1945.*)

Bernhard, Prince. *Het fotoarchief van prins Bernhard.* Amsterdam, 2005

Cahn, Henny. Autobiographical account of 1942 flight to Switzerland. Jewish Historical Museum. Amsterdam, 1990

Dams, F.H. Chr. M., and de Kort, J.D. *Over, door en om de Leytsche Dam.* Leidschendam, 1988

de Jong, Louis. *The Collapse of a Colonial Society. The Dutch in Indonesia during the Second World War.* Leiden, 2002

de Jong, Louis. "Twee gesprekken met Gertrud Seyss-Inquart, Salzburg, 30 September 1952." *Oorlogsdocumentatie '40–'45: jaarboek van het Rijksinstituut voor Oorlogsdocumentatie.* Zutphen, 1989

www.erepeloton.nl, the Waalsdorpervlakte memorial site

www.erfgoedleidschendam.nl, the Leidschendam historical society and its many articles including "Gereformeerde Leidschendam During WWII" by Dick (H.J.Ph.G.) Kaajan

Fuykschot, Cornelia. *Hunger in Holland.* New York, 1995

Hatch, Alden. *HRH Prince Bernhard*. London, 1962

Hefting, Paul. *Ontwerper Henny Cahn*. Amsterdam, 2006

www.hetillegaleparool.nl/ *Het Parool*'s online archive of wartime
  newspapers

Historische Vereniging 's-Gravendeel

Hillesum, Etty. *An Interrupted Life and Letters from Westerbork*.
  New York, 1996

Jewish Historical Museum, Amsterdam

Leidschendam–Voorburg archives

Mechanicus, Philip. *Waiting for Death: A Diary*. London, 1968

Museum Oud Overschie, Rotterdam

National Archives of the United Kingdom, Image Library

Nederlands Instituut voor Militaire Historie, Alexander Kazerne,
  Den Haag, and the diary by Moeskops, Hulpaalmoezenier J.A.,
  28 R.I. chaplain

Neuman, H.J. *Arthur Seyss-Inquart, het leven van een duits
  onderkoning in Nederland*. Utrecht, 1967

Nicholas, Lynn H. *Cruel World: The Children of Europe in the
  Nazi Web*. New York, 2006

www.niod.nl, the Netherlands Institute for War Documentation

Oudheidkundige Vereniging "Het Land van Strijen"

Peters, Maarten; Doepel, Duzan; van Schuppen, Steven.
  "A controversial legacy: The Atlantic Wall from Rhine to IJ."
  The Hague, 2005

Royal Archives, House of Orange-Nassau, The Hague

Ryan, Cornelius. *A Bridge Too Far*. New York, 1995

van der Zee, Henri. *The Hunger Winter: Occupied Holland 1944–45*.
  London, 1982

Verbeek, J.R. "'V2-Vergeltung' from The Hague and Its Environs:
  Deployment of the V2 rockets and the terrors for the city and her
  inhabitants." Den Haag, 2005

Verzetsmuseum, Amsterdam

www.time.com, *Time* magazine's archives

www.vac-acc.gc.ca, Veterans Affairs Canada

www.warmuseum.ca, the Canadian War Museum's online collection of wartime newspaper articles

www.waroverholland.nl, which details the five days of battle across the country

www.westerbork.nl

Wilhelmina, Princess of the Netherlands. *Lonely But Not Alone*. London, 1960